PENGUIN BOOKS

IN DEFENCE

John Bradshaw is a biolo… d
Anthrozoology Institute, …
studying the behaviour of …
five years, and is the auth… pers
and reviews, which have n… dog's abilities
and needs, but have also cha… dogs are understood and
cared for all over the world.

JOHN BRADSHAW

In Defence of Dogs

PENGUIN BOOKS

PENGUIN BOOKS

Published by the Penguin Group
Penguin Books Ltd, 80 Strand, London WC2R 0RL, England
Penguin Group (USA) Inc., 375 Hudson Street, New York, New York 10014, USA
Penguin Group (Canada), 90 Eglinton Avenue East, Suite 700, Toronto, Ontario, Canada M4P 2Y3
(a division of Pearson Penguin Canada Inc.)
Penguin Ireland, 25 St Stephen's Green, Dublin 2, Ireland (a division of Penguin Books Ltd)
Penguin Group (Australia), 250 Camberwell Road, Camberwell, Victoria 3124, Australia
(a division of Pearson Australia Group Pty Ltd)
Penguin Books India Pvt Ltd, 11 Community Centre, Panchsheel Park, New Delhi – 110 017, India
Penguin Group (NZ), 67 Apollo Drive, Rosedale, Auckland 0632, New Zealand
(a division of Pearson New Zealand Ltd)
Penguin Books (South Africa) (Pty) Ltd, Block D, Rosebank Office Park, 181 Jan Smuts Avenue,
Parktown North, Gauteng 2193, South Africa

Penguin Books Ltd, Registered Offices: 80 Strand, London WC2R 0RL, England

www.penguin.com

First published by Allen Lane 2011
Published by Penguin Books 2012
001

Typeset by Palimpsest Book Production Limited, Falkirk, Stirlingshire
Printed in Great Britain by Clays Ltd, St Ives plc

ISBN 978-0-141-98287-8

www.greenpenguin.co.uk

FSC www.fsc.org MIX Paper from responsible sources FSC™ C018179

Penguin Books is committed to a sustainable future for our business, our readers and our planet. This book is made from Forest Stewardship Council™ certified paper.

To Alexis (1970–1984) – a Real Dog

Contents

List of Figures

Acknowledgements

I've spent the best part of thirty years studying dog behaviour, first at the Waltham Centre for Pet Nutrition, then at the University of Southampton, and finally at the University of Bristol's Anthrozoology Institute. Some of what I've learned about dogs has come from direct observation, especially in the early days, but much has been informed by collaborations and discussions with many colleagues and graduate students. The original research described in this book owes much to them, though of course I take full responsibility for the interpretations presented here. In roughly chronological order, they are: Christopher Thorne, David Macdonald, Stephan Natynczuk, Benjamin Hart, Sarah Brown, Ian Robinson, Helen Nott, Stephen Wickens, Amanda Lea, Sue Hull, Sarah Whitehead, Gwen Bailey, James Serpell, Rory Putman, Anita Nightingale, Claire Hoskin, Robert Hubrecht, Claire Guest, Deborah Wells, Elizabeth Kershaw, Anne McBride, Sarah Heath, Justine McPherson, David Appleby, Barbara Schöning, Emily Blackwell, Jolanda Pluijmakers, Theresa Barlow, Helen Almey, Elly Hiby, Sara Jackson, Elizabeth Paul, Nicky Robertson, Claire Cooke, Samantha Gaines, Anne Pullen and Carri Westgarth – and many more too numerous to list. Two deserve a special mention: Nicola Rooney, who in addition to producing consistently world-class research on dog behaviour and welfare for the past dozen years, has also been the social life and soul of my research group; and Rachel Casey, arguably the UK's leading veterinary behaviourist, and unarguably an indefatigable champion of evidence-based dog training and behavioural therapy. I am grateful to Emily Blackwell and Nicola Rooney for their comments on parts of the manuscript. My thanks also to the University of Bristol's School of Veterinary Medicine, and especially Professors Christine

Nicol and Mike Mendl, and Dr David Main, for nurturing the Anthrozoology Institute and its research.

Our research has relied on the co-operation of literally thousands of volunteer dog owners and their dogs, to whom I express my gratitude. Also, much of our research would have been impossible without the facilities and co-operation offered by the UK's leading animal rehoming charities: Dogs Trust, the Blue Cross and the RSPCA.

There are many other academics and dog experts that I've met only briefly, but whose published work has been an enormous inspiration. Many I have been able to mention specifically in the notes. Like any branch of science, the systematic study of dog behaviour embraces many approaches and opinions, and sometimes these can be expressed quite forcefully. Yet there is a crucial difference between canine science and canine folklore; scientists are ready to evaluate evidence gathered by others, and to change their opinions if that evaluation indicates that they should. Canine scientists are not in the business of peddling opinion as if it were fact; they contribute to a body of knowledge which, while never complete, continually gains strength from being the product of many heads and much discussion. I am grateful to them all, even those whose views are now largely discredited or unfashionable. Science advances through the replacement of one hypothesis by another that better fits the data; without the first to act as a stimulus to creative thought, the second might never have been conceived.

Condensing all this science into a book of reasonable length has not been easy, but my agent Patrick Walsh, and Lara Heimert and Will Goodlad, my editors at Basic Books and Penguin respectively, have all taught me a great deal about how to aim for a wider audience than the academic community that I have mainly written for in the past.

I've been amazed and delighted by how my old friend Alan Peters' drawings have brought my descriptions of dogs and canids to life. He's not only a wonderful artist, he's also a skilful gundog trainer (and falconer) and so was able to bring to the task a lifetime's experience of how dogs move and interact.

Finally, to my family. My wife Nicky has been an unwavering source of support throughout all the years of my academic career, and especially during the year or so it has taken me to write this book – I cannot thank her enough. Thanks also to my brother Jeremy for giving me the encouragement to start this book in the first place. Netty, Emma and Pete, thank you for refreshing my brain with music; Tom and Jez likewise but with ales, Rioja and cricket.

Ginger

Preface

The first dog that I became attached to was one I never met. He was my grandfather's cairn terrier, Ginger – a typical long-legged cairn of the early twentieth century, only a few generations removed from his working forebears. Ginger had died long before I was born, and I grew up in a pet-free household: stories about Ginger were, for a while, the nearest I came to having a dog of my own.

My grandfather, an architect, liked to walk. He walked to and from his office in the industrial city of Bradford, and to and from the churches and mill buildings he specialized in, but especially he walked for recreation, whether on the Yorkshire moors, or in the Lake District, or in Snowdonia. Whenever he could, he took Ginger with him. The family maintained that Ginger, who was taller than he should have been for his breed, had acquired his longer than average legs through all this exercise. Actually, in the photographs I have of him he looks quite typical of his breed, and not unlike the cairn chosen to play 'Toto' in the 1939 movie *The Wizard of Oz*. It was not until much later on, when I became professionally interested in pedigree dogs, that I was struck by how much the breed had changed over the intervening decades, including becoming significantly shorter in the leg. I doubt many modern cairns would enjoy the amounts of exercise that my grandfather evidently relished, although cairns today are less prone to inherited diseases than many other breeds are.

Ginger was a genuine Yorkshire 'character', and the family had a fund of stories about him, but what amazed me the most was the freedom he had been given, even though he lived within sight of the city centre. Every lunch time, when my grandfather was at work, Ginger was allowed to take himself for a walk around the neighbourhood. Apparently he had a routine. First he would cross the road into Lister Park, where he would sniff lamp-posts, interact with other dogs and, in summer, try to persuade the occupants of the park benches to part with one of their sandwiches. Then he would cross the tram tracks on Manningham Lane, and amble to the rear of the fish and chip shop, where a scratch at the back door would usually elicit a handful of scraps of batter and some misshapen chips. Then he usually headed straight for home, which involved crossing a busy junction. Here, according to family legend, there was usually a policeman, directing the lunchtime traffic, *who would solemnly stop the cars to allow Ginger safe passage across.*

I have not been to Bradford for many years, but if other cities are anything to go by, Lister Park is probably now ringed with poop-bins, and most of the dogs walked there will be leashed. The Bradford dog-wardens are called out to catch any dog that routinely roams the park, let alone the nearby streets. The trams are long gone of course, and traffic lights have replaced policemen on point duty, but I doubt that, even if he or she wanted to, one of today's stab-vested community support officers would dare to stop a car to allow a small brown terrier to cross the road.

Seventy-odd years have passed since Ginger was allowed to roam the streets and charm his way into the affections of everyone he met, including the local law enforcement officers. During that same period, almost unnoticed, there have been enormous changes in society's attitudes towards man's best friend.

Such attitudes were still quite relaxed in 1970s Britain when I was growing up. My first dog, a Labrador/Jack Russell cross named Alexis, was also a roamer, although he was more interested in the opposite sex than in lunchtime snacks. Despite our best efforts to keep him in sight he would manage to get away once in a while, and so, unlike Ginger, he did end up in police kennels a few times (in those days the police in the United Kingdom still had responsibility for stray dogs), but no one seemed to mind much. Nowadays such tolerance of dogs and their ways is hard to find, especially in cities, and dog ownership is showing signs of retreating to its roots in the countryside. After many millennia in which the dog has been man's closest animal companion, cats are taking over as the most popular pet in many countries, including the United Kingdom. Why is this happening?

First of all, dogs are expected to be much better controlled than they used to be. There has never been a shortage of experts telling owners how to take charge of their dogs. When I took on my second dog, a Labrador/Airedale terrier cross named Ivan, I was determined that he would be better behaved than Alexis. I decided I ought to find out something about training, but was then shocked to discover the approach adopted by the trainers of the day, such as Barbara Woodhouse, who seemed to see the dog as something that needed to be dominated at all times. This simply did not make sense to me – the whole point of having dogs as pets was for them to become friends, not slaves. As I researched, I found that this whole approach to training had stemmed from the ideas of Colonel Konrad Most, a police officer and a pioneer in dog training who, more than a hundred years ago, had decided that a man could control a dog only if the dog was convinced that the man was physically superior. He derived this idea from contemporary biologists' accounts of wild wolf packs, which at that time were considered to be controlled by one individual who ruled the others through fear. Biology, by then my profession, seemed to be at odds with my gut-feeling as to how my relationship with my dogs ought to work.

To my relief, this dilemma has resolved itself over the past decade. The wolf pack, always the touchstone for the interpretation of dog behaviour, is now known to be a harmonious family group except when human intervention renders it dysfunctional. As a consequence, the most enlightened modern trainers have largely abandoned the use of punishment, relying on reward-based methods that have their roots in comparative psychology. Yet for some reason, old-school trainers continue to dominate the media, largely, I suspect, because their confrontational methods make for a more exciting spectacle.

While a more sympathetic understanding of dogs' minds is being applied to training, albeit patchily, their physical health has been progressively undermined. As more and more demands have been placed on the family dog, in terms of hygiene, control and behaviour, the breeding of dogs that might be suited to this ever more demanding niche has been left in the hands of enthusiasts whose primary goal is to produce dogs that look good. Ginger, although he came from pedigree stock, was only ten or so generations away from Scottish and Irish rat-catchers of no particular breeding, and as a result led a long and healthy life. Now, the cairn terrier is in danger of becoming the victim of inbreeding for the show ring, plagued by more than a dozen hereditary complaints such as the exotically named but apparently excruciatingly painful Legg-Calvé-Perthes disease.

Biologists now know far more about what really makes dogs tick than they did even a decade ago, but this new understanding has been slow to percolate through to owners, and, indeed, has not yet made enough of a difference to the lives of the dogs themselves. Having studied the behaviour of dogs for more than twenty years, as well as enjoying their company, I felt it was time that someone stood up for dogdom: not the caricature of the wolf in a dog suit, ready to dominate its unsuspecting owner at the first sign of weakness, not the trophy animal that collects rosettes and kudos for its breeder, but the real dog, the pet that just wants to be one of the family and enjoy life.

Introduction

The dog has been our faithful companion for tens of thousands of years. Today, dogs live alongside humans all across the globe, often as integral parts of our families. To many people, a world without dogs is unthinkable.

And yet dogs today unwittingly find themselves on the verge of a crisis, struggling to keep up with the ever-increasing pace of change in human society. Until a little over a hundred years ago, most dogs worked for their living. Each of the breeds or types had become well suited, over thousands of years and a corresponding number of generations, to the task for which they were bred. First and foremost, dogs were tools. Their agility and quick thinking, their keen senses and their unparalleled ability to communicate with humans suited them for an extraordinary diversity of tasks, hunting, herding, guarding and many others, each an important component of the economy. In short, dogs had to earn their keep, in one way or another; apart from the few lapdogs that were the playthings of the very rich, the company that dogs must also have provided would have been incidental; rewarding, but not their *raison d'être*. Then, a few dozen dog-generations ago, everything began to change – and these changes are still gathering pace today.

Nowadays, an ever-increasing proportion of dogs are never expected to work in the conventional sense; their sole function is to be family pets. Although many working types have successfully adapted, others were and still are poorly suited to this new role, so it is perhaps surprising that none of the breeds that are most popular as family pets have been specifically and exclusively designed as such. Thus far, dogs have done their best to adjust to the many changes and restrictions we have imposed upon them, in particular our expectation that they will be faithful companions when we need them to be, and unobtrusive when we do not. However, the cracks inherent in this compromise are beginning to widen. As human society continues to change, and the planet becomes ever more crowded, there are signs that the popularity of dogs as pets may have peaked, and that they may struggle to adapt as the current century unfolds, especially in urban environments. After all, dogs, as living beings, cannot be re-engineered every decade or so as if they were computers or cars. In the past, when dogs' functions were mostly rural, it was accepted that they were intrinsically messy and needed to be managed on their own terms. Today, by contrast, many pet dogs live in circumscribed, urban environments, and are expected to be simultaneously better behaved than the average human child and as self-reliant as an adult. As if these new obligations were not enough, many dogs still manifest the adaptations that suited them for their original functions – traits that we now demand they cast away as if they had never existed. The collie that herds sheep is the shepherd's best friend; the pet collie that tries to herd children and chases bicycles is an owner's nightmare. The new, unrealistic standards to which many humans hold their dogs have arisen from one of several fundamental misconceptions about what dogs are, and what they have been designed to do. We must strive to better understand their needs and their nature if their niche in human society is not to diminish.

Our rapidly changing expectations are not the only challenge that dogs face today. The ways in which we now control their reproduction also represent a major challenge to their well-being. For much of human history, dogs were bred to suit the roles that humankind assigned to them – but whether their task was herding, retrieving, guarding or hauling, dogs' stability and functionality were considered far more important than their type or appearance. In the late nineteenth century, however, dogs were divided into self-contained breeds, reproductively isolated from one another, and each assigned a single ideal appearance, or 'standard', by breed societies. For many dogs, this rigid categorization has not worked out well; rather, it has worked against their need to adapt into their new primary role as companions. Most breeders strive not to breed the perfect pet, but to produce the perfect-looking dog that will succeed in the show ring. These winning dogs are considered prized stock, and make a hugely disproportionate genetic contribution to the next generation – resulting in 'pure' breeds whose idealized appearance belies their deteriorated health. In the 1950s, most breeds still had a healthy range of genetic variation; by 2000, only some 20–25 generations later, many had been inbred to the point where hundreds of genetically based deformities, diseases and disadvantages had emerged, potentially compromising the welfare of every pure-bred dog. In the United Kingdom, the growing rift between dog breeders and those concerned with dogs' welfare finally became public in 2008, resulting in the withdrawal of the humane charities – and subsequently that of BBC Television, the event's broadcaster – from Crufts, the country's national dog show. While such protests are a start, the dogs themselves will not feel any benefit until the problems brought about by excessive inbreeding have been reversed, and dogs are bred with their health and role in society, not their looks, in mind.

Ultimately, people will have to change their attitudes if the dog's lot is to improve. So far, however, neither the experts nor the average owner have had their preconceived notions challenged by the wealth of new science that is emerging about dogs. Much of the public debate so far, whether it is about the merits of out-breeding versus inbreeding, or the effectiveness of training methods, has amounted to little more than the statement and restatement of entrenched opinions. This is where scientific understanding becomes essential, for it can tell us what dogs are really like and what their needs really amount to.

Science is an essential tool for understanding dogs, but the contributions of canine science to dog welfare have, unfortunately, been somewhat mixed. Canine science, which originated in the 1950s, sets out to provide a rational perspective on what it is like to be a dog, ostensibly more objective than the traditional human-centred or anthropomorphic view of their natures. Despite this attempt at detachment, however, canine scientists have occasionally misunderstood – and even given others the licence to cause injury to – the very animals whose nature they have endeavoured to reveal.

Science has, unwittingly, done the most damage to dogs by applying the comparative zoology approach to studies of dog behaviour. Comparative zoology is a well-established and generally valuable way of understanding the behaviour and adaptations of one species through comparisons with those of another. Species that are closely related but have different lifestyles can often be better understood through comparative zoology, because differences in the way they look and behave mirror those changes in lifestyle. So too can those species that have come to have similar lives, but are genetically unrelated. This method has been highly successful in helping to disentangle the mechanisms of evolution in general, especially now that similarities and differences in behaviour can be compared with differences between each species' DNA, so as to pinpoint the genetic basis of behaviour.

Yet although the applications of comparative zoology are usually benign, it has done considerable harm to dogs, as one expert after another has interpreted their behaviour as if it were, under the surface, little altered from that of their ancestor, the wolf. Wolves, which have generally been portrayed as vicious animals, constantly striving for dominance over every other member of their own kind, have been held up as the only credible model for understanding the behaviour of dogs.[1] This supposition leads inevitably to the misconception that every dog is constantly trying to control its owner – unless its owner is relentless in keeping it in check. The conflation of dog and wolf behaviour is still widely promoted in books and on television programmes, but recent research on both dogs and wolves has shown not only that it is simply unfounded, but also that dogs that do come into conflict with their owners are usually motivated by anxiety, not a surfeit of ambition. Since this fundamental misunderstanding has crept into almost every theory of dog behaviour, it will be the first to be addressed in this book.

Despite the misapplication of comparative zoology, more recent scientific discoveries could, if applied properly, benefit dogs considerably. Although canine science went into eclipse in the 1970s and 1980s, the 1990s saw a resurgence, which has continued to the present day. After nearly fifty years of almost total neglect, this extraordinary uplift in scientific interest in the domestic dog has been driven partly by the increasing role that dogs play in detecting substances such as explosives, drugs and other illicit substances (which they still sniff out more effectively than any machine), and the attendant realization that we need to understand better how dogs perform these tasks. It has also been due to a few primatologists turning their attention from the chimpanzee to the domestic dog, in an attempt to gain fresh insights into the way that animal and human minds work. A further contribution has come from veterinarians and other clinicians who wish to improve the therapies available for treating dogs with behavioural disorders. Finally, it should not be forgotten that many biologists are dog-lovers too. Once the professional stigma of working on a so-called 'artificial animal' has been overcome, such scientists are often keen to apply their skills to improving dogs' lives.

By further pulling back the curtain on dogs' inner lives, the new school of canine science has the potential to provide the average dog owner with new ways of thinking about – and relating to – their pet. Thanks to the efforts of this new community of scientists, we now have a vastly improved insight into how dogs' minds work, how they gather and interpret information about the world around them, and how they react emotionally to varying situations. Some of this research has revealed startling differences between dogs and people, suggesting that it is both desirable and possible for dog owners to 'think dog', rather than simply assuming that, whatever they themselves are sensing and feeling, their dog must be sensing and feeling too.

Although the new science of dog behaviour has the potential to put the dog's role in human society back on track, little of the research has been made available outside obscure academic texts until now. In this book, I attempt to translate for the general reader – and dog-lover – the exciting new developments in canine science. Doing so requires me to overturn a great deal of conventional wisdom about dogs and how we should interact with them. In the first half of the book, I show that the most up-to-date account of the dog's origins, while confirming that the wolf is indeed the dog's only ancestor, reveals an image of the dog's nature very different from what seemed to be the case only two decades ago. Dogs may be constructed from wolf DNA, but this does not mean that they are compelled to behave or think like wolves; indeed, domestication has changed dogs' minds and behaviour to the point where such comparisons can become a hindrance, rather than an aid, to any genuine understanding of our pets.

The new science of dog behaviour has dramatic implications for humans, and for our choice of the best and most humane ways to train our dogs. A word of caution here, though: this book is not a training manual. Rather, its purpose is to show where modern ideas about dog training have come from, so that owners themselves can effectively evaluate whether the training manuals or trainers they have chosen really know what they are talking about.

After revising the story of the dog's origins, I explore what might loosely be referred to as dogs' 'brainpower'. Scientists have recently turned their attention to the kinds of beliefs that owners have about their dogs' emotional and intellectual capabilities, and their findings are showing how accurate – but also how mistaken – these beliefs can be. It is an integral part of human nature to attribute feelings not just to animals, but also to inanimate objects – to speak, for example, of 'an angry sky' or 'the cruel sea' – and yet, until a few decades ago, it was anybody's guess as to what emotions different kinds of animals might have. Many scientists, moreover, used to regard emotions as simply too subjective to be accessible to serious study. While animal intelligence has been studied for over a century, hardly anyone considered dogs worthy of study until perhaps the end of the twentieth century. Since then, research has significantly changed the ways in which we think about dogs' minds. The new canine science reveals that dogs are both smarter and dumber than we instinctively think they are. For example, they have an almost uncanny ability to guess what humans are about to do, because of their extreme sensitivity to our body-language, but they are also trapped in the moment, incapable of projecting the consequences of their actions backwards or forwards in time. If owners were able to appreciate their dogs' intelligence and emotional life for what it actually is, rather than for what they imagine it to be, then dogs would not just be better understood; they would be better treated as well.

Just as canine science can inform human attitudes about dogs' minds, it can also tell us how dogs experience and interpret the world around them. Physically speaking, a dog and its owner live in the same house, visit the same park together for exercise, travel in the same car, meet the same friends and acquaintances. However, the types of information arriving at the dog's brain and the owner's brain in each of those situations are profoundly different. We are visual creatures; dogs primarily rely on their sense of smell. We refer to high-pitched noises that we cannot hear (for example, the squeaking of bats) as 'ultrasound'; dogs would, if they could, scoff at our inability to hear such sounds, which they pick up perfectly. To fully appreciate our dogs' world, we need science to tell us what they can and cannot detect, what they find pleasant and what they would object to if they could. For example, I do not suppose your dog has ever been bothered by the colours you have chosen to decorate your house, but his or her delicate nose was very likely insulted by the odour of the drying paint.

Although our lack of understanding of dogs' nature often compromises their well-being, such offences pale into insignificance beside the problems we have generated for pedigree dogs through excessive inbreeding. Rigid breed standards encourage breeders to eliminate all traits that do not fit the 'perfect' type. In theory this should allow breeders to select for traits that would create healthy and well-adjusted, if rather uniform, animals, but in practice it has led to the appearance of a extensive and widespread range of inherited defects that compromise the welfare of large numbers of dogs in many breeds. Science, thankfully, can help to get dog breeding back on track. While it is beyond the scope of this book to provide a detailed manual of canine genetics, the penultimate chapter addresses the underlying principles that breeders should be following, emphasizing what it is about pedigree breeding that directly affects dogs' well-being.

In the final chapters of the book, I look at how science can help dogs to adjust to twenty-first-century life. Currently, most of the attention given to dogs' breeding has focused on endowing them with superficial, rather than practical, traits. Many pet dogs are essentially breeders' rejects, deemed unlikely to reach the perfection demanded by the breed standard; puppies that look as though they are never going to become champions in the show ring are the ones most likely to become pets. Surely the needs of the pet dog deserve more attention than that? As dog owners and dog lovers, we need to think constructively about how to breed dogs whose primary purpose is not to herd sheep, retrieve game, or win prizes at dog shows – but rather to be rewarding, obedient, healthy, happy family pets.

In writing this book, I have tried to promote a greater understanding and appreciation of the special place that dogs hold in human society. If these aims can be achieved, they should go a long way towards sustaining and reinforcing our relationship with our beloved companions as the next decades unfold.

In Defence of Dogs

I

Where Dogs Came From

'The wolf in your living room' is a powerful image that reminds dog owners that their trusted companion is, under the skin, an animal, not a person. Dogs are indeed wolves, at least as far as their DNA is concerned; the two animals share 99.96 per cent of their genes. Following the same logic, you might just as well say that wolves are dogs – but, surprisingly, no one does. Wolves are generally portrayed as wild, ancestral and primeval, whereas dogs tend to be cast in the role of the wolf's artificial, controlled, subservient derivative. Yet dogs are, in terms of sheer numbers, far more successful in the modern world than wolves. So, what do we gain from knowing that wolves and dogs share a common ancestor? Many books, articles and television programmes about dog behaviour have claimed that understanding the wolf is the key to understanding the domestic dog. I disagree. My view is that the key to understanding the domestic dog is, first and foremost, to understand the domestic dog, and it is a view I share with an increasing number of scientists worldwide. By analysing the dog as its own animal rather than as a lesser version of the wolf, we have the opportunity to understand it – and refine our dealings with it – as never before.

To be sure, it is undeniable that dogs share many of their basic characteristics with other members of the Dog family (the Canidae) of which the wolf is a part. Dogs evolved from canids, and they owe such qualities as their basic anatomy, their refined sense of smell, their ability to retrieve and their capacity to form lasting social bonds to this evolution. To some extent, then, comparing dogs to their wild ancestors can be illuminating – but when the wolf is taken as the only available point of reference, our understanding of dogs suffers.

At the most fundamental level, dogs are unique because, unlike wolves or other canids, they have adapted to live alongside human beings, the result of the process of domestication. As dogs have been altered by domestication, many of the subtleties and sophistications of wolf behaviour appear to have been stripped away, leaving an animal that is still recognizably a canid, but no longer a wolf. Domestication has altered the dog considerably, more than any other species. It is self-evident that dogs come in a wide range of shapes and sizes; indeed, there is actually more size variation among domestic dogs than in the whole of the rest of the Dog family put together. Yet this is by no means the only profound effect of domestication. Perhaps the most important one, for both us and our dogs, is their ability to bond with us and understand us, to an extent that no other animal can match. Understanding what has happened during domestication is therefore a key element in understanding the dog.

To understand the domestic dog fully, we need to look beyond the process of domestication – beyond even the wolf – to examine the dog's entire history. We need to know where the dog came from and what all its ancestors were like, not just its closest living relative, the wolf. Of course, it is ultimately impossible for us to know precisely how the domestic dog's ancestors behaved, whether we are examining its immediate forebears (wolves that lived more than 10,000 years ago) or its more distant ancestors (social canids, the precursors of the wolf, in the Pliocene era several million years ago). They are all extinct. We can, however, get some idea of how they might have behaved by examining the range of behaviour that is characteristic of today's social canids. Indeed, a detailed examination of the behaviour of those species would not only shed light on to the dog's earliest ancestors, but also help us to work out why it was that, apart from the wolf, none of the canids was successfully and permanently domesticated.

DNA analysis leaves us in no doubt that the dog is descended only (or at least almost entirely) from the grey wolf, *Canis lupus*. The first comprehensive sequencing of the maternal DNA of dogs, wolves, coyotes and jackals, published in 1997, produced no evidence that dogs had ancestors in any species other than the grey wolf.[1] None of the dozens of investigations performed since then have contradicted this; however, there is still a relative lack of data on paternal DNA, which is more difficult to analyse, so it is still possible that a few types of dog could claim descent from other canids through their paternal line.

Genetically, dogs and wolves have a great deal in common; but the mere fact that two species have considerable overlap in their DNA does not mean that their behaviour will be the same. Indeed, many animals with similar DNA are drastically different from one another, especially in terms of behaviour. We know this thanks to the DNA 'revolution', which has led to the sequencing of the genomes of humans, canines, felines and an increasing number of other species. Many of these sequences exhibit a remarkable degree of similarity. For example, your DNA and your dog's are identical for about 25 per cent of their length, which is perhaps not surprising given that you are both mammals – roughly the same 25 per cent is also found in mice. The other 75 per cent accounts for why dogs, mice and people look – and behave – very differently from one another.

Species that are much more closely related to one another than we are to dogs can share almost their entire DNA sequences, and it is tempting to assume that they must therefore be restricted to the same range of behaviour. But DNA does not control behaviour directly; rather, it specifies the structure of proteins and other constituents of cells, and a tiny change in DNA can lead to a huge change in behaviour. For example, there is no 'blueprint' for the brain; each nerve cell in the brain emerges out of interactions between thousands of DNA sequences. A change in one 'letter' in those sequences could have an enormous effect on the way the brain functions, or none at all – we simply do not know enough yet about how DNA and behaviour interact. Take two closely related apes: the chimpanzee and the bonobo. Common chimps share 99.6 per cent of their DNA with bonobos, and yet the social behaviour of these two kinds of great ape could not be more different. Common chimps are omnivorous, often hunting other kinds of monkey, and their social groups are based on coalitions between males, which are highly aggressive to outsiders and may even murder them if they get the chance. Bonobos, on the other hand, are vegetarian, live in societies centred on groups of related females, rarely show aggression, and have never been seen to murder in the wild. Genetically almost identical, the two species are vastly different in behaviour.

Like bonobos and chimpanzees, dogs and grey wolves share most of their DNA – but there seems little reason to presume that, based on this fact, they must inevitably share the same social systems as well. In fact, domestication appears to have dissolved away much of the detail of wolf-specific behaviour in dogs, leaving them with a behavioural repertoire that has much in common with that of slightly more distantly related species, such as the coyote *Canis latrans*, and even some more distant relatives in the same family, such as the golden jackal *Canis aureus*.

Even to early biologists, the differences between dogs' behaviour and that of wolves were obvious. Many of these differences are manifested socially: dogs, for instance, are clearly not pack animals (even when they form groups these do not behave in a coherent way), and they are much more adept than wolves are at forming relationships with people. Over the years, many eminent biologists, including Nobel Prize-winner Konrad Lorenz and even Charles Darwin himself, have been struck by the flexibility of the dog's behaviour, as well as by the enormous size difference between the smallest and largest breeds. Both suggested that domestic dogs must be some kind of hybrid between two or even several of the canids. Lorenz, in his charming book *Man Meets Dog*, was convinced that wolves were far too independent in nature to explain the indiscriminate friendliness shown by many dogs, and proposed that most of the breeds that had originated in Europe were predominantly jackal in origin. He later retracted this idea, having realized that there was no evidence for spontaneous cross-breeding between dogs and jackals (as readily happens between dogs and wolves), and that the details of jackal behaviour did not fit that of the dogs (the jackal's howl, for example, is nothing like any dog's).

Despite these scientists' best efforts to determine why dogs are so different from wolves in their behaviour, the puzzle was not resolved, and remains largely unanswered to this day. Yet perhaps some clues can be gathered if we look further back in evolutionary time, thinking of our domestic dog as a product not of one species, the grey wolf, but of a whole family, the Canidae (also referred to as the Dog family, but they will be 'canids' here to avoid confusion with the domestic dog). Many of the canid species have sophisticated social lives, which – when they overlap with those of dogs – can potentially shed light on the origins of dog behaviour; coyotes, for instance, are more promiscuous than wolves, a characteristic shared with dogs. Although the behavioural traits of other canids are not as well understood or well publicized as those of the grey wolf, they nevertheless have a great deal to tell us about when – and how – dog behaviour may have originated.

Tracing the canids back to their origins reveals that their social intelligence was probably one of the early traits that set dogs' ancient ancestors apart. Canids probably first evolved some 6 million years ago in North America, where they eventually replaced another type of dog-like mammal, the borophagine. This was a large, hyena-like animal that specialized in scavenging and had massive bone-crushing jaws to match. The original canids, which probably looked more like foxes than dogs, must have been little Davids to the cumbersome borophagine Goliaths, out-competing them in speed, cunning and intelligence, and ultimately helping to drive them to extinction. If we then fast-forward a mere 1.5 million years, we find that the surviving canids had spread all over the world, and split into several types, one of which was the ancestor of today's dogs, wolves and jackals – collectively referred to as *Canis*.[2] Subsequently, further diversification produced three strands of evolution, any one of which could potentially have culminated in a domestic animal, for there is nothing in the behaviour of any of the canid lineages to suggest that they could not have produced an animal that was suitable for domestication. Indeed it is likely that at least two of the three did produce domestic animals, and entirely possible that the wolf was not the only species in its lineage to be domesticated.

The first evolutionary break within the *Canis* genus occurred in North America, and eventually (about 1 million years ago) gave rise to today's coyote, still confined to that continent. Another group emerged in South America, where they live to this day, and are classified as *Dusicyon* rather than *Canis*. Rather misleadingly, they are collectively known as South American foxes, though they are only distantly related to the much better known red fox of hunting fame. The other six species of *Canis* all evolved in the Old World, most likely in Eurasia, although some possibly in Africa. Four of these are jackals, although one of these, the Simien jackal, is sometimes confusingly referred to as the Ethiopian wolf; they include the golden jackal that Lorenz thought might have been the origin of some breeds of dog. Another is the grey wolf *Canis lupus*, the ancestor of our domestic dogs. Of the Eurasian canids, only the grey wolf reached North America, migrating across the Bering land bridge some 100,000 years ago during one of the periods when Alaska was joined to Asia.

Many of these species superficially seem to be potential candidates for domestication, thanks to a number of social tools that they share with the domestic dog. All can, when conditions are favourable, live in family groups or 'packs'. All seem to be able to adapt their lifestyles – specifically, whether they live alone or in small or large groups – to the circumstances they find themselves in.[3] (Nowadays, the most important such 'circumstance' is often the activities of our own species, whether direct persecution, or incidental provision of food at rubbish-dumps.) The current consensus is that the canid genome is rather like a Swiss Army knife,[4] a social toolkit that has remained resistant to evolutionary change and which can be used to cope with a wide variety of circumstances, ranging from solitary living when times are hard, to complex societies when food is plentiful and persecution is at a minimum. The success of the domestic dog in adapting so successfully to life with humans can therefore be seen not as a specific set of changes that began only with the grey wolf, but rather as a new use for this ancient canid social toolkit – one that allowed the dog to socialize not just with other members of the same species, but also with members of ours.

While we are now certain that the grey wolf is the domestic dog's one and only direct ancestor, the dog shares its earlier ancestors with many other still-living relatives, each of whom may offer us a new perspective on these ancient forebears. The dog's lineage, after all, goes back much further than that of the grey wolf, to canids that are now extinct, but were themselves the ancestors of all of today's living canids Each of the latter has something to tell us about the ways that canids can adapt to fit different circumstances – that is, how they construct their social groups – and therefore each provides a different set of clues as to what the canid 'toolkit' may have looked like, as it emerged some 5 million years ago. As all of these canids carry the same 'toolkit', the fact that none apart from the wolf has been permanently domesticated will also need to be accounted for.

The golden jackal, *Canis aureus*, is one of the dog's most social relatives, and therefore a seemingly ideal candidate for domestication. It is the only jackal to be found in the Fertile Crescent, the cradle of civilization, where many other domestications, including sheep, goats and cattle, occurred; all the other jackals are restricted to Africa. Like many of the other canids, the golden jackal shows considerable flexibility in its social arrangements. A few hunt alone, but most live in male-female pairs, often bonding for life, which in practice can be six to eight years. If one partner dies, the other rarely finds a new mate. Very often, some of the first litter that a pair produces will stay with their parents until the next litter is born the following year, and will then help to bring them up, before leaving to find their own mates a few months later. They protect the young at the den while their parents are off hunting or, if they catch something themselves, will often bring it back to share with the cubs. Cubs are more likely to survive if their elder brothers and sisters stay on to help, so their contribution is valuable. Jackals often hunt in pairs, enabling them to tackle larger prey than they could alone, and sometimes the helpers may hunt with them to make up a pack of three or four. The family members have a rich vocabulary for communicating with one another, just as wolves do. Based on its wealth of social skills, there seems little reason why the golden jackal could not have become domesticated as the grey wolf did.

Golden jackals

In fact, a recent archaeological find provides hints that the golden jackal may, indeed, have been domesticated in Turkey. Gobekli Tepe, an Early Neolithic hilltop site to the south-east of that country, appears to be a temple, an arrangement of huge stones erected a staggering 11,000 years ago, more than twice as old as Stonehenge. These stones, which predate agriculture and metal tools, are covered in highly stylized carvings of people, animals and birds. Some of the stones are T-shaped, with the head of the T representing the head of a person, and the upright part the body. Many of the animals portrayed are potentially menacing – lions, snakes, spiders, vultures, scorpions. The absence of domesticated animals is unsurprising; these stones were carved by hunter-gatherers, long before any animal was domesticated

A T-shaped stone pillar, thought to represent a man's head and torso, at Gobekli Tepe, an archaeological site on the borders of modern Turkey and Syria. The arm carved into the vertical stone appears to be holding a canid.

for food. A few of the carvings clearly depict dog-like animals, which archaeologists have labelled as foxes, just another sort of potentially harmful animal. Yet on one stone, a 'fox' is depicted in the crook of a man's arm, more the place for a pet than an enemy, making it unlikely that the drawing depicts a red fox, as that animal is solitary and therefore a very unlikely candidate for domestication. And although it is hard to be sure, the carving does not look much like a wolf, either; its fox-like features and bushy tail make it much more likely to be a jackal, and the only jackal native to that area is the golden jackal. Perhaps Konrad Lorenz's idea of a jackal origin for dogs was only half wrong: maybe jackals were domesticated once, more than 10,000 years ago, but were less well adapted to living with humans than wolves were, and so died out or returned to the wild.

To find a similar example of a failed domestication, but one that survived into recorded history, we need to travel to South America. Coincidentally, this example also involves a 'fox', one of a group of fox-like dogs that evolved in South America some 3 million years ago. One of these, the culpeo fox *Dusicyon culpaeus*, was domesticated – or at least tamed (living with people, but still only breeding in the wild). These animals came to be known as Aguara dogs. At the end of the eighteenth century, the English soldier turned scientist and explorer Charles Hamilton Smith noted that these dogs could be found in hunter-gatherer villages. They would accompany the men on hunting trips, although they appear not to have made themselves particularly useful, and would often come home on their own after a few hours. In the villages they would scavenge for food, or go off on short hunting expeditions of their own, where they would eat almost anything they could find, including fish, crabs, limpets, lizards, toads and snakes. By the middle of the nineteenth century, however, Aguara dogs had disappeared, replaced by the much more biddable and useful dogs that the Europeans had brought with them to the continent. It is difficult to work out why the Aguara dog did not progress to full domestication, because very little is known about the habits of its wild ancestor, the culpeo fox. However, none of the South American foxes regularly form groups of more than two, so it is likely that their social abilities were simply too undeveloped to be adapted to include relationships with humans.

Culpeo fox

In North America, the most likely candidate for domestication, apart from the immigrant grey wolf, is the coyote (*Canis latrans*). The traditional image of this member of the dog family is that of a solitary hunter, but the coyote is in fact a highly social animal, whose appetite for livestock has led it to be persecuted by humans. Left to their own devices, coyotes live in pairs, and, as with the golden jackal, these can turn into small packs when one year's offspring remain with their parents to assist with the next litter. This is most likely to be possible when large prey, such as elk and white-tailed deer, are available, providing both the necessity and the opportunity for the coyotes to hunt as a pack. In this, they may rival the wolf in terms of the sophistication of their social lives; nevertheless, neither they nor, as we shall see, the wolves of North America, ever appear to have been domesticated. The reason may simply be that by the time humans colonized North America they already had dogs and thus no need for any alternative. It is possible, however, that some coyote genes have found their way into modern American dogs. The reverse has certainly happened, inasmuch as about 10 per cent of 'wild' coyotes carry genes from domestic dogs.

Although it is possible that these are the progeny of matings between female coyotes and male dogs, it is unlikely that a domestic dog would be sufficiently bold to impress a wild coyote bitch. More likely, they are the result of male coyotes forcing themselves on female dogs, whose puppies then escaped and joined the local coyote population. The more tractable of these offspring might have subsequently bred with other dogs, inserting coyote genes permanently into the dog population.

A family of coyotes

Finally, our journey takes us to Africa, the birthplace of our own species, and an area in which domestication would therefore seem highly plausible. This continent is rich in canids, including four species of jackal (the golden jackal among them), as well as the African wild dog, undoubtedly a rival for the grey wolf's claim to be the most sociable of the canids. The African wild dog's packs are larger than the wolf's; up to fifty individuals have been seen hunting together, although the typical number of adults in a pack is eight. In the open grasslands which the African wild dog favours, co-operative hunting is essential for survival. Only a pack can defend kills against other large predators, such as lions and hyenas. (Not that African wild dogs are particularly small themselves – they are the size of a small German shepherd, but with a brindled coat and huge upright ears.) After they have made a kill, the food is shared amicably between all pack members; if there are cubs back in the den, each dog will eat more than usual and regurgitate some to feed the young upon returning home.

A pack of African wild dogs

For most of the year, relationships between the members of a pack of African wild dogs are friendly. Every morning and evening, they engage in a greeting ritual, running around excitedly, thrusting their noses into each other's faces (a mimicry of the begging behaviour that they used when they were cubs), and producing a squeaking noise that make them sound more like a troop of monkeys than a pack of dogs. Once the adults have become sufficiently hyped up by all this chatter, they run off together on the hunt. Pack members will occasionally quarrel with one another, but serious fighting is rare – until one of the females comes into season. When she is ready to mate, the dominant female becomes seriously aggressive towards the other adult females, and it is not unknown for her to inflict serious injuries on them. As a result, she is usually the only female in the pack to produce a litter each year; if one of the other females also produces a litter, the dominant female may try to kill her cubs, though sometimes all the cubs get mixed up together and both mothers look after them.

Despite this occasional violence within groups of African wild dogs, the high level of co-operation in wild-dog packs suggests that they should be easy to domesticate. For example, they have a complex vocabulary of vocalizations – twitters, begging cries, gurgles, yelps, squeals, whimpers, whines, moans, 'hoo's, growls and barks — that would seem ideally suited for communication with such a vocal species as ourselves, far more so than the rather more taciturn wolf. Yet there seems to be no evidence that any attempt was ever made to domesticate this species. Considered in the broader context of domestication as a whole, however, this failure may be less surprising. Despite mankind having evolved in Africa and therefore having a much longer history there than anywhere else, almost all the significant domestications of animals have taken place on other continents. It has been suggested that the human race needed to get outside its evolutionary 'comfort zone' before becoming sufficiently motivated to domesticate animals (or indeed plants). Perhaps the African wild dog was simply in the wrong place to become part of our world.

While the histories of the canids vary from place to place and species to species, two of the dog's distant cousins – the golden jackal and the South American culpeo fox – provide tantalizing glimpses of domestications that seem to have been begun but never completed. Each occurred on a different continent – one in Eurasia, the other in South America – and in very different societies. This points again to the importance of the 5-million-year-old canid 'toolkit' – a flexible sociality, a good nose, expertise in hunting – as being the key to the suitability of canids for domestication. And yet neither of these experiments in domestication was, in the long run, successful.

Domestications only occur when a human need meets a suitable species, and the need is backed up by sufficient resources to see the process through. Such conditions seem to occur only very rarely, as attested by the tiny number of mammalian species that mankind has fully domesticated, a number which barely scrapes into double figures. It seems entirely possible that all the species discussed so far could have been domesticated, except that the conditions for domestication were never as ideal, or could not be sustained for long enough, as those of the domestic dog.

*

Finally, we must turn to the grey wolf, as the only one of the canids to have been domesticated successfully – if by successfully we mean surviving into the modern world. Indeed, the domestic dog is very successful: the 400 million or so dogs in the world outnumber wolves over a thousandfold. A few hundred years ago there were probably about 5 million wolves in the world; today there are only 150,000 to 300,000. If we set aside the artificial distinction of 'domestication' for a moment, we could say that the wolf has evolved into the dog, leaving behind a few, highly totemic vestiges of its past that hang on by a thread in the wild. Some wolves were able to take advantage of man's domination of the globe, and became dogs. Others were not, and stayed wolves.

A family of grey wolves

No account of dog behaviour can afford to ignore the wolf, if only because many books on dogs place such emphasis on the dog's wolf-like nature – but wolves themselves have, as it turns out, been fundamentally misunderstood. A great deal has been written about the grey wolf, but much of that is either misconceived, or at least unhelpful when it comes to understanding the behaviour of modern domestic dogs. In the past, the wolf has been portrayed as the quintessential pack animal, and its packs have been portrayed as being essentially despotic, rigidly and aggressively controlled by an alpha pair. Logically, therefore, as a descendant of the wolf, the dog was thought to be the same under the skin, undoubtedly less aggressive in nature but nevertheless born with the expectation that it must eventually seek to 'dominate' all those around it, canine and human alike. The past decade has seen a radical reappraisal of the wolf pack, however – regarding both how it constructs itself, and the evolutionary forces that drive it. Our conception of the dog is therefore overdue for revision. If wolves are not despots, as we now know, then why should we assume that domestic dogs are impelled to take control of their owners?

Like most other canids, grey wolves are highly social animals, and have a strong preference for living in groups. This is not to say that individuals do not live alone from time to time, but it is not usually from choice. A lone wolf may have been driven out of its pack, or may have been forced to forage on its own when there was not enough food available to feed two wolves travelling together. But wherever possible wolves try to live collectively. Even wolves that scavenge from rubbish-dumps do so in groups, usually with between three and five members. (The wildcat, the domestic cat's ancestor, has also occasionally been observed feeding on rubbish, but always alone.) It is undoubtedly this thirst for company that, among other factors, made it possible for wolves to be domesticated.

Although they are fundamentally sociable animals, wolves are also remarkably adaptable when it comes to their living arrangements – another trait that, perhaps even more than sociability itself, makes them especially good candidates for domestication. Wolves come together when local conditions permit, and go their own ways in times of adversity. They can live alone or in small groups; when conditions are right, larger groups comprising from six to ten adults can form. As a rule, these larger groups occur only when the main prey available is also large, typically moose, caribou or bison. Although a solitary wolf could probably kill a caribou, especially one that was old, young or sick, the wolf would risk getting injured itself, and would thus be more apt to seek smaller, less dangerous prey. Pack hunting is most likely a safer and more efficient way of hunting large animals, but this appears not to be the key to why packs can exist. What is probably more important in determining the formation of large packs is that a kill of one of these large animals provides far more food than a single wolf could consume. In summer, when alternative prey is often available, these larger packs tend to fragment into smaller units, perhaps coming back together again in autumn. It is flexibility such as this that is now seen as a second crucial factor allowing wolves – at least, a few of them – to adapt to living with humans.

The nature of wolf packs is crucial to understanding the social behaviour of wolves, and thus the behavioural inheritance of domestic dogs, but until recently wolf packs have been wrongly thought of as competitive organizations. It is now known that the majority of wolf 'packs' are simply family groups. Typically, a solitary male will pair up with a solitary female – either or both will most likely have recently left a pack – and raise a litter together. In many species the young leave or are chased away when they are old enough to fend for themselves, but not so in wolves. Provided that no one is starving, the cubs may stay with their parents until they are fully grown. Once they are experienced enough, they will participate fully in hunting, and thus a pack emerges. Often the younger members will still be part of the pack when the next litter of cubs is born, and will help their parents to raise their brothers and sisters, bringing food back for them and babysitting them when the other members of the pack are out hunting. Contrary to many notions of wolf behaviour, co-operation, not dominance, seems to be the essence of the wolf pack.

Modern biology demands explanations for the seemingly selfless behaviour exhibited by the younger adult wolves operating within a pack. Logically speaking, a gene that influences one animal to help another to breed should die out, since it will be the animals not carrying the 'unselfish' version of the gene that will leave the most offspring. Co-operative breeding must therefore have long-term advantages that outweigh its disadvantages. Biologists have been arguing for the past five decades as to what the finer points of those advantages might be and how they are expressed, but the theory of kin selection, first proposed in the 1960s, robustly accounts for why co-operative breeding is much more likely to occur in families than in random assemblages of individuals.

By ascribing a benefit to the co-operation observed within wolf packs, scientists have been able to use the theory of kin selection to make sense of behaviour that would otherwise be unintelligible. Offering co-operation to an unrelated animal carries risks, even in animals as smart as wolves; there is a danger, after all, that the favour may not be returned. On the other hand, performing a favour for a close relative, say a son or a daughter, has genetic advantages; even if that favour is never returned, the helper is still promoting the survival of some of his or her own genes, specifically those versions that are identical in their relative. (In a son or daughter there will be a 50 per cent overlap, the other half coming from the other parent.) This advantage does not seem sufficient to promote lifelong abstinence from breeding – the only mammals which exhibit such abstinence are naked mole-rats, which burrow beneath harsh deserts where a single breeding pair is unlikely to survive for long, even with the others' help. Nevertheless, kin selection does seem to be powerful enough to sustain temporary abdication from breeding, making it worthwhile for offspring to help their parents until the family group gets too large to sustain itself, and the offspring leave to start families of their own.

Kin selection explains that, when the younger members of the pack appear to deliberately put their own breeding rights to one side, they are actually acting in their own interest – but the advantages of this behaviour are not purely familial. In addition to the advantage they gain from kin selection, it is also safer for the wolves themselves not to leave their pack while they are still young. Their lack of experience means that their chances of forming their own pack are actually rather slim. This accounts for the rare occasions when unrelated wolves have been recorded as joining existing packs; they often seem to be recruited as a replacement when one of the most experienced members of the pack, maybe one of the original founders, leaves or dies.

Packs that form naturally, in the wild, are usually harmonious entities, with aggression being the exception rather than the norm. As in any family, there are occasional conflicts of interest within wolf packs, but in general the parents have to do very little to keep their grown-up young in order. The young are essentially volunteers – they could leave the family and set up on their own, but they choose not to, preferring to stay safely within the family unit until they are older and more experienced, and hence more likely to survive the risks of finding a mate and a new place to live. They regularly reinforce their bond with their parents, and at the same time reassure them that they are helpers, not rivals, by performing a special ritual. The youngster crouches slightly as it approaches the parent, ears back and close to its head, and tail held low and wagging. It then nuzzles the side of the parent's face, an imitation of the food-soliciting behaviour that it used when it was a cub. (This is very similar to the greeting ritual of the African wild dog, and so possibly a very ancient canid behaviour, predating the evolution of both wolf and wild dog.)

The image of a harmonious pack is not the picture of wolf society that you will find in most books on dog behaviour. Wolf biologists originally based most of their ideas on captive packs, which were easy to observe. Some of these packs were random assemblies of unrelated individuals, while others were fragments of packs, usually with one or both of the parents missing – basically composed of whatever individuals were available for the zoo to make an exhibit. What almost all of these packs had in common was that their structure had been irrevocably disrupted by captivity, so that the wolves were thrown into a state of confusion and conflict. Moreover, unless their human captors decided to separate them, none had the opportunity to leave. As a result, the relationships that emerged were based not on long-established trust, but on rivalry and aggression.

The true picture of wolf society emerged only as wolves became protected, allowing packs to form and thrive over several years, without becoming fragmented by continual persecution. At roughly the same time, better technology for tracking and observing wolves in the wild became available: GPS, miniature radio transmitters with batteries robust enough to allow tracking over a whole season, and so on. Within a decade, descriptions of wolf society had changed from the image of the hierarchical pack run by two tyrants, one male, one female, to that of the harmonious family group, where, barring accidents, the younger adults in the family voluntarily assisted their parents in raising their younger brothers and sisters. Coercion was replaced by co-operation as the underlying principle.

This radical change in our conception of pack behaviour has required that we also reappraise the social signals that wolves use. Under zoo conditions, signals that wolf parents would normally use to remind their offspring to co-operate instead became the precursors of out-and-out fighting, and were labelled 'dominance indicators'. Similarly, the cohesive behaviours that the adult young wolves would normally use to bond with their parents were now being used in desperate attempts to avoid conflict, and so came to be labelled as 'submission'.

Contrary to long-standing theories of wolf behaviour, it is now believed that 'submissive' behaviour may be nothing of the sort. An effective 'submissive' display should, by definition, indicate to an attacker that the attack is not worth pursuing – and, indeed, when wolves from two different packs happen to meet, the smaller one will try to avoid being attacked by performing such a display. This rarely works, however, and if the smaller wolf fails to run away, it will be attacked and often killed by the larger. Wolves from different packs have no common interests; they compete for food and are probably only very distantly related, if at all. Nevertheless, if the 'submissive' display was truly an indication of submission, it ought to work in these circumstances, since the attacking wolf is putting itself at risk of injury, even if it wins. The fact that this display does not work under these circumstances indicates that it is not a 'submissive' display at all. Moreover, when it is performed between members of the same family, for the most part it is not preceded by any form of threat from the recipient. Rather, it usually appears spontaneously, reinforcing the bond between the members of the pack. Only in artificially constituted 'packs', kept in zoos, do 'submissive' displays come to be a standard response to threat. Presumably the younger, weaker wolves learn by trial and error that such displays (sometimes) work under these unnatural circumstances, where pack loyalties have been totally disrupted, and there is nowhere for them to escape to.

Wolves perform two signals that used to be labelled 'submissive': 'active' and 'passive'. Domestic dogs perform very similar signals, and these, too, are conventionally referred to as 'active submission' and 'passive submission'. One might expect that any reinterpretation of these signals in the wolf would have been quickly followed by a reappraisal of what they mean when performed by dogs, but this has been slow to happen.

*A wolf (*left*) performing the affiliation display*

The 'active' display is the more common of the two in wolves, and rather than being a sign of submission, is in fact a bonding signal that scientists now refer to – much more appropriately – as the 'affiliation display'. In the affiliation display, the wolf approaches with a low posture, holding its tail low; its ears are pulled slightly back, and its tail and hindquarters wag enthusiastically. This display forms part of what is called the 'group ceremony', which occurs when the pack reassembles, or as a precursor to a hunting trip. Under these circumstances it can be performed by the parents (the so-called 'alphas') as well as by their offspring, confirming its role as a mechanism whereby affectionate bonds are reinforced. It is actually difficult to work out how this display was ever labelled as 'submissive' behaviour. A wolf performing the affiliation display is actually in rather a good position to attack its recipient – a swift twist of the head and it could sink its teeth into the other's throat. Therefore accepting the performance of the affiliation display is, if anything, more of an expression of trust on the recipient's part than on the performer's. It is undeniable that the younger members of the family perform the affiliation display towards their parents much more frequently than vice versa, but this is typical of all parent–offspring relationships, and does not mean that the offspring are allowing themselves to be 'dominated' by their parents. Indeed, it simply reflects the asymmetry of the relationship between parents and offspring. These are the only parents that the young wolves will ever have, and therefore their attachment is total. The parents may – indeed probably do – have other offspring, so their attachment to each cub must unavoidably be a shared one.

Also in urgent need of reinterpretation is the wolf's other, less common submissive display, 'passive submission'. Unlike the affiliation display, this may be an actual sign of submission, one that is derived from an infantile behaviour, in which cubs roll over to allow their mother to groom their belly and stimulate urination, which the cubs cannot yet do on their own. This display, which seems to have been adopted by adults as a way of deflecting possible attack, involves one wolf lying down, rolling on to its back, and exposing its abdomen for inspection by another. Some wolf biologists now refer to it as the 'belly-up display', which is more descriptive and presumes nothing about its function. Nevertheless, this display has precisely the characteristics that one would expect of submission, since the wolf that performs it is placing itself in a position where it is at the mercy of the other.

The belly-up display

In wolves, the belly-up display is much rarer than the affiliation display, and is more commonly seen in captive wolves than in the wild. When observed in zoos, it is most likely to be performed by wolves that are on the fringes of the captive 'packs', are often involved in fights, and rarely participate in group-howls. These are the very wolves that would almost certainly have gone off on their own if the fence surrounding their enclosure had not been there.[5] Continually stressed by being forced to remain in close quarters with other wolves that threaten to attack them at every turn, these outcasts will try any tactic that might deflect aggression. In cases where the affiliation display fails, behaving like a helpless cub evidently works, so they learn to use it when they are in desperation. Thus in wolves this display may be an artefact of captivity – not a normal part of adult behaviour at all, but rather a signal artificially carried over from infancy into adulthood, under unnatural circumstances.

Studies of wild wolf packs have made clear that the traditional interpretations of wolf submission – both aggression within the pack, and the 'submissive' behaviour that is an attempt to defuse or deflect this aggression – reflect artefacts of captivity, and therefore cannot be applied to wolves as a species. Wolf packs that have not been manipulated by man, and are allowed to manage their own affairs, so to speak, are generally peaceful. This is not to say that all of what has been written about aggression between wolves is wrong; for instance, it is an undeniable fact that wolves – captive or not – can be very forceful and aggressive when they want to be. In the wild, even though relationships within packs are usually congenial, aggression towards outsiders, though infrequent, is unrestrained and potentially fatal. In captivity, however, pack 'identity' is either non-existent or severely disrupted, resulting in the expression of behaviour that would normally be seen only in skirmishes between members of different packs.

Observations of captive wolf packs have led not only to mistaken assessments of wolf behaviour, but also to fundamental misunderstandings about the structure of wolf families themselves, misunderstandings that have warped the popular conception of dogs as well. In captive wolf packs, the breeding pair are conventionally referred to as the 'alpha male' and the 'alpha female'. Many dog trainers, borrowing from this conception, insist that owners must impress their own 'alpha' status on their dog, which would otherwise be driven to seek 'alpha' status for itself. Thanks to our new understanding of the way that wild wolves construct their packs, however, it has become clear that 'alpha' status comes automatically with being a parent. The term 'alpha', as applied to a parent wolf in a normal pack, does not thus describe much about the wolf's status beyond its role as a parent.[6] It is meaningful only when used to describe the eventual victor of the warfare that is endemic to captive groups of wolves, which lack the family ties that would ensure peace in a natural pack. Which of these two models points to the most appropriate way to understand pet dogs and their relationships with their owners? Is it the 'alpha' model, based upon the unnatural captive pack, or the 'family' model, based upon the behaviour of wolves that have been allowed to make their own choices as to who or who not to live with? The family model is the product of millions of years of evolution, allowing the formation and refinement of an elaborate set of signals that serve to keep the peace. The alpha model emerges only in artificial social groupings that evolution has never had the opportunity to act upon, and in which individual wolves have to draw upon every ounce of their intelligence and adaptability just in order to survive the relentless social tensions inherent in such groupings.

Putting aside these objections about popular conceptions of wolf hierarchies for a moment, we should note two further reasons why understanding wolf behaviour cannot be the be-all and end-all for understanding dog behaviour. Scientists have (inadvertently, to be fair) studied the wrong wolves; on the wrong continent, and 10,000 years too late.

The American timber wolf, which is a sub-species of the grey wolf, is the most studied wolf of all, and has long been used to interpret the behaviour of dogs.[7] Until very recently, researchers tacitly assumed that the American timber wolf was closely related to the domestic dog, and therefore that studies of American wolves were highly relevant to understanding what makes dogs tick. However, the advent of DNA technology has forced a reappraisal of this comparison between dogs and American timber wolves.

Apart from deliberately bred wolf-dog hybrids, it has not been possible to trace the DNA of any of the dogs in the Americas to North American wolves, not even the 'native' dogs that were there before Columbus. This lack of evidence has not been for want of effort. The first such genetic analysis was done on the Mexican hairless dog, or xoloitzcuintli. The Spanish conquistadors discovered this dog when they first arrived in Mexico, where it was used for a variety of purposes, including companionship and food; it was also believed to have healing powers. To avoid contamination of these supposed properties through cross-breeding with European dogs, xolos were reportedly bred secretly in isolated locations dotted throughout western Mexico, and their descendants survive to this day. Could these dogs be relics of an ancient domestication of New World wolves? Their mitochondrial DNA (inherited through the female line) proves otherwise: it is most similar to that of European dogs (and wolves), bearing much less resemblance to that of American wolves.

Although the xolo's genetic makeup suggested that this breed originated in Europe, not South America, the possibility still remained that the American continents had produced other native dogs. Indeed, the modern xolos examined by scientists might conceivably not have belonged to an ancient breed at all, but instead might have been facsimiles re-created by breeders from crosses between European breeds – a possibility that would explain why the modern xolos' DNA is European in type. So genetic researchers next turned their attention to other native American dogs; to DNA extracted from the marrow of 1,000-year-old (or older) dog bones taken from archaeological digs in Mexico, Peru and Bolivia, and also from the bones of dogs buried in the permafrost of Alaska prior to the discovery of that area by Europeans in the eighteenth century. In both cases, the DNA was much more similar to that of European wolves than to that of American wolves.

While research into the origins of modern dogs is far from over, the available evidence makes it clear that comparisons between domesticated dogs and American timber wolves should be treated with caution, to say the least. With one proviso: the research has so far been focused almost entirely on maternal DNA; therefore, the descendants of a mating between a male American wolf and a female domestic dog would not be picked up. Some American dogs may therefore carry American wolf genes from one or more long-distant male ancestors; research should be able to resolve this soon. What is clear, however, is that no female American timber wolves were successfully domesticated. It is impossible to determine, thousands of years after the event, whether the reason for this was that American wolves were intrinsically difficult to domesticate, or that the first human colonizers of the Americas, having brought their own dogs with them from Asia, saw no need for further domestication and rather, being hunters, would have perceived the local wolves as competitors. Whatever the explanation, the fact remains that the vast majority of domestic dogs are only very distantly related to the American timber wolf, separated as they are by 100,000 years of evolution.

This is the first reason why comparisons between wolf behaviour and dog behaviour need to be treated carefully: most studies have been done on a type of wolf that, if it was any more distantly related to domestic dogs, would probably be considered a different species.

Scepticism about comparisons between wolves and dogs is further warranted by the fact that, although the DNA analysis indicates that dogs descended from Eurasian grey wolves, none of the wolves that have been studied over the past seventy years or so, American or European, can possibly be considered the ancestors of the domestic dog: the two certainly had a common ancestor many thousands of years ago,

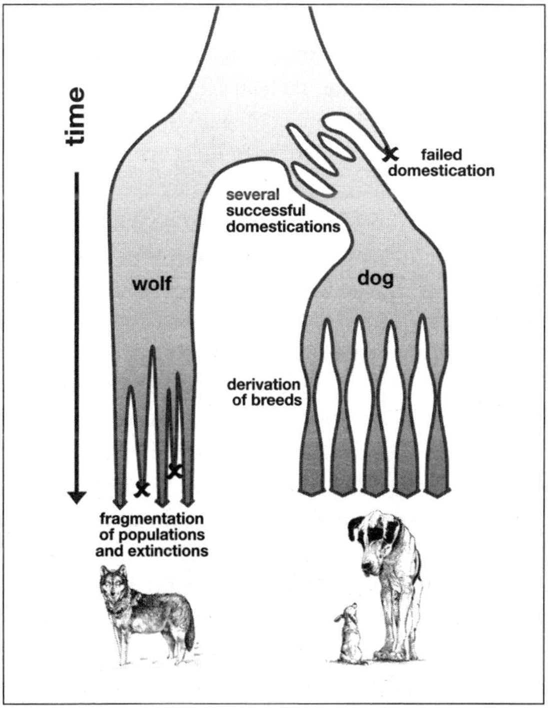

A simplified representation of the evolution of the wolf and the domestic dog. Genetic 'bottlenecks' occurred: at each of the domestications (one failed domestication is shown); when dogs were divided into breeds; and when many local wolf populations went extinct, leaving the survivors isolated from one another in different parts of the world.

but there is no evidence to suggest that modern wolves closely resemble these common ancestors. Indeed, logic dictates precisely the opposite.

Wild wolves, as they exist today, are almost certainly quite different in behaviour from their – and dogs' – ancestors. As soon as agriculture began in earnest, all wolves that had not been domesticated would have inevitably become a threat to the newly formed herds of livestock, and so they would have been persecuted by humans. Until firearms became widely available in the eighteenth century, human efforts to eradicate wolves were fairly ineffective, but thereafter it became possible to exterminate wolves from whole areas. For example, the wolf population in Norway and Sweden declined dramatically from the 1840s onwards; the DNA of today's Scandinavian wolves shows that they are descended from immigrant Russian animals, which had hung on in isolated areas throughout the twentieth century, until the modern conservation movement gave them the space to move into areas recently vacated by their cousins. This pattern of local extermination, or at least severe population reduction, was repeated throughout Europe; the few wolves that survived must inevitably have been those that were the most wary of people. Today's wolves are therefore the descendants of the wildest of the wild, whereas today's dogs must be derived from a much more tameable sort of wolf, one that is no longer found in the wild and about which we know almost nothing.

So, although the DNA of dogs tells us that they are, indisputably, wolves, much of the scientific study of wolf behaviour conducted in the twentieth century must now be regarded as of dubious significance to our conception of dog behaviour. Most of the wolves that were studied were kept under conditions that we now know were not only highly artificial, but also highly stressful for many of the individuals concerned, thereby inducing highly abnormal behaviour. Furthermore, we have no reason to suppose that any of these wolves precisely resemble the type of wolf that was originally domesticated. Such wolves no longer exist; they are far from extinct, since they have millions of living descendants – our dogs – but they no longer exist in the wild. Their nearest wild equivalents are probably feral dogs, domestic dogs that have reverted to a wild or semi-wild existence; these, too, are at the same time the direct descendants of the wild ancestor of the dog, and they live a similar, independent, lifestyle.

Since comparisons with the wolf are no longer as valid as they seemed as recently as a decade ago, my approach is to widen the search for the biological characteristics that make up the dog's true nature. Some of the characteristics that facilitated domestication may indeed be much more ancient even than the wolf, going back many millions of years to long-extinct species that were themselves the ancestors of wolves, jackals and wild dogs. All of these current species have features in common, features they most likely share with their common ancestors: they live in family groups, where the young adults often help their parents to raise the next round of offspring, have excellent noses, are highly intelligent and adaptable, and are either hunters, or scavengers, or both.

Ultimately, there may be nothing special about the wolf that singled it out for domestication; perhaps it just happened to be the social canid that was in the right place at the right time.[8] Unfortunately both that place and that time are currently shrouded in mystery, but what is certain is that the aberrant and atypical behaviour of modern, captive wolves is highly unlikely to be of any value in understanding either the behaviour of these ancestral wolves or that of domestic dogs. Rather than focusing exclusively on the grey wolf, we should regard the dog as a canid whose closest living relative happens to be a wolf. It is the possession of the canid toolkit that was vital to the successful domestication of the dog – a story whose roots are intimately twined with those of our own.

2

How Wolves Became Dogs

The story of the dog's domestication – its evolution from wolf to its own unique sub-species of canid – parallels that of our own emergence into civilization, from the hunter-gatherers of the Mesolithic through to the modern age. There were domestic dogs well before any other animal was domesticated, so arguably the dog is likely to be more altered relative to its ancestors than any other species of animal on earth. The process of domestication has stripped away much of the detail of the ancestral species, but dogs nonetheless retain some of the characteristics of the more ancient lineage that gave rise to jackal, coyote and wolf alike. Dogs are somewhat like each one of these, but they are also unique, the only fully domesticated canid, and much of what makes them unique was introduced by that very process of domestication. The story of that domestication therefore makes an essential contribution towards understanding what our dogs are, and what they are not.

Over the last decade, we have learned a great deal about the domestication of the dog. The sequencing of the DNA of hundreds of individual dogs has forced a reappraisal of all the previous evidence regarding the process of domestication. While there are undoubtedly more surprises to come, the broad scope of how it happened, as well as much of the detail, is now fairly well established.

In addition, we have new perspectives on when and where the dog may have been domesticated. We can be reasonably sure that there were several, possibly many, attempts at domestication of the grey wolf in various parts of the world, but that ultimately the products of some of those domestication events – in places other than North America – ultimately endured, whereas others did not. The process of discovery is still ongoing; ancient bones and fossils that were formerly identified as unequivocally belonging to wolves are being re-examined, in case they might actually have come from early wolf-like dogs. The evidence has been clear enough, however, to place the separation between wolf and dog further back in their evolution, by thousands of years, giving more time for wolf and dog to diverge, an analysis that further undermines the idea that the behaviour of the dog is simply a subset of that of the wolf.

While we are gaining a better understanding of the ways in which dogs are different from wolves, we are also learning more about how we, as humans, have helped to make the dog different. The domestication of dogs has been revealed as a complex process, more convoluted than that of any other animal, leading not only to radical changes in the shape and size of their physical bodies, but also to an almost complete reorganization of their behaviour. Furthermore, while mankind has guided that process, it is only in the past century and a half, and only in the West, that we have taken control of it completely. For 10,000 years or more, as the purposes for which dogs were valued changed and proliferated, dogs have coexisted and co-evolved with us. Essentially, they domesticated themselves as much as we domesticated them.

When was the dog domesticated? Until fifteen years ago, the answer was thought to be simple. The oldest remains of dogs found by archaeologists were carbon-dated to be no more than 12,000 years old, 14,000 at most. This timeline placed the first dogs before the beginnings of agriculture about 10,000 years ago, and well before the domestication of any other animal. So the dog was, for this reason alone, considered a special case: the pioneer for all subsequent domestications, such as goats, sheep, cattle and pigs. Because the dog was domesticated so early in the history of humans, there is little detailed evidence as to how wolves became dogs, a paucity of information that has left a great deal of room for speculation as to why and where this first occurred. Until fifteen years ago, however, at least the 'when' seemed well established; no bones had been found that had both unequivocally belonged to a dog and were more than 14,000 years old, so domestication must have occurred no earlier than about 15,000 years ago.

Then, in 1997, a team of scientists from the United States and Sweden made an astonishing claim: they had sequenced DNA from living dogs and wolves, and the findings indicated that domestication could have taken place more than 100,000 years earlier.[1] If this was true, it would mean that dogs were man's companions not just at the birth of agriculture, but right at the dawn of our own species – as soon as modern humans had emerged from Africa, where they had evolved, and encountered grey wolves (which do not occur in Africa) for the first time. This announcement triggered a minor epidemic of speculation about the possible co-evolution of man and dog. Most archaeologists rejected the idea, pointing to the complete lack of dog remains that could be dated any earlier than 14,000 years ago. But there was nothing intrinsically wrong with the DNA data, even though its interpretation was still open to debate. Dogs, it seemed, joined us during our pre-agricultural origins.

Since 1997, there has been a steady flow of more detailed studies of dog and wolf DNA, and, as a result of these, our conclusions about the exact moment of the dog's domestication have changed, and are still changing today. DNA technology is relatively new, and while it may give unequivocal answers when used for 'fingerprinting' (for example when confirming the parentage of a particular puppy in a dispute over pedigrees), its use in reconstructing events long past is much more open to interpretation. Different types of DNA can give different answers; for example, that contained in the nucleus of most mammals' cells (the subcellular organelle where paternal and maternal DNA mix) often tells a different story to DNA from other parts of the cell, such as the mitochondria (which contains only maternal DNA). As new analyses have appeared and been integrated into the picture, the estimate that dogs might have been domesticated more than 100,000 years ago has since been revised down considerably – now to between 15,000 and 25,000 years ago.

One reason for this drastic downward revision is that problems have been found in the method used to calculate how much time has elapsed since two animals had a common ancestor. The DNA most commonly used for this purpose comes not from the nucleus but from the mitochondria (whose genetic content is abbreviated as mtDNA). Very occasionally – only once every few thousand years – mitochondrial

DNA mutates, so that mother and daughter, who would otherwise have identical mtDNA, exhibit sequences that differ at just one location (this applies only to mothers; fathers do not pass on any mtDNA to their offspring, male or female). Unlike other kinds of mutation, these changes have no effect on the health or fecundity of the animal, and so are passed on 'silently' down the generations, spreading throughout all the daughter's descendants. By counting the number of differences between two individual animals' mtDNA, scientists can estimate the amount of time the two individuals' lineages have been diverging – and can thus form an idea of how long ago their most recent shared female ancestor lived. The bigger the number of distinct mutations, the older the two animals' joint lineage must be.

Errors slip into this sort of mtDNA dating when scientists, having determined how many unshared genetic mutations exist between two individuals, attempt to work out just how often these mutations may have occurred in both animals. The regularity of these mutations varies from one kind of animal to another. However, scientists know from the fossil record and from carbon dating that the dog's ancestor, the wolf, diverged from the coyote about a million years ago. A simple comparison between the number of differences between dog and wolf, and the number between wolf and coyote, suggests that the dog and the wolf have been separated for about one-tenth of that time – in other words for about 100,000 years. This calculation, however, relies on the mutations in mtDNA occurring at the same rate in domestic and wild animals. Since the 1997 study, it has become apparent that mtDNA mutations occur more frequently in domesticated animals than wild ones. The same comparative method used in the 1997 study has consistently overestimated the time since domestication for virtually every animal to which it has been applied: for example, the DNA of the pig, probably first domesticated 9,000 years ago, suggests a domestication of between 500,000 and 60,000 years ago; that of the horse, more than 300,000 years ago instead of about 6,000. The mutation rate must therefore be faster during domestication than in the wild, speeding up the rate at which mtDNA changes from once every few thousand years to once every few hundred. Studies of other species suggest that this accelerated rate may be a side effect of chronically high levels of stress hormones, caused by living in crowded conditions and in close proximity with man. Thus the estimate of 100,000+ years is highly likely to be an overestimate, perhaps by a factor of five or more, bringing the interval since the dog's domestication down to a much more realistic 20,000 years or so.

In addition to comparing the dog's DNA with that of the wolf, scientists can also examine how much variation there is between different types of dog, as a way of determining how long they have been around. However, this procedure, too, superficially seems to suggest that dogs were domesticated much earlier than 20,000 years ago. A recent analysis of the DNA that codes for the dog's immune system has produced an estimate of several hundred thousand years since domestication, a figure even more unlikely than the 100,000 years indicated by the mtDNA, since it predates the evolution of our own species. On the other hand, such an estimate assumes that mutation is the only source of variation, and that all dogs are descended from a single pair of wolves. A similar degree of diversity could occur if, say, several wolves had been domesticated, each of which had distinctive DNA. But this is likely to be the case only if each of those wolves had lived in a different part of the world, a supposition which in turn implies several domestication events.

The apparent contradictions between the archaeological evidence and DNA evidence can be reconciled if we posit not just one domestication event, but several, in different parts of the world. It is now becoming possible to examine the DNA of fossilized dog teeth taken from Neolithic burial sites. While only a few dozen individuals have been sequenced so far, the results tend to confirm that wolves were indeed domesticated at several, possibly many, locations.

Scientists have also begun to find proof for multiple domestications by looking at a different type of DNA, extracted from living dogs. The DNA that codes for the immune system is inherited from both parents, not just the mother, as mtDNA is. The much greater diversity in the DNA for the immune system suggests that dogs have far more forefathers than foremothers; in other words, dogs overall seem to have many male wolf ancestors between them, but only a few female wolf ancestors. Thus the genetic material from the 'extra' males must have been introduced after domestication had started. The early domestic dog bitches would presumably have been attractive to, and so occasionally mated by, wild male wolves. Moreover, their puppies would have been born in close proximity to humans, and, provided the genetic contribution of their wolf father did not make them too intractable, they could have survived to contribute to the dog genome. There is no reason why a mating between a male dog and a female wolf should not also produce puppies, but they would be born in the wild, and hence would be more likely to contribute to the wolf's genome than to the dog's.

Thanks to recent scientific developments, we now know that the diversity of the modern dog's genome is not hopelessly incompatible with the archaeological evidence surrounding the dog's domestication. Nevertheless, there is still a discrepancy – possibly as large as 5,000 to 10,000 years – between the most likely date suggested by the DNA (20,000 or more years ago) and the oldest date that most archaeologists will agree to (14,000 years). The reason for this discrepancy probably lies in the type of evidence that archaeologists will accept as evidence for domestication. Human remains and the bones of wolves have been found together at sites going back half a million years, long before modern humans evolved, but archaeologists do not accept these joint burials alone as signs of domestication. Rather, they look for evidence of domestication either in the remains of animals that are clearly distinguishable from wolves (for example, those having a wider skull, a shorter muzzle or smaller teeth), or in signs that the animals, even if otherwise indistinguishable from wolves, had a special place in human society – and preferably both.

Probably the earliest well-established archaeological example of a dog that is both biologically distinct from wolves and specially connected to humans is the burial, about 12,000 years ago, in what is now northern Israel, of a human with one hand resting on the body of a puppy. Not only does the position of the puppy show that it had a close relationship with that person, but its teeth are also significantly smaller than those of any wolf that lived nearby at that time, indicating that it must have come from domestic stock.

Neither the physical signs of domestication in this puppy, so distinct from its wild counterpart, nor the evident bond between the animal and its owner, can have arisen overnight. Rather, the puppy must have been preceded by many generations of dogs that made up the transition from wild wolf to domesticated pet. Such transitions may be virtually invisible to archaeology, but the subsequent rapid emergence of dogs all over the Old World is compatible with the idea that there was not one domestication, but several. In the next two millennia after this 12,000-year-old burial, other similar burials – either of humans and dogs together, or of dogs on their own – occurred in various parts of Europe. These sites have been found in, among other places, the United Kingdom, suggesting that dogs had also spread quickly from their points of origin, which are thought to be far to the east. It is thought that, at roughly the same time, humans were taking other domestic dogs, probably from another focus of domestication in East Asia, out of Siberia and into what is now Alaska. (At the time, both were part of a single land mass, known as Beringia, which, depending on the period, stretched as far as 600 miles from north to south.) These dogs moved with one of the early waves of colonists down the west coast of North America, and then into the interior: the earliest confirmed dog remains in the Americas, in Danger Cave, Utah, are perhaps 10,000 years old. Meanwhile halfway across the world, humans took dogs with them as they moved into the furthest reaches of south-east Asia; the DNA of the 800,000 street dogs found in Bali today shows that they are the descendants of dogs that arrived there overland, before Bali became an island 12,000 years ago.

This rather rapid appearance, in the archaeological record, of dogs all over the globe can, at a stretch, be explained by many independent domestications taking place almost simultaneously – but it is also plausible that domestication of the dog did actually start much earlier than the archaeology indicates. The point at which archaeologists can be sure that the dog had already become a domesticated animal may actually reflect not the beginning of the transition from the wolf, but rather the culmination of a fundamental change in the relationship between man and dog, one that had already taken thousands of years to develop. This process could not be complete until the dog had become an integral part of human culture, and also until it no longer needed to maintain the physiognomy of the wolf, because many of its essential needs were being taken care of by its owner. Thus the 5,000-year discrepancy between the date of domestication as shown by the archaeological record and that indicated by the dog's DNA can be accounted for by positing an extended period over which domestication took place gradually. These earliest dogs, or proto-dogs as they are sometimes called, would have been indistinguishable from wolves in the way they looked, and were probably treated in a strictly utilitarian way. For example, they may have been communal 'property', as today's village dogs are, rather than having a single 'owner'.

To be sure, any pre-domestication theory that suggests several thousand years of coexistence between wolves and people before the transformation to domestic dogs must account for the lack of archaeological evidence over this period, say from 20,000 to 15,000 years ago. If dogs existed during this period, possibly even earlier, why are they absent from human burials for the whole of this period, but then suddenly start appearing in burials, all over the globe, over the course of 'only' a couple of millennia? The archaeological record itself may hold the answer.

The earliest known dog burial is more than 14,000 years old. Located in Bonn-Oberkassel in Germany, it was discovered in a quarry in 1914, and seems to have consisted of a partial skeleton of a dog, buried alongside two humans. Unfortunately the outbreak of the First World War led to the loss of much of this material; yet a single piece of the dog's jaw remains, the arrangement of its teeth showing that it was clearly not from a wolf. Archaeological evidence suggests that from then on, dog burials become almost commonplace (other kinds of animals were occasionally treated in this way, but nowhere near as frequently as dogs[2]). Some dogs were buried alongside people, others had their own dedicated graveyards. In what is now the south-eastern United States, dog burials were so common during the period between 9,000 and 3,000 years ago, that it is their relative infrequency from later burial grounds that archaeologists feel they need to explain, rather than the other way around.

Mankind had been burying its dead for tens of thousands of years before dog burials began. Many ancient human graves contain animal remains; some may have come to be there accidentally, but many were obviously included deliberately, indicating a powerful emotional link between early humans and the animals they found around them. Consider this description of the contents of a grave, dug 28,000 years ago in Russia, that contained the remains of a boy, a girl and a sixty-year-old man. Buried with them were thousands of pieces of deer's antlers, polar foxes' teeth and mammoth ivory, which had probably been incorporated into necklaces or as decoration on their long-disintegrated clothes. Alongside the boy was a sculpture of a mammoth, itself carved from mammoth ivory. In another grave nearby there was a small ivory sculpture of a horse (a hunted animal at this point, not domesticated). These people had clearly had an important relationship with their local animals, one that included representing them in their art, and possibly featuring them in their religion. This relationship, however, seems to have been exclusively that of hunter and quarry.

The absence of dogs in known burial sites older than 14,000 years almost certainly means that dogs were, before then, rather rare. If the culture represented in this group grave in Russia had used dogs for hunting, it seems likely that there would also be evidence of dogs in this or similar graves – either bones, or, as with the horse, some kind of representation. That there are no such traces indicates that the society from which these people came did not have domestic dogs. If they had, these dogs' remains would have probably been indistinguishable from those of wolves, but in fact there is no trace of any wolf-like animal, domestic or wild, in the Russian group grave, even though wild wolves would have almost certainly have been in the vicinity. Indeed, very few graves hold traces of ancient wolves.

Unlike dog burials, which as noted were quite common after they first appeared in the archaeological record, wolf burials – whether alone or accompanying human burials – seem to have been extremely rare throughout ancient human history. (If common, they might have provided evidence for the early stages of domestication, when the bones of proto-dogs would have been indistinguishable from those of wolves.) Wolf teeth do feature, alongside those of other predators, in many burials of humans, but their significance is usually unclear, and in any case many probably come from animals that were killed for their pelts. The close emotional relationship that hunter-gatherers evidently had with the animals they hunted seems not to have been extended to their competitors in the hunt, including wolves. Thus there is very little archaeological evidence indicating any kind of relationship between hunter-gatherer man and wolves, either wild animals or those already on the path to domestication, until dogs suddenly appear in burials, some 14,000 years ago.

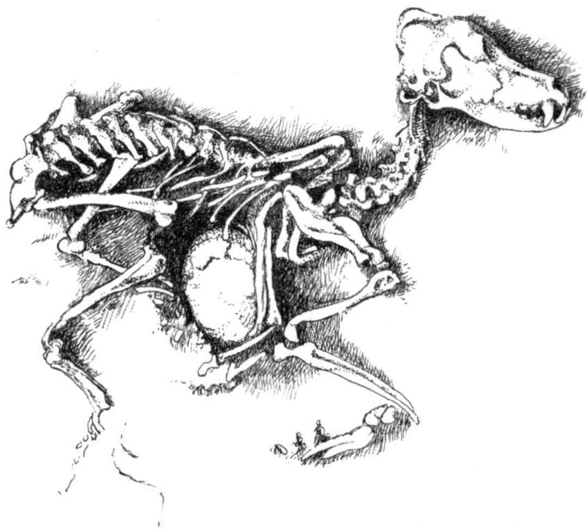

A wolf burial from near Lake Baikal in Siberia: its limbs enfold a human skull

Among the very few wolf burials that have been discovered, one is particularly odd, and may provide evidence for the transition from wolf to dog. Russian archaeologists recently discovered, in a cemetery near Lake Baikal, what they have identified as a wolf, buried with a human skull between its paws. The burial probably dates from only about 7,500 years ago, by which time there may well have been dogs in this area. What is remarkable about this wolf is that it was not local; it appears to be a tundra wolf, and if so must have travelled several thousand miles before ending its days in this grave. But what if the animal is not a wolf at all? Rather than a far-flung tundra wolf, the wolf buried near Lake Baikal is, I believe, more plausibly the descendant of a 'socializable' tundra wolf that had been adopted, many generations before, as a pet. Under this interpretation, such a burial gives us a tantalizing glimpse of the process of domestication in action. Domestication is very unlikely to have involved a steady transition from one group of wolves to today's dogs; on the contrary, it was more likely to have been a more haphazard process in which several domestications occurred, in different places and at different times. The 'wolf' in the grave may in fact be a proto-dog, the product of a late attempt at domestication in the frozen north, brought south, where it lived and died alongside its more 'domesticated' cousins – the progeny of earlier domestications – that were, by then, recognizable as dogs.

Archaeologists have found a few other burials of 'wolves' that may in fact be proto-dogs. For example, 8,500 years ago in what is now Serbia, a small type of domestic dog was used for food, as attested by the many broken leg-bones and skulls found in rubbish pits there. Another (larger) type of dog from the same area and at about the same time was buried unharmed in proper graves, implying a role that included companionship. Even more pertinent, however, is evidence – from the same location and period – of the remains of what appear to be wolves. These may have been wild, but it is also possible that they were a third type of dog, which, unlike the other two, had not changed much in appearance from its wild ancestor.

Few traces of proto-dogs have been found in human burials, but is there anything in the fossil record to support the idea of gradual and haphazard domestication? Until recently, archaeologists were reluctant to identify wolf skulls more than 14,000 years old as belonging to anything other than a wolf, so any possible proto-dogs that were found were not labelled as dogs. The earliest distinct dog skull, from Eliseevich, in the Russian plain, was excavated from the edge of a pile of mammoth skulls, and it, too, has been dated to about 14,000 years ago; roughly the size of a husky's skull, its burial seems to have been accidental rather than deliberate. However, three new skulls have recently been found that are intermediates between those of wolves and early dogs, such as the Eliseevich dog. All three are very similar to today's Central Asian shepherd dog. The oldest of these skulls, from Goyet in Belgium, is a staggering 31,000 years old, more than twice the age of the oldest dog burial. The other two, from Ukraine, are probably only about 13,000 years old, roughly contemporary with the first dog burials. The Goyet specimen is therefore something of an anomaly. Could it have been a direct ancestor of today's dogs? Or is it our only record of a very early domestication of the wolf – one that failed, hence the absence of any trace of dogs for the next 17,000 years?

There is one more small piece of evidence that suggests a relationship between man and dog going back more than 20,000 years. Deep in the Chauvet cave in the Ardèche region of France, which is famous for its prehistoric art, a 50-yard trail of footprints made by an eight-to-ten-year-old boy, alongside those of a large canid, hints at a close relationship between the two. The footprints of the canid are intermediate between those of a dog and a wolf. Soot from the torch that the child was carrying dates the event at 26,000 years ago, making these probably the oldest human footprints in Europe. With a little imagination, one can picture a boy and his faithful (proto-)hound, venturing into the cave to view the spectacular representations of wild animals, painted on its walls 5,000 years previously.

Single footprints of a child and a canid in the Chauvet cave, in the Ardèche region of France

Evidence such as the foregoing is, ultimately, too flimsy to give us any firm idea of when or where domestication of the wolf began. Nevertheless, this process does appear to have been repeated several times, in several locations in Europe and Asia, over a period of many thousands of years, to the point where domestic dogs may already have been established in some parts of the world at the same time that wolves were being taken from the wild in others. Some of these attempts must have succeeded; others almost certainly failed, leaving no trace in today's dogs. The habit of burying dogs with humans seems, for some reason that is still unclear, to have been adopted only after domestication was well advanced, otherwise there would be human graves from somewhere between 25,000 and 15,000 years ago that contained the bones of proto-dogs, indistinguishable from those of wolves.

We can say for certain, however, that the earliest confirmed dogs, at 14,000 years ago, logically represent not the beginning of domestication, but rather the end of its first phase, marking the point at which dogs became physically distinct from wolves. Before that, there must have been changes in the brains of wolves that made them suited to living with people but which left little or no trace in their skulls for archaeologists to find today. The question still remains as to how long those changes took, how many of those first alliances between dogs and wolves failed, and how many leave their traces in the dogs of today.

Since we can account for the diversity of the dog's DNA only by hypothesizing that individual domestications of wolves occurred in different parts of the world, these different 'proto-dog' populations must initially have been isolated from one another, and probably remained so for thousands of years. As domestication progressed, however, these early dogs would have eventually become manageable enough to travel with people on large-scale migrations, thereby allowing individuals from one proto-dog population to meet up with, and begin interbreeding with, individuals from another. The resultant churning of the dog's gene pool probably started more than 10,000 years ago, such that even dog remains that are old enough to be fossilized may have originated in wolf populations many hundreds or even thousands of miles away.

Thanks to this complicated timeline of domestication, the location of the original domestication events has proved impossible to pin down. The wolf itself is a highly mobile animal, even though it has not benefited from being transported around by man. Migrations of wolves, even since the dog was domesticated, have resulted in the incidence of almost identical DNA among individuals in regions as far apart as China and Saudi Arabia. Thus the DNA of modern wolves gives only very weak clues as to where domestication might have taken place.

Leaving the wolf to one side and approaching the locational problem from the opposite end, other biologists have recently analysed the DNA of local 'village dogs'. The scientists' hope was that these dogs would be the direct descendants of the first wolves to be domesticated in the area, and the assumption was that, as dogs dependent on humans, they were much less likely than wolves to have travelled long distances since then.[3] One recent study has suggested that, because the village dogs of southern China have the most varied DNA found so far, that was where domestication must have occurred – but since then it has been discovered that village dogs are almost as diverse in Namibia, where the nearest wild wolf is 3,000 miles away.[4] To have got that far, and to have become so widespread (there is little difference between the DNA of village dogs in Namibia and Uganda), these village dogs must have had considerable help from mankind; perhaps they accompanied humans on their various migrations around Africa. There also appears to have been a substantial amount of interbreeding between apparently localized village dog populations, resulting in a gradual trickling of greater diversity into their DNA – even in places as isolated as Namibia.

Village dogs

Despite all this considerable – and continuing – research, there are still no firm answers to the question of where the dog was domesticated. It must have happened in areas where wolves occurred naturally, yet North America has been ruled out, since the DNA of North American wolves is quite different from that of domestic dogs. This leaves most of Europe and Asia as possible locations. Beyond this consensus, there is a great deal of conjecture, even disagreement, among the various researchers pursuing a definitive answer.[5]

The most likely scenario is that wolves were domesticated at several different locations, possibly across Asia, including the Middle East, although one or more additional European origins also seem plausible. Taken at face value, the archaeological evidence points to at least one early origin in the Fertile Crescent, and this is the preferred scenario of some of the DNA experts. However, one interpretation of the DNA points to the earliest domestication as occurring in South China, where far less archaeological investigation has taken place. Each of the teams of DNA experts have their own samples of dogs and wolves, and so far these have led them to different conclusions. Their accounts are not easy to reconcile at present, but the most likely conclusion is that there was no single point of origin, but rather that wolves entered human society at several far-flung locations across Asia and Europe. Some left few or no descendants; others prospered, and eventually interbred as humans began to take dogs with them as they travelled.

Although we still do not know where, exactly, the dog originated, it is clear that our modern dogs do not trace their ancestry back to any one particular kind of wolf. Dogs are the result of a mixing of many different kinds of wolves from across Asia and Europe; the only wolf that is definitely missing from the recipe is the American timber wolf. Thus there is no wolf alive today that can act as the perfect model for understanding dogs and the way they behave. Moreover, the long period over which domestication occurred means that dogs have had the opportunity to change radically since they became separate from wolves, 10,000 or more generations ago. During the same period their environment, too, has undergone a considerable transformation.

The dog's evolution did not occur all at once, and the forces driving it have themselves altered over the dog's long period of coexistence with man. Indeed, over the same span of many thousands of years, we have changed almost as much as dogs have. The dog's history is bound up in our transition from hunter-gatherer to modern city-dweller, and its roles have changed during that time, as well. Unlike that of some other species, the domestication of the dog has served more than just a single purpose. Dogs have fulfilled many functions within human society, and so the story of their domestication is necessarily complex: a series of steps without a coherent underlying plan, but each one significant to our understanding of the dogs we have today.

Unfortunately, the early stages of the dog's domestication occurred so long ago that we know little of how they occurred. Given that the dog was the first domestic animal of all, deliberate domestication seems far-fetched – where, after all, would such a radical idea have come from? The most likely scenario is that associations between man and wolf appeared spontaneously, in several places, over thousands of years, long before the archaeological record shows any dogs that were distinct from wolves in appearance. Many of these associations would have died out, perhaps as environmental conditions or human customs changed. Others – probably only a small minority – lasted long enough for the 'village wolves' to turn themselves into the prototypes for domestic dogs. The 'village wolf' would have looked so much like a wild wolf that the two would be indistinguishable in the archaeological record.

Despite the difficulties of understanding the process by which dogs became domesticated, we can gain some insight by studying the process in other animals, where the evidence is more detailed and better preserved because domestication occurred later. The history of the pig is one instructive example. Our modern domestic pigs are descended from the wild boar: while the archaeological record points to a single domestication in Turkey, the DNA indicates six other domestications, each independent of the next and stemming from a different population of boars. Did seven different civilizations each domesticate the pig independently of one other, or did one think of it first, after which the idea of domesticating pigs spread from one area to another, each turning to its local population of wild boars for the raw material? It turns out that this is the wrong question, because both alternatives are based on the concept that domestication is a deliberate and cumulative process.

The first few domestications appear, with the benefit of hindsight, to have been haphazard affairs, progressing in fits and starts and occasionally going into reverse. This scenario certainly applies to the domestic pig. More than 2,000 years elapsed between the first pigs that were distinguishable from wild boars, and the pigs that showed clear evidence of being farmed (for example, a high adult female-to-male ratio, since culling of males when they are young maximizes productivity). That it took nearly a hundred generations of humans to accomplish a single domestication doesn't suggest much of a plan. Rather, the gradual changes in the bones of the pigs recovered during this period suggest that, initially, pigs were scavengers around human settlements, where they would also have served as a useful walking larder when hunting failed. They may also have been useful in cleaning up human wastes, including faeces: the 'pig-toilet' is still found in some parts of Goa (India) and China, and was probably once widespread throughout Asia.

The likely origins of the pig's domestication shed important light onto the process in general; domestication is almost certainly as much the agency of animals as of humans. In the case of the pig, every human settlement near to a population of wild boars was a potential source of domestication: once the settlement had grown to a suitable size, a few boars with the right temperament to tolerate the proximity of humans moved in, exploited the new food source, and were themselves exploited as food. In many cases these arrangements would have died out temporarily, perhaps when food shortages resulted in the consumption of all the pigs in the village. But the whole cycle could easily have started again in better times, if there were still wild boar in the vicinity. Domestication could have followed much later, presumably when the conditions were right among the local people – for example, when their culture allowed for individual or family (rather than communal) ownership, which would protect the animals against slaughter when food was in short supply. The next stage would have been the evolution of husbandry methods such as enclosure to protect the captive pigs from predators, and the selective culling of the more belligerent males, reducing the risk of injury to their human captors.

Since there is no indication that dogs were initially domesticated as food animals, the details of their story are likely to be different from those of the pig, but the transition from wild to domesticated was probably just as piecemeal and haphazard. If the pig took 2,000 years to change from hanger-on to agricultural animal, most likely the dog took just as long, perhaps even longer. With no prior experience in domestication, humans are unlikely to have deliberately begun the process of domesticating wolves; a much more probable scenario is that the wolves themselves started the process. Indeed, I am firmly of the opinion that the pioneers of the long road to today's dogs were wolves that were simply exploiting a new niche, a new concentration of food provided by man, as humans began to live in villages rather than being constantly on the move. These wolves then evolved to fit our new lifestyle, which would have demanded capabilities very different from hunting on the open range.

Living near human settlements would have required a tolerance of the proximity of humans that no modern wolf can manage, and probably few ancient wolves could have either – but humans would almost certainly have aided in selecting for this trait. Initially, those wolves that were suited to scavenging from man would have prospered and produced offspring, whereas those wolves that were unsuited either did not, or left to rejoin their wild cousins. It is difficult to imagine how hunter-gatherer humans could have actively intervened in this process; selecting which male would breed with which female, for instance, would have been unlikely at such a tenuous stage. However, humans probably did intervene, in a much less deliberate way – one that nevertheless speeded up the separation between village and wild wolves.

Humans must have at least tolerated the wolves that were gravitating to their settlements, because otherwise such a transition could never have taken place. There must have been times, of course, when having a large well-armed carnivore hanging around would have been dangerous. The very young and the infirm would have been at particular risk from an animal, perhaps only a few generations removed from a wild hunter, that had run out of food to scavenge. Any wolf that threatened to injure a human must have been driven away or even killed; only wolves that posed no apparent threat would have been allowed to remain in the village for very long.

The domestication-by-scavenging hypothesis is a start, but it cannot be the whole story, for it seems unlikely that wolves would have been able to survive entirely on the by-products of early human settlements. Modern village dogs can get most of their food by scavenging, but they are much smaller than wolves, and modern villages are a lot bigger and more productive than hunter-gatherer villages must have been. The scavenger theory depends, critically, on whether hunter-gatherers regularly produced enough surplus food to make scavenging worthwhile. Wolves are large and require a great deal of energy – about 2,000 calories a day, equivalent to two-and-a-half pounds of meat. It seems unlikely that, 20,000 years ago, any human settlement would have produced that much surplus meat day after day. It must be remembered, however, that wolves are not strictly carnivorous; they are perfectly capable of subsisting on a diet of plant material supplemented with the occasional bone or scraps of meat. They may even have contributed to village hygiene by performing the same function as today's toilet pig; however unsavoury this idea may seem to us today, it would explain the unfortunate penchant that some modern dogs have for eating faeces.[6] Whether or not the village wolves exploited this insalubrious source of calories, however, it is hard to imagine that several wolves, even a pair, would do well enough – and survive for long enough to produce offspring – by relying entirely on scavenging. Indeed, it seems illogical that any animal would give up hunting, a way of life for which it had evolved over millions of years, for the uncertainties of scavenging from a species that was not yet as skilful at obtaining meat as it was.

Thus scavenging, while a plausible contributor, is not nearly sufficient by itself to account for a transition from hanger-on to domestication. Scavenging around hunter-gatherer encampments is unlikely to have provided a reliable source of food even for small wolves, and I strongly suspect therefore that there must have been some deliberate feeding by the hunter-gatherers themselves. Of course, such behaviour on the part of humans requires explanation: why would humans give up their own resources to animals that served no clear purpose within the community?

If humans encouraged wolves to stick around by deliberately feeding them, then part of the motivation behind this might possibly lie in the apparently universal human trait of keeping animals as pets.

Pet-keeping is not just a modern phenomenon; it is widely practised among contemporary hunter-gatherer societies, and was probably a feature of many pre-agricultural societies as well. In contemporary contexts, these 'pets' are usually obtained as very young animals from the wild, perhaps when a nest or den is discovered by the hunters, and are brought back to the village and hand-reared by women and children. As they grow, some of these animals will escape back into the wild; others will become too large or boisterous for comfort and will be driven out, or even killed and eaten. It is apparently rare for the 'pets' to breed successfully within the village, so each generation has to be newly obtained from the wild. These are therefore not really 'pets' in the usual of the word, but the hunter-gatherers lavish on them the same level of care when they are young as does the owner of a new kitten or puppy in the developed world.

Modern hunter-gatherers have remarkably varied pet-keeping tastes. In some of today's hunter-gatherer societies, such as the Penan of Borneo and the Huaorani of the Amazon rainforest, there seems to be no particular preference for one animal over another. Virtually any young bird or mammal of manageable size may be adopted, such that at any given time there may be dozens of different species within a single village – parrots, toucans, wild ducks, raccoons, small deer, assorted rodents, opossums and monkeys. Other societies may attach particular importance to one particular species. For example, the Guaja of Amazonia are a matriarchal society, in which all the women keep monkeys as pets; the headwoman will have several, while adolescent girls will usually look after just one. They treat their monkeys at least as well as, possibly even better than, their own children. The newly collected infant monkeys are suckled at the breast, are constantly fed choice titbits, and are carried everywhere – the matriarch will usually have two or three draped over her head and shoulders as a sort of living robe of office. In other such cultures, for example in Polynesia, Melanesia and the Americas, it is dogs that are treated in this way, including the nursing of puppies alongside human infants.

Thanks to contemporary evidence, the most direct of which comes from the indigenous Aboriginal peoples of Australia, we can guess that our ancestors found puppies just as appealing as we do today. There are no grey wolves or other wild canids in Australia; in their place there are dingoes, which are actually the descendants of dogs that reverted to the wild several thousand years ago. Aboriginals were hunter-gatherer-cultivators until recently; they had no domesticated animals, but do have a long tradition of taking dingo puppies from the wild, and keeping them as pets. Some were collected from litters found accidentally, during hunting trips, others were taken deliberately, as part of religious ceremonies. These puppies were highly valued and well cared for, but as they grew into adults they became a nuisance, stealing food and becoming over-boisterous, and were usually driven away soon after they had become sexually mature. So a separate population of domesticated dingoes never emerged – and yet the tradition continues to this day.

The persistence of the dingo-keeping tradition in Australia suggests that, in the absence of (or sometimes in spite of) practical considerations, humans will keep puppies purely for their cuteness. Dingoes are clearly a drain on human resources, not an asset. Originally, scientists speculated that Aboriginal Australians kept dingoes to serve as hunting companions, but in fact dingoes interfere with hunting, to the point that Aboriginals bring home more meat if they leave their dingoes behind. Furthermore, dingoes often outnumber the human inhabitants of a village, and accordingly have to compete for food; their scavenging can be so intense that they have to be deliberately excluded from mealtimes. Nevertheless, the habit of taming large numbers of these animals has persisted for hundreds, probably thousands of years, so they must have some redeeming features in the eyes of their hosts. Indeed, dingoes feature more in the Aboriginals' art and spiritual narrative than any other animal, with the possible exception of snakes. Although respect for dingoes of all ages has long been encapsulated in Aboriginal culture, the habit of keeping young dingoes must surely have started as an exaggerated susceptibility to the cuteness of puppies.

It seems entirely possible, therefore, that, in one or two locations, perhaps 20,000 years ago, there were hunter-gatherer groups in which wolf cubs taken from the wild came to have a social significance similar to that of contemporary hunter-gatherers' pets. The feeding and care of the young wolves, so difficult to account for if their parents had been merely scavengers, would instead have been performed by the villagers, initially for their own enjoyment, and subsequently to gain social esteem, much as, for example, the keeping of monkeys as pets brings status to women of the Guaja. Additionally, the intimate relationship between the cub and its carer would have enabled the cub to become socialized to people, as well as to its own kind – provided, of course, that it had the capacity to do both.

There is one very important way in which the dog is different from other hunter-gatherer pets. Whereas the dog eventually became domesticated, these other 'pets' – from rodents to parrots to monkeys – are really just tame animals, many of which have been raised in isolation from their own kind and probably would not know how to breed even if given the opportunity: hence the need for these 'pets' to be continually replenished from young born in the wild. The wolf, however, became domesticated because it stayed near humans by choice, forming a reciprocal relationship. For domestication to begin, a wolf would need to be raised by humans from a cub, and then stay in (or return to, but that seems unlikely) the village to produce its own first young. (Village habitation would be necessary only for the females; the cubs could just as well be fathered by wild wolves, but it would be essential for the females to be completely tame so that the cubs could be born in the village.)

In fact, by comparing today's wolves and dogs, we can see that dogs have adapted to the human presence in a remarkable way. Perhaps the most striking difference between dogs and wolves today, apart from their appearance, is the ease with which domestic dog puppies adopt a dual identity, something today's wolf cubs seem incapable of. This capacity for the dog to adopt a dual identity – part human and part wolf – is essential in accounting for the transition from primitive pet to truly domesticated animal. Perhaps it is the key attribute that singled out the grey wolf, from all the other possible candidates among the canids, for successful domestication. Perhaps its unique transformation to domestic animal has little to do with its ability to form packs, or to communicate by body-language (neither of which, as we have already seen, are traits unique to the grey wolf anyway). Perhaps the grey wolf was simply able to form social bonds with humans, whereas other canids were not.

It is entirely possible that some accident of genetics – some sort of mutation – gave a few wolves the ability to socialize to two species simultaneously, to direct their social behaviour to mankind *and* to other wolves, while their sexual preferences remained steadfastly directed at their own species. Until man came along, this hereditary change would have been of no advantage (or disadvantage) to the wolves that carried it. But as hunter-gatherer societies in places where there were also wolves developed to the point where the 'pet'-keeping habit became established, those local wolves with the altered socialization mechanism would have been pre-adapted for coexistence with mankind. On the one hand, then, societies that serendipitously happened to adopt wolves in the locations where their socialization mechanisms had been altered, were presented with animals that could breed successfully within a man-made environment.[7] On the other hand, societies that fixed on other canids – such as the golden jackal – as their prototype pet of choice, could tame them as individuals, but could never succeed in breeding them, because their socialization mechanisms were still suited only to their original wild lifestyle.

What evidence is there for the existence of these special, easily socialized wolves? Simple – it is all around us, in the form of modern dogs. They are the only living descendants of the socializable wolves that, I suspect, existed 20,000 years ago. Modern wolves are, of course, quite different from the earlier wolves I am describing; today's grey wolves are very difficult to tame, let alone socialize to people. Even tame wolves do not seem to form specific attachments to individual humans. Modern wolves, however, are not the descendants of the wolves that became dogs.

Today's dogs are, if my hypothesis is correct, the descendants of a small fraction of the original wolf population, products of a mutation that separated these wolves from the majority of their species by allowing them to socialize with both humans and other wolves. While this small fraction of wolves went on to live among humans and eventually turned into dogs, most wolves could never follow this path, because they displayed a natural wariness of man. In essence, what I am suggesting is that this ability to socialize to humans is not, as it is usually assumed, a consequence of domestication. Instead, I conceive it as the crucial, if accidental, pre-adaptation that opened the door to domestication in the first place.

The key difference between a dog and a wolf is not what it looks like but how it behaves, and especially how it behaves towards people. DNA and bones cannot tell us how these early dogs behaved, or what their everyday interactions with people were actually like. Domestication affects outward appearance, certainly, but at the very earliest stages this is incidental. What defines an animal such as a dog is what goes on under the skin – specifically, how the behaviour of its ancestors has been altered to enable it to live comfortably in man-made environments.

Although we know a great deal about the behaviour of today's American timber wolves, and an increasing amount about the relict wolf populations of Europe, this information gives us little insight into the behaviour of the first domestic dogs. Modern wolves are only very distantly related to the domestic dog, and they have been under intensive selection pressure, especially over the past few hundred years, from those who wished to exterminate them. It is therefore unsurprising that today's wolves are very difficult to socialize, and that tame wolves tend to remain unpredictable and potentially aggressive towards people throughout their lives. By persecuting wolves, we have selected those individuals that are naturally wary of us. It is therefore very difficult to derive any knowledge about early dogs from what we know about contemporary wolves. Moreover, this means that we cannot even replicate domestication, by taking wolves out of the wild and selectively breeding them to become more like dogs. Since the wolves that were the direct ancestor of domestic dogs are, in their original form, extinct, that would be impossible.

One recent modification of a canid is widely held to provide pointers as to how wolves might have changed into dogs. This is the silver fox, a colour variety of the wild red fox, that is bred in fur-farms. Silver foxes are usually kept in cages and are scarcely tame, let alone domesticated, but in the 1950s a group of Russian scientists began to breed them selectively, using only the tamest individuals in each generation.[8] At first, few of the foxes could be handled, even by a person offering a tasty food treat. After a few generations of breeding only from individuals that would tolerate handling, however, some individuals emerged that would actively seek contact from people. Indeed, after thirty-five generations, most of the foxes were behaving in a remarkably dog-like way – wagging their tails, whimpering to attract attention, sniffing and licking their handlers' hands and faces. Some were even taken home as pets by the staff, who reported that these animals could be as obedient and loyal as domestic dogs. The geneticists' objective of producing a fox that was easier to handle seemed to have improved its welfare too. Freed from the relentless fear and anxiety of having to encounter an alien species (us!) every day of their lives, the new 'tame' farm-foxes exhibit levels of stress hormones four times lower than those in the original 'wild' version. A similar reduction in reactivity, and susceptibility to stress, is evident when dogs are compared with wolves – a reduction traceable to changes in the hypothalamus, a part of the brain that is, among several functions, concerned with emotional reactivity. Such changes are probably a direct consequence of selection for tameness, so in this respect the tame farm-foxes may well be similar to the wolves that adapted to living near, and scavenging from, human settlements.

The most interesting finding of the Siberian fox experiment was that the farm-foxes became easier to tame because the period before they became frightened of new experiences was effectively lengthened. Most young mammals go through a period of their lives in which they are naturally inquisitive and trusting. And it is usually during this stage that they are still being looked after by their parents, who are on hand to make sure that this characteristic does not get them into trouble. As they get older and more independent, the offspring become much more suspicious of anything unusual, and much more likely to run away after an initial inspection. In the farm-foxes, selection for tameness corresponded with an extension of this 'trusting' phase, which ends when wild foxes are about six weeks old, but lasts for about nine weeks in the 'tame' variety. That extra three weeks is enough to allow regular handling to take effect, producing a fox that trusts, rather than fears, the people who look after it.

Another finding of the Siberian experiment has been used to posit the effect of domestication upon canids' appearance, though this is largely unsubstantiated. The appearance of some of the tame foxes produced in the experiment is different from the wild variety; a few, though by no means all, of the tame foxes have unusual dog-like features, such as curly tails, floppy ears and white patches on their coats. Some authorities have claimed that such features are part and parcel of domestication, that selection for tameness inevitably brings with it all these changes in appearance. Unfortunately the data do not really support this idea. True, more 'tame' foxes have floppy ears than do the 'wild' ones, but they are still in a tiny minority – fewer than a quarter of 1 per cent. Fewer than one in ten of the tame foxes has a curly tail. Fewer than 15 per cent have a white 'star' on their forehead. Exactly how these changes became slightly more common in the 'tame' foxes is still something of a mystery, but they are still rare, and probably tell us little or nothing about domestication.

While the Siberian experiment produced tame foxes, there is a significant difference between these foxes and domestic dogs in terms of the extent to which they are – or, it seems, can be – 'domesticated'. In dogs, the process of acclimatizing to humans does not disrupt normal social relations with other dogs. By contrast, when the foxes develop a relationship with humans they seem to lose interest in socializing with other foxes. Red foxes – the same species as the farm-fox – are rather sociable animals, often living in groups of four to six animals. Yet the tame farm-foxes are solitary animals; as devoted as dogs, but as independent as cats. This contrasts with the domestic dog (and the domestic cat), whose social relationships can and indeed normally do develop simultaneously both with humans and with members of their own species (and potentially other species as well).

If the tame foxes can tell us anything useful about the dog, it is that tameness, while a useful first step, is not the same thing as full domestication. Tameness permits the replacement of one set of social responses – directed at members of the same species – with another – directed at humans. Dogs, by contrast, need to retain both, in order to continue functioning as members of their own species while simultaneously establishing and maintaining relationships with their human owners. Nothing in the farm-fox experiment sheds any light on how this capacity might have come about during the domestication of the dog.

The farm-fox experiment does show that selection for tameness can be extremely rapid – indeed, it seems to be fast enough to suggest a plausible first stage in the domestication of the wolf. The key difference between the two animals is, of course, that the foxes were a captive, isolated population that was deliberately selected for tameness. The wolves that were sufficiently tolerant of humans, on the other hand, selected themselves to be the ancestors of domestic dogs: those that were easily tamed could start breeding in the proximity of humans; those that could not, rejoined the wild population. The appearance of dog-like behaviour in the tame foxes, such as licking humans' faces and hands, and whimpering, also supports the idea that the dog's social repertoire is drawn not from that of the wolf exclusively, but rather from an ancestral palette of possibilities inherited from the canids as a whole.

The farm-foxes tell us that natural variation in tameness within a species can be sufficient, in at least one of the canids, to produce individuals that could be the ancestors of a domestic animal. This experiment thus provides us with a model for the initial separation between wild wolves and those that were naturally tame enough to live alongside people. The resources that the naturally tame wolves were able to obtain from humans must have been sufficient to allow them to adopt a new way of breeding. Instead of hiding them away in a den, the intrinsically 'tame' mother wolves must somehow have allowed their cubs access to humans, so that taming, and selection for tameness in subsequent generations, could proceed further. Underlying the onset of tameness are changes in the production of and reactivity to stress hormones, alterations that are evident from tame farm-fox and dog alike. However, the farm-foxes tell us nothing about the way that dogs gained the capacity to sustain social relationships simultaneously with their own species and with ourselves. Nor do they tell us anything about how dogs achieved their remarkable diversity of shapes and sizes – and yet this very diversity permits another, very different, approach to understanding the subsequent phases in the domestication of the dog, once tameable wolves had begun their association with mankind.

Instead of comparing dogs with wolves, or trying to reconstruct the domestication process, we can find important information about how dogs came to be by examining the differences between breeds and types of modern dogs. The ways in which they differ from one another can provide clues as to how those changes in appearance might have come about. Since different-sized dogs appeared very early in the history of domestication, at least 10,000 years ago, it is possible that the processes that led to the diversification in body shape are the very same as those that permitted domestication to proceed beyond tameness. And since many of the differences between breeds and types of dogs are known to arise through alterations in the rates at which the body and behaviour develop in early life (alterations that are reflected both in the outward appearance of the dog, and in the way its behaviour is organized), the emergence of these superficial differences is arguably the most important underlying process that has produced today's dogs.

Dogs come in so many shapes and sizes that they have long been a puzzle to zoologists, but in fact many of the changes can be accounted for simply by a common biological mechanism, the technical term for which is *neotenization.* Roughly speaking, this refers to the phenomenon whereby growth in some parts of the body stops, while other parts continue to grow at the normal rate. If the whole skeleton stops growing earlier than usual, but the internal organs continue to mature, then the result is a smaller-than-usual animal that is still capable of reproducing. For example, the skeleton of an adult Lhasa apso is similar to that of a Great Dane puppy, but the Great Dane will continue to grow for many more months before it becomes sexually mature. If the growth of the skeleton is altered selectively, the end result is a change in shape as well as a reduction in size. The skull of an adult Pekinese has essentially the same proportions as that of a wolf foetus, but its body is more dog-like. In 'toy' dogs, the growth of the whole skeleton stops at what would be, for a wolf, a very early stage. In flat-faced dogs, the growth of parts of the skull is slowed to maintain the proportions of that of a foetal wolf.

We are now coming to understand even more about the physiology that underlies these differences in canid appearance. It turns out that the skull and skeleton of the wolf change shape dramatically between their genesis in the foetus and their final form in the adult, under the control of various hormones. Much of the size variation in today's dogs probably comes about through changes in the growth stages during which these hormones are produced, how much is produced, and how effective they are at doing their job. Thanks to all the work that is going on to unravel the canine genome, it should soon be possible to identify how these changes work.

The very same principle of selective arrested development that governs dogs' growth can also be used to explain how domestication moulded the dog's behaviour. For example, dogs continue to play even when they are adult, unlike most animals. Because the behaviour of juvenile wolves is more flexible than that of the adults, the dog has been likened to a wolf that has never grown up, except in the important sense that it becomes sexually mature and so can reproduce. Its behavioural development has, in a sense, been arrested. The farm-fox story sheds important light on this process by telling us that tameable wolves probably differed from untameable wolves in having a delayed period of social learning at the beginning of their lives, such that tolerance of human contact had time to develop. Dogs, for their part, are like tameable wolves in which development of behaviour has been slowed down further still, to the point that it becomes arrested at the (wolf's) juvenile stage, where behaviour is more flexible and can therefore be adapted much more easily to the requirements of humans. Some simple resetting of the dials that control the development of brains and behaviour can, in theory, account for much of the transition from wild wolf to tame, from tame to domestic, and then to the diversification of dogs into types of different sizes and shapes.

One further difference between dogs and wolves can also be accounted for by a selective change in the development in the two animals: dogs become sexually mature somewhat earlier than wolves. Dogs are also fertile throughout the year, unlike wolves, which are sexually active mainly in the winter, leading up to the birth of the cubs in the spring. Both of these differences are likely to be consequences of the transition from the wild, with its seasonal but predictable food supply, to early human societies where food was more plentiful on average but also more unpredictable; proto-dogs that could breed any time after their first birthdays would have out-competed those that waited, as wolves do, until their second winter.

For the same reason that they need to be much more opportunistic in grasping opportunities for breeding, dogs are also much less choosy than wolves in their choice of sexual partners. This is evident from the Y-chromosome (paternal) DNA of today's dogs, which is much less diverse than their mitochondrial (maternal) DNA. Because wolves pair-bond, males and females are about equally likely to contribute to the DNA of the next generation. Given the promiscuous tendencies of male dogs, some males can potentially sire more than a hundred litters in their lifetime, while many others leave no offspring at all. Bitches are constrained by the fact that they can produce only one litter per year. Moreover, the variability in male reproductive success appears to have been set up well before the creation of the modern breeds in the nineteenth century, suggesting that male promiscuity is an ancient, not a recent, trait of dogs.

The promiscuity of the male dog must have been one of the factors that helped man, first accidentally but then increasingly deliberately, to impose his own selection pressures on the species. Some of these choices might have been simply fanciful, such as a preference for a particular coat colour, or an especially 'cute' face – qualities of no particular consequence for the process of domestication. Other aspects of human behaviour – such as taking special care of the offspring of a bitch prized for her trainability and loyalty – might have pushed the process of domestication along.

At the early stages of domestication, certainly up to the point that dogs became physically distinct from wolves, human intervention in breeding is unlikely to have been a conscious process, and indeed may have been haphazard, as it remains to this day in village dogs. The archaeological record indicates that dogs may have disappeared entirely from some societies, only to be replaced hundreds of years later by immigrants from elsewhere. Other societies may have rejected dogs even when they were available: although Japan was first colonized by mankind about 18,000 years ago, there is no record of dogs in that country until about 10,000 years ago – presumably Japan's new inhabitants considered the dogs available in ancient China unsuitable, for some now impenetrable reason.

Despite the almost certain lack of early deliberately applied selective pressures from humans, over the course of several thousand years wolves must have made some kind of faltering progress towards becoming an animal that had many of the behavioural characteristics of today's dogs, even if it still looked much like a wolf. Certain physical changes, however, would almost certainly have begun to occur during this time. Dependence on man for what was probably a rather erratic supply of food would have favoured a reduction in body size. As dogs were transported into warmer climates, those with shorter, paler coats would have out-competed those with the wolf's long, darker fur, producing a conformation that survives in village dogs to this day.

Many of the other conformations that we see in today's dogs are also ancient. By 10,000 years ago, dog-keeping and therefore dogs themselves had spread throughout much of Europe, Asia, Africa and the Americas; soon after this, and in many parts of the world, recognizably distinct types of dog appear. Over the next couple of thousand years, dogs diversified rapidly, so that by the time representational art became commonplace some 5,000 years ago, there were already dogs for many purposes. Long-limbed, long-nosed sighthounds, superficially similar to the modern saluki or greyhound, were used for hunting.[9] Heavy, large-headed mastiff types were used for guarding and general intimidation. Hounds were developed that hunted mainly by scent, suited to finding and following large game in thick cover. Subsequently, larger dogs were found to be useful as pack animals, either carrying loads on their backs or – as widely practised by some Native Americans – pulling a travois. Small terrier-like dogs were used for keeping rats and mice at bay, and for hunting animals that go to ground, such as rabbits and badgers. Lapdogs, similar to today's Maltese dog, are first recorded from Rome more than 2,000 years ago, but there were probably already lapdogs in China by this time, probably among the ancestors of today's Pekinese and pug. The arrival of lapdogs completed the process of generating the dog's remarkable variation in size; any that became smaller, or larger, would probably not have been biologically viable in the days before veterinary care. Lapdogs were also the first dogs bred solely for companionship, though for many centuries these through-and-through pets would have been rare compared to dogs kept for more utilitarian purposes.

We can be reasonably sure that there was a deliberate element in

Native American dog travois

the breeding of all these dogs, over at least the last 5,000 years, by the simple expedient of allowing bitches to mate only with chosen males of similar type. Some males were evidently favoured over others: molecular biologists have found much more variety in the (maternal) mitochondrial DNA of dogs than in the Y-chromosome (paternal) DNA, indicating that, during the entire history of the dog, far fewer males than females have left surviving offspring. Favoured males must therefore have been prized and taken to mate with many bitches, much as happens today within pedigree breeds. The choice of male must sometimes have been based on body conformation (for example in dogs bred for food) but mainly it would have been based on whatever kind of behaviour was desired in the puppies, whether that be suitability for herding, hunting or guarding.

Although dogs were almost certainly being bred deliberately 5,000 years ago, matings based on the dogs' own preferences would have kept the dog population diverse. Since dog-keeping would have been much more chaotic than it is today, many matings would also have been unplanned – and if the resulting offspring turned out to be useful, they would have been retained. Taboos against raising puppies that were not 'purebred' would have been rare, unlike the situation today.

So without any deliberate planning, a healthy level of genetic variation was maintained within types, as well as between. Transfer of dogs from one location to another by traders would have ensured that most local populations were not reproductively or genetically isolated from one another, maintaining diversity at the local as well as global levels. In the absence of veterinary knowledge, natural selection would have continued as a major force directing the development of dogs in general; the rates of both reproduction and mortality would both have been much higher than they are today, at least in the West. Dogs that were prone to disease or infirmity, or carried other disadvantages, such as difficulty in whelping, would have left few offspring, and their lineages would eventually have died out.

As the modern world developed, so did the degree of deliberate breeding, for purposes that were at the same time both increasingly diverse and narrow in definition. For example, further specialization within the existing range of sizes and shapes occurred in medieval Europe, where the importance to the new aristocracy of hunting led to the breeding of many specialist kinds of hound, each with its own

Medieval dogs

local variations – deerhounds, wolfhounds, boarhounds, foxhounds, otterhounds, bloodhounds, greyhounds and spaniels, to name but a few, although these are not necessarily the direct ancestors of the breeds that bear the same names today.

The mtDNA of some existing breeds shows that their identity extends back in an unbroken line at least 500 years, and possibly much longer. Some of these ancient breeds are oriental, including the shar-pei, Shiba Inu, chow-chow and Akita. Others, including the Afghan hound and saluki, have Middle Eastern origins. A third group (malamute and husky) are Arctic dogs, while an African breed, the basenji (recently confirmed from its Y-chromosome DNA as both unique and ancient), forms the fourth. Some of the North Scandinavian breeds, such as the Norwegian elkhound, have probably been derived from interbreeding wolves with dogs, several hundred and possibly as long as a few thousand years ago.

Speciality breeds may have originally had other uses besides the standard ones, such as tracking and hunting. Several types of dog, such as the chow-chow and the fat Polynesian types, were developed specifically for food; others, such as the Manchurian long-haired types, were probably bred for their fur as well. Breeding dogs is not a particularly efficient way to obtain nourishment or something to wear, so we have to presume that there was always some social significance attached to these uses: dog meat may have been prized as a delicacy, and dog fur may have carried a higher social cachet than the hide of hunted animals such as gazelle.

Whatever one may think of such uses for dogs, they are a testament to the dog's extreme adaptability to the twists and turns of human civilization. Dogs have been adapted, or have adapted themselves, to all kinds of roles, in a way unmatched by any other domestic animal, and such flexibility must lie at the heart of the enduring power of the human–canine relationship. Although today most dogs are valued primarily for their companionship, at least in the West, we must also remember that historically many dogs were kept first and foremost because they were useful. Some of these functions must have come and gone in just a few centuries; just a footnote to the dog's association with man, they are now almost forgotten (see box – 'The Turnespete'). Others – such as hunting, shepherding and guarding – persist today.

THE TURNESPETE

The sole purpose of this British 'breed' of dog was to run in a mousewheel-like contraption, which, through a system of belts and pulleys, slowly turned a joint of meat roasting over an open fire. This device was first mentioned in the mid-sixteenth century and had disappeared by the mid-nineteenth, replaced by more efficient ways of roasting meat without burning it. Actually, purely mechanical methods of turning spits had become available in the seventeenth century – Leonardo da Vinci had sketched one – so the continued use of dogs for this purpose for a further 200 years may reflect not a strictly utilitarian consideration but a British preference for using dogs wherever they could. The dogs were certainly given names – Fuddle, one of the

turnspit dogs at the Popinjay Inn in Norwich, even had a poem written in his honour. On Sundays, it was apparently the custom to take them to church where they would act as foot-warmers on cold winter days. Incidentally, there is no evidence that the Turnespete was ever a specific breed in the modern sense of a closed gene pool; short-legged and stocky, turnspit dogs were probably selected from a variety of terriers, including, according to one record, badger-hunting dogs. However, the one surviving specimen, a stuffed dog displayed at Abergavenny Museum in Wales, is more reminiscent of a dachshund.

Modern sensibilities would be offended by such a use of dogs today.

Imagine how frustrated these dogs must have felt, endlessly running nowhere while the tantalizing aroma of roasting meat was all around them. Yet their continued use even when mechanical substitutes had become available could be explained by an affectionate attitude towards these dogged little workers, rather than simply a reluctance to embrace new technology. And don't we still give running-wheels to caged mice, hamsters and gerbils, on the grounds that they 'need exercise'?

European breeding restrictions were comparatively lax at first, and developed relatively late. The fact that the few genetically isolated 'ancient' breeds come from such far-flung locations (and none from Europe) suggests that they are relics of dogs that were carried, by human migration, out of Asia and south-eastern Europe, and were subsequently not interbred with more recent migrants, the most notable of which would have been the diverse types of dog developed in Europe in the Middle Ages and subsequently spread by colonialism. Such genetic isolation indicates a greater degree of human intervention in reproduction than for many other types of dog, although it is not possible to tell how much of this would have been achieved by selecting purebred partners for mating, and how much by culling or simple neglect of accidentally cross-bred puppies. By contrast, the DNA of modern dogs indicates that cross-breeding between different types of dog was commonplace in Europe and America. While much of this was probably accidental, historical records also indicate some deliberate breeding of unlikely combinations of types, just to see whether some useful new type might emerge.

Aside from the few genetically isolated 'ancient' breeds, cross-breeding of dogs continued apace in Europe and North America until the middle of the nineteenth century. The idea that a dog should be mated only with other identical dogs is a comparatively new one, dating back only about 150 years in Europe, the same notion then spreading rapidly to other countries. Nowadays, if a dog is to be registered as a particular breed, its parents, grandparents and so on for many generations must also have been registered as the same breed – a restriction known as the 'breed barrier'. Although many mongrels and cross-bred dogs continue to be born in the West, they are much less likely than pedigree dogs are to find homes and leave offspring of their own.

Pedigree breeding is the third phase of the transition from wolf to modern dog, each phase of which having been abetted by a different selective pressure. The first was the initial selection for tameness, from wolves that were already pre-adapted to scavenging from man. As we have seen, this process must have been essentially passive: the wolves that could tolerate interaction with man gradually isolated themselves reproductively from their wild cousins and became proto-dogs. In the second phase, deliberate selection by man for specific functions then began to become a factor, through attempted isolation of one type of dog from another. However, this was rarely, and then only locally, the factor controlling which dogs had descendants and which did not, given that deliberate selection occurred as isolated exceptions against a background of some deliberate, and much accidental, interbreeding. By contrast, the third and most recent stage of the transition from wolf to dog has seen an explosion of deliberate selection. Dogs are mated with other, virtually identical dogs, in an attempt to create 'ideal' breeds – most of which are cherished for their appearance, not their functionality.

Domestication has been a long and complex process, and despite the self-evident differences between types of dog, every dog alive today is a product of this transition. What was once another one of the wild social canids – the grey wolf – has been altered radically, to the point that is has become its own unique animal. In the course of this change, the dog has shed many of its wolf-like attributes, so much so that there is no reason to presume that the characteristics that define today's dogs are derived specifically from wolves; most of these are either products of domestication or general features of canids that predate the evolution of the grey wolf.

Whatever the selective pressures governing them, many of the characteristics that separate domestic dogs from the wild canids can be ascribed to changes in the rates at which the body and behaviour mature. As noted earlier, dogs are in many respects similar to juvenile canids; although they grow into adults in the narrow sense that they become capable of reproducing, they also remain immature in many other respects – a sort of arrested development that neatly accounts for the way they depend on their human owners for the whole of their lives.

Despite the differences between breeds, dogs are recognizably dogs – and not just as far as we humans are concerned. Dogs evidently recognize other dogs as such, even when the disparity in size and shape between them makes it seem implausible that they could. Dogs of all breeds, or almost all, must therefore retain some common social repertoire, enabling them both to recognize one another as dogs and to engage in some at least rudimentary communication. The question, then, is to what extent the dog's social capabilities are a product of domestication, and what has been inherited directly from the wolf – or possibly from even further back in the canids' evolutionary history.

3

Why Dogs Were – Unfortunately – Turned Back into Wolves

Today's dogs are clearly not wolves on the outside, but their behaviour is often interpreted as if they were still wolves on the inside. Indeed, now that we know for sure that the wolf is the dog's only ancestor, it seems impossible to avoid such comparisons. The idea that dogs retain most of the wolf's essential character is not only out of date, but also reflects some deep-seated misconceptions about wolf behaviour that science is only now beginning to overturn. Despite these holes in the dog-wolf theory, however, it is still widely used to inform dog training, with unfortunate consequences for dog and owner alike.

For more than fifty years, the concept of a dog as a wolf dressed up in a cute package dominated dog training and management, with results that were – to say the least – mixed. Some parts of the advice that logically flowed from this misconception are harmless, but others, if applied rigorously, can damage the bond between dog and owner. Moreover, equating dogs with wolves allows trainers and owners to justify physical punishment of the dog, by the mistaken analogy that wolf parents achieve control of their offspring through aggression.

The concept that dog behaviour is little changed from that of wolves does not sit well with the self-evident friendliness of the large majority of dogs. Most dogs love meeting other dogs, and most love people. This may seem a blindingly obvious statement, but, from a biologist's perspective, it is one that demands explanation. After all, neighbouring cats often spend their whole lives avoiding one another, whereas many dogs will try to greet every dog they come across. Where does this general affability come from?

The dog's sociability is even more remarkable when compared to that of its ancestors. Wolves from different packs try to avoid one another; if they do meet, they almost always fight, sometimes to the death. This is not unusual; modern biologists view all co-operative behaviour as exceptional, because the default behaviour of every animal should be to defend itself and its essential resources – its food, its access to mates, its territory – against all others, and especially against members of its own species, since these must be its most direct competitors. Wolves are no exception to this rule, and any wolf that failed to compete in this way would, all other things being equal, produce fewer offspring than its neighbours. Logically, therefore, any gene that predisposes a wolf to put the interests of other wolves first should eventually disappear. Of course, kin selection means that wolf packs composed of family groups do co-operate, because this co-operation enables them to propagate their genetic material most effectively. But unrelated groups, which share far fewer genes, will either avoid one another, or fight, if they do happen to meet.

Dogs, unlike wolves, are extraordinarily outgoing – yet even this trait has been interpreted as fitting into the idea of dogs' underlying wolfishness. Dogs that are self-evidently unrelated – say, from different breeds – are usually perfectly happy to meet when out being exercised by their owners. Yet many old-school trainers and dog experts would argue that dogs are friendly only because they are trained to be so. Within every dog, they maintain, lurks a savage wolf that could spring at any moment for the throat of any dog it meets, unless its owner remains in vigilant control. Despite having being comprehensively discredited by biologists and veterinary behaviourists more than a quarter of a century ago, this idea continues to have a surprisingly wide currency. Many training manuals still emphasize the need for constant vigilance against the moment when young dogs begin their inexorable attempts to dominate or control all around them, dog and human alike. The only answer, they say, is to make sure from day one that dogs know that their owner is boss – a stance that humans are supposed to be able to achieve by mimicking the way that dominant wolves control their packs.

Clearly, dogs' easy sociability requires further examination. Inasmuch as we do not have access to the world of the ancient, tameable, wolves from which dogs are descended, perhaps it would be best to set aside the origins of the dog altogether. Put simply, the question could be: how would dogs organize their lives if they had the choice, away from mankind's interference? Of course, this is not an easy question to answer because there are very few dogs who live free from human supervision. Dogs rarely survive for long far from human settlements, not least because domestication has all but destroyed their ability to hunt successfully. Although some elements of hunting behaviour have indeed been retained in some working breeds, few dogs, if any, possess the innate ability to put all these elements together, in order to locate, hunt, kill and consume prey on a regular basis – and certainly not when competing with other predators.

Although it is rare to find dogs that are not controlled by humans, there are enough of them for us to begin forming a picture of what a dog-run society might look like. All over the world there are millions of dogs, generically referred to as ferals or 'village dogs', that are just outside man's direct control. They live on the fringes of human society, scavenging from rubbish-dumps and begging for handouts, but they are otherwise independent of people and certainly show no allegiance to any human owner. Such dogs are commonplace in the tropics and subtropics: they go by different names, such as the pariah or pye dogs

Urban scavengers

of India, the Canaan dog from Israel, the Carolina dog from the southeastern United States, and the basenji-like village dogs of Africa. Their DNA suggests that many are indeed native to their areas. (By contrast, that of dogs from tropical America suggests descent from escaped purebred European dogs.) There are also a number of ancient types unique to a particular location, such as the New Guinea singing dog, the kintamani from Bali, and the Australian dingo, the only completely wild dog known to have originally descended from domestic dogs.

Because of its uniqueness, the dingo's story offers a tantalizing example of the social systems that dogs form when left to their own devices. Sometime between 5,000 and 3,500 years ago, a single, pregnant, domestic bitch – probably descended from the medium-sized dogs that originally evolved from wolves in Asia – arrived on the Cape York peninsula, the northernmost tip of mainland Australia, and escaped into the bush; later, her offspring were joined by a few others, transported by traders across the Torres Strait from New Guinea, as she must herself have been. On arrival in Australia, these escaped dogs found little competition from local (marsupial) carnivores, and rapidly became the dominant predator. They were thus able to, and still do, adopt several types of canid social structure; many individuals remain solitary outside of the breeding season, while others form packs of up to a dozen individuals.

Although their re-adaptation to the wild offers a compelling glimpse of how dogs might organize themselves in the absence of human intervention, the dingo is a problematic case study. The social behaviour of dingoes has been studied in detail only in captivity, where they maintain a pack structure in which sometimes only one pair breeds. As with wolves, this restriction of breeding could be an artefact of captivity, and of the enforced mixing of unrelated individuals. Moreover, dingoes have experienced several thousand generations of living in the wild, long enough to become undomesticated and to lose the characteristic behaviour of their village-dog forebears. What we know of the dingo is therefore not ideal for understanding how domestic dogs would organize themselves if they were allowed to do so unconstrained by captivity. Better would be studies of dogs that have not reverted to the wild so comprehensively.

Until about ten years ago, the few studies of ferals or 'village dogs' that had been published painted a misleading picture of their social organization. Their groupings appeared to be mere aggregations, with little co-ordination of activity. No compelling evidence was found for co-operative behaviour within feral dog 'packs'. Instead, researchers witnessed dogs fighting over food that could not easily be shared. Similarly, pregnant females would leave their packs to have their young, returning only when those puppies could stand up for themselves, and males played no part in looking after the young.

The reason these early studies of feral dogs revealed such competitive social 'systems' was, with a dash of hindsight, obvious. Most of the studies had been conducted in Western countries such as the United States, Italy and Spain, where feral dogs are generally regarded as a nuisance, and are never allowed to settle anywhere for long enough to develop their own social culture. The 'packs' that do form are generally composed of unrelated individuals, with none of the mutual assistance from close kin that benefits the typically interrelated wolf pack. Constantly at risk of being shot, trapped or poisoned, and prevented from accessing their food supplies (such as rubbish-dumps), these dogs probably never have the time to establish permanent relationships with others, let alone to develop a culture of co-operative behaviour. To flourish, co-operative behaviour relies on exactly the right circumstances – regular interaction with the same individuals, access to sufficient food and consistent shelter, and a structure based on family ties. Only then will a group be sufficiently coherent to act together against other groups without disadvantaging any of its own members. Because of the environments in which these early studies of feral dogs were conducted, they gave no indication as to where the enormous affability of domestic dogs had originated.

In short, a proper understanding of the sociable behaviour of domestic dogs required studies of feral dogs that were not persecuted, and so could form stable groups without a fear of man. Scientists found what they needed in West Bengal,[1] where villagers allow feral dogs to live alongside them, generally tolerating their presence even if the dogs choose to rest just outside a house's front door. Dogs like those in modern West Bengal appear to be little different from the dogs that lived in the Fertile Crescent of the Near East, where modern civilization is thought to have arisen some 10,000 years ago. Their behaviour may therefore be similar to that of some of the earliest domesticated dogs. In addition to scavenging, these 'pariah dogs' are also occasionally given food. But feeding does not constitute ownership; these are independent animals, living a commensal lifestyle like that of a city pigeon.

The independence of West Bengal's pariah dogs, maintained over many generations, gives them every opportunity to demonstrate the dog's natural social structure, some aspects of which mirror that of wolves. A given town may support several hundred individuals, but the dogs tend to cluster into smaller family groups numbering five to ten members, just like wolves or indeed other canids. Yet they forage singly, since there is no large local prey available that requires communal hunting, and so it is perhaps slightly misleading to refer to such groups as 'packs' in the wolf sense. However, they do share a communal territory, which they will defend against the members of neighbouring groups. So far, so much like wolves.

While some aspects of wild dogs' social structures are similar to those of wolves, their sexual behaviour and parental behaviour are radically different. Taken as a whole, the reproductive behaviour of these feral groups is quite unlike that of the grey wolf, and much more like that of other species from the dog family with far less structured social lives, such as the coyote. In a wolf pack, only one male and female will breed; they are conventionally referred to as the 'alpha' pair. But when each female pariah dog comes into heat, she is courted by many males, mostly from outside her own pack, with up to eight males fighting for her attention. Although she rejects some, several others may be judged worthy, and she is likely to copulate and 'tie' with each, sometimes even more than one on the same day. After mating is over, one of these males will often pair up and stay with her until after the pups are born. Some paired-up males will even go so far as to assist with feeding the litter by regurgitating food for them. Whether the male of a pair is usually the father of all, some or even *any* of the pups is unclear, so his reasons for investing his time in staying with the female can only be guessed at. Perhaps his hope is that if he helps with this litter, she will give him exclusive mating rights next time. Thus every 'pack' of pariah dogs annually fragments into pairs, each looking after their offspring separately, until they and their adolescent young rejoin the group. When the next mating season arrives, each adult may form a pair different from that of the previous year. Unlike in wolf packs, there is no apparent consistency in the family structure, nor do young adults help their parents in raising the next year's litter.

Pariah dogs

Pariah dog packs are, in many ways, quite unlike wild wolf packs – nor do they resemble the artificial wolf packs that are often assembled in zoos. Many groups contain several adult females, and they are usually tolerant of one another, even in the mating season. Unlike captive wolves, none seems to want to monopolize the best of the males, or to prevent others from breeding. Wolf-like ritualized indicators of dominance or submission are apparently never used by either males or females, although the dogs do seem to recognize one another – an ability essential to maintaining a group's cohesion – and regularly exchange what appear to be subtle greeting signals. However, there does seem to be some sort of hierarchy; the oldest breeding pair is the most aggressive, especially towards any unpaired males. Possibly the male of the pair sees these unpaired males as potential future rivals, while the female may be concerned for the safety of her pups.

A further striking difference is that neighbouring groups of pariah dogs seem to be able to coexist amicably, whereas adjacent wolf packs try to avoid one another whenever possible – and when they do meet, they almost always fight. Although aggression between members of different groups of West Bengal feral dogs does occur from time to time, in many such encounters both dogs defer to each other and then return to their core areas. These dogs do not appear to be motivated by any desire to dominate or displace their neighbours, who must occasionally compete with them for food, even those that they are presumably sure are unrelated to them. In short, the highly competitive nature of unrelated wolves seems to have been completely erased from feral dogs.

The West Bengal studies tell us a great deal about the way that dogs might prefer to organize their lives. They do not seem to be able to adopt the 'family pack' structure that is typical of the wolf. Although they do form bonds with family members, these bonds are far looser than among wolves; more important are the bonds between mother (and to some extent father) and their dependent young. As they grow to adulthood, the young share territory with their parents, but do not help them to raise their younger brothers and sisters. While dominance hierarchies are evident, they predict only which dogs get priority of access to food and shelter, not who breeds successfully. So despite the comparatively crowded conditions in which many feral dogs live, they behave like captive wolves no more than like wild wolves. There is not the slightest shred of evidence that they are constantly motivated to assume leadership of the pack within which they live, as the old-fashioned wolf-pack theory would have it.

The affability of dogs who are not related to each other and are not part of the same pack must have been a necessary component of domestication. For instance, domestic dogs live much more closely with one another than wolves do, a characteristic that must be a product of their adaptation to exploiting a new, more centralized food supply. Large predators such as wolves cannot afford to live at high densities, because they would never be able to find enough food. Wolf packs rarely have more than twenty or so members, and they defend very large territories. The dogs that accompanied hunter-gatherers, only recently domesticated from wolves, may have been equally intolerant. However, as soon as humans began to live in large permanent villages, dogs would have needed to evolve ways of coexisting with unrelated animals, the debilitating alternative being constant wariness and frequent fights. Although they exhibit this very characteristic today, and therefore illuminate the domestication process, the situation of the pariah dogs is, needless to say, a long way removed from that of a pet dog living in a typical household. Indeed, pet dogs are usually neutered, and even dogs kept primarily for breeding are not generally allowed to form long-term pair-bonds with the partner of their choice.

Given that pariah dogs do not organize their societies in the same way that wolves do, it seems unlikely that pet dogs would do so either, but the remote possibility does remain that pet dogs might somehow have re-evolved the desire for dominance that characterizes wolves in zoos and is so beloved of some old-school dog trainers. In order to examine this possibility, my students and I worked at a sanctuary for unhomed dogs in Wiltshire.[2] Such dogs serve as a useful intermediate between the feral and the pet dog, because they all started their lives in domestic circumstances, before being allowed unrestricted access to other similar dogs. At any one time the sanctuary contains about twenty dogs, usually castrated males whose behaviour towards people is judged to be too unpredictable for them to be homed. At night they sleep in spacious kennels shared by four or five dogs, but during the day they have the run of a large paddock planted with trees and bushes, littered with toys, and equipped with tunnels through which they can run from one part of the paddock to another.

If any group of pet dogs had the opportunity to establish a wolf-type hierarchy, it would be at a sanctuary like this one, where the dogs have eight hours a day of unregulated interaction with their own kind. However, many hours of observation failed to reveal anything of the sort. There was plenty of competitive behaviour to record: dogs would growl or bark at one another, pretend to bite each other's necks, attempt to mount one another, or chase one another around the paddock. Others would react by crouching, looking away, licking their lips or running off. Yet most of this behaviour took place between a minority of the dogs, whom we ended up calling 'The Insiders'. Three dogs, 'The Hermits', kept out of the way of all the others, and consequently almost never interacted, so it was difficult to know what their 'status', if any, might be. Seven others, 'The Outsiders', did not actively avoid The Insiders, but always gave way to them. Relationships between The Insiders themselves were inconsistent – it proved impossible for us to construct any kind of hierarchy from our data, let alone any of the types of hierarchy thought to occur among wolves. Over a third of the interactions took place between just four pairs of dogs

– Ronnie with Benson (both collie crosses), Jack (a springer) with Eddie (rough collie), Mickey Brown (German shepherd cross) with Branston (collie/spaniel), and Dingo (another shepherd cross) with Tarkus (a Weimaraner). Exactly why these pairs of 'buddies' had formed was unclear – none, as far as we could tell, were related – but these attachments were certainly not predicted by any aspect of wolf behaviour. They do, however, emphasize that dogs, unlike wolves, find it easy to establish harmonious relationships with dogs that they are not related to and have not met until both were adult.

Our study of the sanctuary dogs failed to uncover any evidence that dogs have an inclination to form anything like a wolf pack, especially when they are left to their own devices. This reinforces all the other scientific evidence indicating that domestication has stripped dogs of most of the more detailed aspects of wolf social behaviour, leaving behind only a propensity to prefer the company of kin to non-kin – a propensity shared by many animals and certainly not restricted to wolves or even canids. Nevertheless, many experts on dogs and dog training persist in alluding to the wolf as the essential point of reference for understanding pet dogs, despite the fact that the wolf they refer to is not the wild wolf, which values family loyalties above all else, but rather the captive wolf that finds itself in a constant battle with the unrelated wolves with which it is forced to live.

Despite all the evidence indicating that dogs and wolves organize their social lives quite differently, many people still cling to their misguided and outdated comparisons between dogs and wolves. The question therefore has to be asked once again: does the behaviour of the wolf have anything useful to tell us about the behaviour of pet dogs?

The misconception that dogs behave like wolves might not matter if it did not seriously misconstrue the dog's motivations for establishing social relationships. The most pervasive – and pernicious – idea informing modern dog-training techniques is that the dog is driven to set up a dominance hierarchy wherever it finds itself. This idea has led to massive misconceptions about their social relationships, both those between dogs within a household, and those between dogs and their owners.

Every dog, conventional wisdom holds, feels an overwhelming need to dominate and control all its social partners. Indeed, the word 'dominance' is used widely in descriptions of dog behaviour. Dogs that attack people they know well are still universally referred to as suffering from 'dominance aggression'. The term is sometimes even used – incorrectly – to describe a dog's personality. Consider this quote from the American Dog Trainers Network website: 'A dominant dog knows what he wants, and sets out to get it, any way he can. He's got charm, lots of it. When that doesn't work, he's got persistence with a capital "P". And when all else fails him, he's got attitude.'[3] Actually, this is just a description of an unruly, untrained, yet somehow charming, dog. It says nothing about what that dog's relationships with other dogs are like – nothing about its relationships, 'dominant' or otherwise. Other inaccurate or misleading uses of the term 'dominance' abound in dog training. For example, celebrity trainer Cesar Millan has referred to dogs trying to 'dominate' cats, and even a dog chasing the light from a laser pointer has been described as trying to 'dominate' it,[4] behaviour that a biologist would immediately classify as predatory, not social.

Used properly, 'dominance' means something quite different from these meanings assigned to it by dog trainers. The term simply describes a relationship between two individuals at a particular moment in time; it makes no predictions about how that situation arose, about how long it is likely to last, or about the personalities of those individuals. Indeed, a biologist would be likely to point out that if you put the dominant one of the two in another social situation, it might well end up *not* being 'dominant'. Moreover the term is just a description – it says nothing about whether the two animals involved are in any way themselves aware that theirs is a 'dominance' relationship.

Calling dogs 'dominant' also suggests that their relationships can be fitted into hierarchies. The concept of 'hierarchy' is the corollary of 'dominance', whenever a group consists of more than two individuals. If each pair can be observed to have a dominance relationship, and if those relationships can be arranged in a linear fashion, such that each individual is subordinate to all those above it, a hierarchy can be determined. Sometimes no such hierarchy can be constructed; this is the case, for example, when individuals that should be 'low down' in the hierarchy according to most of their relationships nonetheless 'dominate' an individual that 'dominates' many others and should therefore be 'high up' in the hierarchy. Furthermore, just as the dominance relationships between all the pairs that make up the hierarchy may not be appreciated as such by the individuals involved, so too the hierarchy may not be visible to those within it, even if one is evident to an outside observer.

There is little evidence that hierarchy is a particular fixation of dogs, either in their relationships with other dogs or in those with their owners. Let us first examine what hierarchy *is*. Let us assume that dominance relationships are based on how much of a single attribute – say, fighting ability – a dog possesses: the dog with the most of that 'quality' should be dominant over all the other dogs in its household, and might be labelled the 'alpha'. The dog with the second largest quantity of fighting ability should be dominant over all the others, except the alpha, and is conventionally labelled the 'beta'. The dog with the least fighting ability – the one subordinate to all the other dogs – is labelled the 'omega'. In a four-dog household, the hierarchy might look like this:

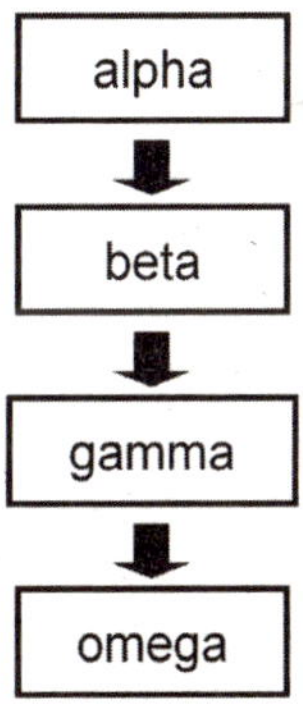

Linear hierarchy

Relationships between real animals are usually not as simple as this neat hierarchical arrangement. Some relationships may have been resolved by fighting; others, through superior problem-solving ability. Still others may be historical in that the 'subordinate' dog was brought into the household as a puppy and has never challenged any of the older adults. When such complexities apply, it may be possible to distinguish consistent relationships between pairs of dogs, but impossible to arrange them in a hierarchy, like this:

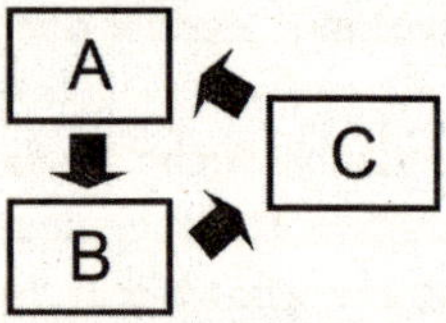

Circular 'hierarchy'

Traditional thinking presumes that the dog's hierarchy stems from the wolf's, and more specifically, from that of the captive wolf – but we now know that this conception is fundamentally misguided. The typical structure of a captive wolf 'pack' was thought to be made up of two hierarchies, one for each sex, although in larger packs these are not entirely linear, since dominance relationships between the juveniles and between the cubs are often indistinct. However, these 'hierarchies' are now thought to be an artefact of captivity, whereas the structure of a natural pack depends largely on family allegiances in which no aggression-based hierarchy is apparent at all.

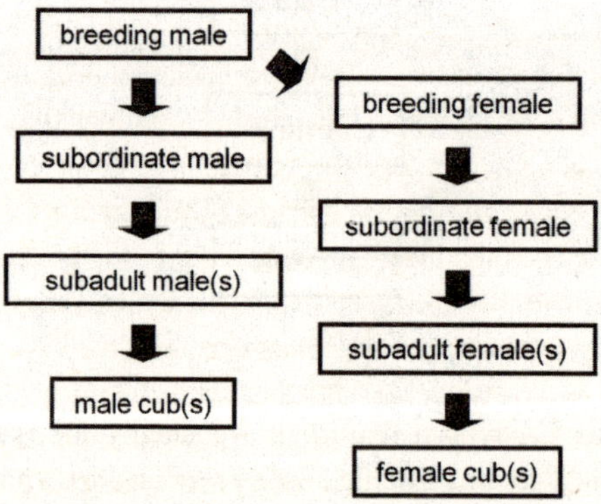

Captive wolf-pack hierarchy

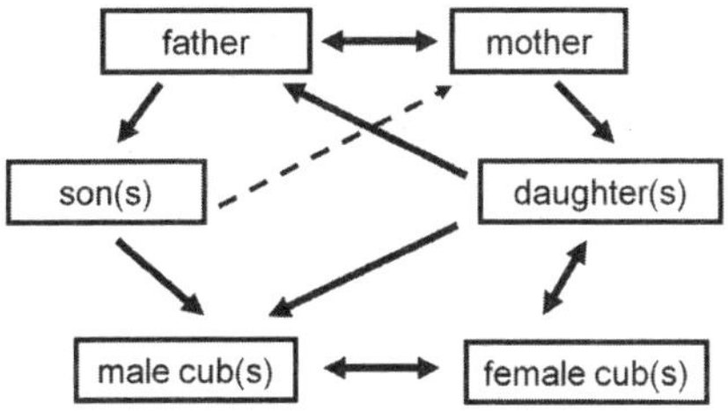

Wolf-pack family structure

In the wild, then, a dominant, or 'alpha', wolf is just the wolf that leads the pack, usually because it is the mother or father of most or all of the other members of the pack. The normal way for a wolf to become a 'dominant' animal is simply to become sufficiently mature and experienced to be able to find a mate, and then to breed. The term 'dominant' thus becomes synonymous with 'mother' or 'father', or occasionally 'stepmother' or 'stepfather', if one of the breeding pair dies and is replaced before the pack breaks up.

Since it is clear that modern wolves are almost certain to be much more wary of man than were the domestic dog's wild ancestors, we should logically consider whether the social grouping preferred by modern wolves – the family-based pack – is likely to have also been the preferred social structure of the wolves that became dogs, tens of thousands of years ago. It is, of course, impossible to be sure about how these ancient wolves organized their societies, because social structures do not fossilize. However, we can be confident that wolves lived in packs then as now, because the family unit is the basis for packs wherever they occur among the canids; family groups are inherently more stable than groups formed by unrelated individuals.

Since it was probably shared with ancient wolves, the canids' intrinsically family-based structure is almost certainly the raw material that domestication had to work with. In that case, the most likely explanation for how we have been able to domesticate dogs is that we have been able to insert ourselves into that family structure. By this, I do not mean 'family' in the genetic sense; that is clearly impossible. I mean 'family' in the sense of a group whose members live together and are able to co-operate because they know one another well. Family members do not have to be genetically related to one another in order to function effectively; for instance, as an adopted human baby grows up, it behaves towards its adoptive parents as if they were its genetic parents. Although such babies may eventually come to know that they have other, biological parents, this knowledge does not displace the bond they have with the adults who have cared for them. The reason is that, in our species, recognition of immediate family members is largely based upon familiarity, even though we come to overlay this with more conscious knowledge of our actual genetic relationships. Biologically, as a species with a long period of childhood dependency, we are set up to base our family bonds on who looks after us and is affectionate towards us; our instinctive ability to distinguish who is actually related to us genetically is comparatively weak (much weaker than in species with little or no parental care).

Much as human children bond to their carers, regardless of their biological connection, as puppies grow they come to regard both their canine and human carers as 'family'. This capacity must be a product of domestication, for while dogs can bond to humans in this way it is difficult to get wolves to do the same, even if they are separated from their mother and siblings and hand-reared by people. Domestication must have introduced a much greater fluidity into the process whereby 'family' allegiances are learned, such that humans can be incorporated as well as other dogs, whether or not those dogs are actually genetic relatives.

Since wolves and other canids share a fundamentally co-operative social structure – and since this social system was probably critical to our domestication of dogs – it is illogical to suggest that the process of domestication replaced this co-operative system with a 'dominance' structure based on self-interest and aggression. If anything, domestication, by requiring dogs to live in close proximity to one another, should have made dogs more tolerant of one another, and certainly not less so. For this reason alone, concepts of 'dominance' and 'hierarchy', so beloved among much of the dog-training community, are fundamentally implausible. Moreover, such hierarchical behaviour is not readily apparent in natural wolf packs, and studies of feral dogs have also failed to find hierarchical structures – most of feral dogs' competitive behaviour is seasonal, and seen in the context of mating and breeding, not in establishing permanent 'dominance' relationships. As a whole, the terms 'dominance' and 'hierarchy' can, it seems, no longer be justified to account for the behaviour of pet dogs.

Rejecting the idea of dominance as a natural driver of dog behaviour is not the same as saying that dogs are never competitive – of course they are, when they have to be. Put several un-neutered dogs of the same sex that do not know one another into a small space, and they are likely to set up a temporary 'hierarchy' based on threats, or even fighting, especially if they can sense that there is a member of the opposite sex nearby. This outcome would occur with almost any species, having nothing to do with the dog being descended from the wolf (although it does resonate with the conflict seen in some artificially constructed captive wolf packs). However, such situations are very unnatural, in that they seem almost designed to provoke conflict, telling us nothing about what goes on in dogs' heads when they live in a multi-dog household, or when they meet another dog in the park – or, for that matter, how they perceive their human owners.

The old 'dominance' model of dog behaviour is based on three concepts, each of which is now known to be false. First, it is derived from how wolves behave when they are living in unnaturally constituted groups in captivity, and not from the natural behaviour of wolves living in wild packs. Second, ferals or 'village dogs', when allowed to establish family groups, do not behave like wolves at all, neither captive nor wild. These feral dogs, which are much closer to the ancestors of our pet dogs than any wolf, are much more tolerant of one another than any other modern canid would be if it lived at such high density; initially, this tolerance was a consequence of domestication, and it has been maintained by the necessity of remaining tolerant in order to survive around people. Third, although dominance based on competition and aggression does occur among wolves in captivity, dogs kept under similar conditions do not establish hierarchies.

Ultimately, the behaviour of captive wolves is of little or no relevance to understanding dog behaviour. Not only is the behaviour of captive wolves now known to be unnatural, but it is also clear that domestication has radically altered the social repertoire of the wild species. Dogs have taken an evolutionary path quite different from that of the wolf, so, if we are to understand dog behaviour, we shall need to do so on fundamentally different terms.

Since the practice of explaining the behaviour of dogs by referring back to one of their ancestors, the wolf, has been discredited, some alternative is needed if we are to understand not only why dogs behave the way they do, but also how they interpret and respond to our behaviour. In recent years, much of our understanding of how to relate to dogs has revolved around the notion of hierarchy. Indeed, many animals, not just wolves, appear to construct their groups in a hierarchical way. But often those hierarchies are constructed by scientists for their own purposes, for example, to test whether the animals that fight the most are also the most successful at breeding (and, more often than you might expect, they are not). The fact that a hierarchy can be observed by scientists does not mean that any of the animals involved have any awareness of that hierarchy. In short, the use of any hierarchical model, wolf or otherwise, presumes that the animals behave in the way they do because they are responding to their own conception of that hierarchy.

The question of whether or not dogs understand the notion of hierarchy – and their own place within it – has a very profound implication for the way that we relate to them. If dogs do understand this concept, then training methods based on concepts like 'status reduction' and 'putting the dog in its place' have a logical foundation, and thus should be effective. But if dogs have no concept of their own status, then such methods are likely to convey a different message to them than that which was intended. Many of these methods are based on inflicting punishment on the dog. The question of whether or not dogs understand hierarchies is not just an academic exercise, therefore; it may have real consequences for their welfare.

To ascertain whether dogs understand the concept of hierarchy, we need to refine our analysis. Rather than trying to second-guess what dogs are thinking, based on an outmoded concept of what they might have inherited from their wild ancestors, it is perhaps more useful to go back to first principles: dogs' fundamental objectives in life. We know what dogs need. At the most basic level, they need food and water and opportunities to mate and raise offspring, thus ensuring the survival of their genes. In domestic situations, all of these needs are taken care of by humans. So the next question is, what do dogs want? These desires will generally connect back to something dogs needed during their evolutionary history (but not necessarily currently), and will involve both the things they required for survival and the means of achieving them. For example, a hungry carnivore wants (and needs) to eat, but even if it is not hungry, it will often want to look for food, in case its luck is about to run out and it does not find anything to eat for a while. On a longer timescale, it may also want to maintain a foraging territory where it has exclusive rights to hunt. As a youngster, it may want to play with objects, which may ultimately improve its hunting skills, even though it is almost certainly never aware of this connection: the 'want' is enough to promote its survival. Some of these 'wants' can be satisfied without disadvantaging any other member of the species. For example, play-fighting between littermates is mutually beneficial; both participants improve their competitive skills, and, because they are closely related, the survival of their genes improves twofold.

Many of dogs' 'wants' bring individuals into conflict with one another. Two animals cannot satisfy their hunger if there is only enough food for one; if all the available space is already occupied, a newcomer cannot gain an exclusive territory without displacing an existing territory-holder. The dominance framework describes one set of ways in which such conflict is avoided; some individuals, by being able to impose themselves on others, guarantee themselves priority of access to all resources – their 'wants' are met first. However, the dominance concept is unnecessarily restrictive in the context of thinking about how conflict can be resolved without coming to blows.

One alternative to the dominance model can better explain how dogs avoid potential disputes: the Resource Holding Potential (RHP) model. According to this model, whenever a conflict of interests arises, each dog is thought to make its decision based on the answers to two questions: how much do I want this resource (food, toy, etc.), and how likely is it that the other dog is going to beat me if we fight for it? One factor that the individual dog should take into account when answering the latter question is, how much does it look as though my opponent wants the resource? This opens the door to the possibility of cheating; animals that threaten first and most emphatically may win even when they are no bigger than their opponent. If two dogs know each other, their memories of previous disputes are also available to be taken into account. If not, they may use information they have gathered during encounters with similar-looking dogs, perhaps even during disputes between other dogs they have watched. So, prior acquaintance is not absolutely necessary: the RHP model can be used just as well when the two dogs are meeting for the first time.

The RHP model can therefore be applied to many more situations than the dominance model can. Studies done in my research group[5] have shown that dogs do indeed take account of how much another dog wants (or at least appears to want) a particular thing. Within groups of dogs that live together, it is male dogs especially that exemplify this principle. For example, in one group of French bulldogs, one of the four bitches appeared to have priority of access to food, even though she was not the oldest or the mother of the most recent litter (a finding that also contradicts the wolf model). The single male deferred to her over food, but usually had priority of access to toys, and to the first sniff of any unfamiliar male dog. Among five Shetland sheepdogs, both of the males would allow any of the three females to feed first, but not give priority of access in any other context, including access to people and other dogs, male or female. Observations like these provide further evidence that pure 'status' cannot be the guiding principle for dogs' competition over resources; if it were, one of the dogs in these groups should have enforced the right to prior access to everything, for fear that if it did not, it would be showing weakness, inviting a challenge from one of the others. In this respect, dogs seem to be obeying one main 'rule' of the RHP model: if another dog seems to want something badly, and you do not, then it is not worth getting into an argument over it.

The basic RHP model has one significant drawback when applied to dogs. Dogs seem to try diligently to assess others' intentions, but many appear not to have heard about the other main 'rule' of RHP: do not pick a fight if your opponent is a lot bigger than you are. Most animals are extremely good at gauging the size and strength of their opponent, even when the difference is quite small: picking unnecessary fights with those that are bigger than you are is, of course, likely to result in injury. One might expect this rule to apply even more so to dogs, given the enormous range of sizes between the biggest and the smallest breeds, greater than in any other species of animal – but it does not. At some time or other, everyone will have witnessed a small feisty dog meeting a larger dog in the park, and forcing it to retreat. More systematic studies that I have contributed to have borne this out:[6] neither the way that two dogs first approach one another nor the outcome (which one retreats first) depends upon which is the larger or heavier of the two. Nor did size appear to have had any influence on the relationships between the dogs that we observed in the Wiltshire sanctuary. Unusually among the whole of the animal kingdom, dogs seem to pay little attention to size in considering whether or not to start a challenge with another dog that they do not know. Instead, individual dogs vary in terms of how bold they are in such situations, as if it were a part of their 'personality'. The RHP model therefore has to be modified if it is to be applied to dogs: when one dog is deciding how to proceed in an encounter, the apparent motivation of the other dog seems to be given greater weight than its actual size and hence likely strength.

Dogs' lack of attention to size when competing over resources may be a product of domestication. In the wild, aggression emerges when much is at stake, that is, when an animal is in danger of losing its territory, when it is very hungry or thirsty and another is preventing it from eating or drinking, and when it is competing with others for the opportunity for access to a receptive member of the opposite sex. Today's dogs encounter these problems far less frequently, if at all; access to all these key resources is controlled by people, and so the requirement to be very careful before starting an unwinnable fight, imposed on wild animals by natural selection, is no longer as important for dogs. Nevertheless, starting fights under any circumstances is risky for dogs, for three reasons. First, because they may get seriously injured, which could, before the advent of modern veterinary surgery, have had life-threatening consequences. Second, because their human masters, for most breeds at least, value tolerance of other dogs, and tend to breed from animals that were tolerant of the proximity of other dogs. Third, because dogs with high general thresholds for aggression pose the least risk to humans, especially to children.

Because of the various incentives not to start fights, aggression is unlikely to be the default strategy for any normal domestic dog when it meets another of its own kind. Most owners are able to exercise their dogs in public areas without fear that they will try to 'dominate' every unfamiliar dog they come across. Even at first encounters, most dogs prefer to use signalling to defuse any potential aggression: hackles may be raised briefly, but are then lowered again as the two participants decide either not to get too close to one another, or to approach one another to sniff since the associated risk is low.

As two dogs get more familiar with one another, they will learn to look for specific signs that predict how the other is going to react to any given action. For example, if a puppy is brought into a household that already contains an older dog that likes its food but has little interest in toys, the puppy will learn that trying to steal food gets a warning growl, but that grabbing a toy from under the other dog's nose does not. A harmonious relationship should build up between the two, in which each knows and respects the other's preferences and quirks. The way this happens need not, and probably does not, involve highly sophisticated intelligence on the part of either dog; simple learning is probably sufficient. If there are three or more dogs in the household, however, it is likely that each dog can rely on its observations of the other two interacting, as well as its own interactions with them, as part of the information that it can use to predict how they will behave in a particular situation.

Importantly, when dogs are learning about other dogs, they do not do so in the same way we humans do when we are establishing our own relationships. Dogs are unlikely to be able to associate events (unless they occur within a few seconds of each other) or to perform mental time-travel. We have no evidence that dogs can actually think ahead in order to predict what another dog will do next, or even recall specific incidents from the past that involved that dog. Rather, they seem continually to refine simple 'rules of thumb' that enable them to get along with one another – 'avoid that other dog when he's eating', or 'playing a tugging game with this dog is fun because he lets me win sometimes, but it's not fun with that one because he always wants to take the toy away'.

Further observations of dogs' interactions can provide more clues about how they manage their own behaviour when encountering other dogs. Each cycle of refinement of dogs' 'rules of thumb' has a slightly smaller effect than the previous cycle; or, to put it another way, the first few encounters can be crucial in determining the form of a 'rule'. For example, if the older dog had been unwell or in pain when the puppy first came into the house, it may have responded by snapping at the puppy when it came near. The puppy, in its next few interactions with the older dog, might then recall the tinge of fear it felt in those first few encounters. If by then the older dog was well, and able to behave in a more friendly way, that fear would soon be forgotten. However, transfer this scenario to a dog that the puppy meets only occasionally, perhaps a neighbour's dog, and the fear may become a permanent fixture of the relationship. Not only that, but the puppy may generalize its fear to all other similar dogs: 'medium-sized brown dogs with bushy tails make me scared'. This feeling may become very persistent if nothing happens to counteract it, emphasizing the need for owners to be careful when introducing a puppy or young dog to other dogs. It can also explain why two otherwise quite well-behaved dogs fight when they first meet, if each has previously developed a fear that is triggered by the appearance of the other. A Labrador that has previously been attacked by a small brown terrier will start to feel anxious whenever it sees a similar dog, and this will quickly become evident from its tense body posture. Moreover, if the terrier that has unwittingly triggered this anxiety has a history that makes it fearful of black dogs, and neither is in a position to back down (for example, they meet on a narrow path), then both may try to alleviate their fear by turning to anger and attacking the other.[7]

Dogs that live in the same household can usually overcome such setbacks; they literally learn how to get along, in ways that the theory of 'dominance' overlooks. To observers, the relationships that arise can look like a set of 'dominance relationships', which taken together look like a 'hierarchy'. In my study of French bulldogs, one of the bitches could be described as 'dominant' because the other bitches usually (but by no means always) deferred to her. But we have no evidence that the dogs themselves saw it this way. It is much more likely that the other three bitches in the group, one the daughter of the 'dominant' one and the others older, unrelated animals, each individually remembered her as being grumpy towards them when food appeared. Recalling this would not make them anxious, because their owner saw to it that they got enough to eat, so it would not – and, indeed, did not – cost them anything to give way.

The ways that dogs interact with each other when they meet can thus be explained without reference either to 'dominance' in general, or to the captive wolf-pack model in particular. Even in groups of dogs that live together, what might appear to be a hierarchical structure is almost certainly a projection of our preconceived notions of canid relationships. There is no evidence that suggests that all dogs are motivated by the desire to achieve 'status' over other dogs; although some dogs undoubtedly appear more competitive than others, in all likelihood they are simply more strongly motivated to compete for things they happen to value highly – toys, for example – without being even slightly aware that they are thereby achieving something that we might (misleadingly) label 'status'. Of course, we cannot be certain that wolves have this capacity either, so it is quite possible that their 'hierarchies' are also apparent only to us, and not to the wolves themselves. As predicted by the RHP model, each individual dog (or wolf) is likely to be using its experience of previous encounters to gauge how to behave, each time it interacts with another of its own kind; these 'rules of thumb' enable it to coexist comfortably with every other individual in its group. The range of experiences each individual can call upon will vary depending on how familiar it is with the other dog, but whether the other individual is totally unknown or one of its lifelong companions, the dog will use what information it has available to judge the other's behaviour and proceed in the safest but most effective way possible. Consideration for its own safety will inhibit aggression, which is dangerous to both parties, while its experience of previous encounters will cause it to focus on gauging whether the other dog appears interested or uninterested in the resource in question. The majority of encounters between dogs pass without incident, with neither of the participants knowing or caring that its 'status', as some experts would have it, may have been affected.

Unfortunately, the idea that dogs see everything in terms of 'status' has been embraced most emphatically in interpretations of relationships between dogs and their owners. In the popular conception of these relationships, the dog perceives the owner as just another member of the pack – and as an obstacle to the dog's accumulation of 'status'. By encouraging owners to believe that their dogs will, at some point, try to 'dominate' them and take control of the household, this idea promotes the use of 'status reduction' techniques, and physical punishment if these fail. But if the dog has no concept of 'status' – and we have reason to believe it does not – then none of these techniques is going to achieve precisely what is intended. Some techniques (especially the punishment) will alter the dog's behaviour, but not necessarily in the desired direction.

Many dog trainers still rely heavily on the idea that most dogs try to control the human families that adopt them. In this way of thinking, dogs must conceive of humans as members of their own species, albeit rather strange two-legged ones, and their behaviour towards people must therefore be derived from what occurs in wolf society; this has been termed the 'lupomorph' model.[8] There may be some truth in this model; after all, if it were completely false, such that dogs think of humans as completely distinct from them, then it seems likely that dogs would have to have evolved a totally novel set of behavioural responses towards humans, at an early stage in domestication. But that conclusion seems implausible, given how much overlap there is between how dogs interact with humans and the ways they interact with each other. Still, some dog trainers have taken to the extreme the notion that dogs think of humans as being similar to themselves.

The model adopted by many dog trainers has generally followed the outmoded view of dogs as constantly struggling to assert dominance, over their own kind and hence over humans as well.[9] In order to account for the generally harmonious nature of most dog-owning households, these trainers assume that some dogs automatically 'respect' the superior status of their human pack members, possibly because they come to realize that humans are smarter than they are, or alternatively, simply because the humans evidently function like parents in providing food. However, they portray other dogs as attempting to achieve, or actually achieving, dominance over one or several family members and repeatedly exhibiting aggressive behaviour in order to affirm their position in the 'social hierarchy' of the 'pack'. In this view, the undivided attention that dogs give to their owners and families is unwavering surveillance for an opportunity to move upwards in the hierarchy.

Many dog trainers and behaviour experts still wholeheartedly support this concept – despite the fact that science has almost completely repudiated it – and have even come up with rules designed to thwart dogs' supposed attempts at domination. According to these trainers, the 'dominant dog' constantly gives himself away by his body-language. If he puts his chin or paw on his owner's knee, it means he thinks he is taking control of his owner's behaviour, and is therefore on the road to becoming the pack leader. To forestall this attempt at 'domination', they go on to assert, owners should always move the dog's paw or chin off their leg. However, for some reason such trainers make exceptions for small dogs: if these are used to sitting on their owners' laps, this does not necessarily mean the dog thinks he is dominant. As an additional measure to prevent dogs from assuming dominance, owners are urged always to go through doors and gates in front of their dog.[10] Some trainers have even come up with elaborate lists of these 'commandments' – such as those in the following example – that are supposed to stop your dog from thinking it is dominant over you.

1. Do not allow your dog to eat its meal until you (the top dog) have eaten first.
2. Do not allow your dog to leave the house (den) before you (the top dog) have passed through the doorway first.
3. Do not allow your dog to climb onto the sofa or bed (only top dogs are allowed to rest in the cosiest places).
4. Do not allow your dog to climb your stairs, or to peer at you from the top of the staircase.
5. Do not allow your dog to peer into your eyes.
6. Do not cuddle or stroke your dog.
7. Do not interact with your dog unless you are involved in some kind of training.
8. Do not greet your dog when you come home from work or from the shops etc.
9. Do not greet your dog first thing in the morning; it should be the one to greet you (the top dog).
10. Do not allow your dog to keep the toy at the end of a game; it will interpret this as winning.[11]

The effects of these 'commandments' vary greatly, but none of them are especially constructive. Indeed, if dogs do not have a concept of 'status', and there is no evidence that they do, then some of these recommendations will be either harmless or incidentally beneficial to the dog–owner relationship. For example, many owners will prefer not to encourage their dogs to go upstairs, or sleep on their beds with them, though there is no evidence that allowing either would in itself have any effect on their relationship in general. Other 'commandments', however, such as the admonishment against cuddling or stroking the dog, seem aimed at taking much of the pleasure out of keeping a dog, turning dog-keeping from a joy into a challenge.

Some of these 'commandments' have been investigated scientifically, but none of those examined were supported by the research. In one study by my colleague Dr Nicola Rooney, dogs were allowed to win tug-of-war games played with a person, over and over again; understandably, this made the dogs more keen to play with people than when they were forced to lose every time, but there were no signs indicating that any dog became 'dominant' as a result. In another of her studies, owners reporting that they always let their dogs win games were found to be no more likely to have disobedient dogs than owners who always insisted on winning, whereas dogs whose owners liked to play contact games, such as rough-and-tumble, were noticeably more attached to their owners than those that were usually kept at arm's length. Not only were dogs that had been allowed to break the ten commandments listed above not in control of their owners' behaviour, but they were also no more aggressive, which they should have been if their owners had inadvertently given them the green light to take over the household.[12]

There is one more problem with the dominance theory of training, and it is especially significant: even if wolves themselves are inclined to dominate each other, it seems unlikely that domesticated dogs would have retained this desire to dominate. Even if we believe that dogs can only perceive us as if we were other dogs (or wolves), and even if we accept the dubious assertion that canids have a drive to dominate other canids, there is no logical basis for assuming that they would automatically want to control us. Domestication should have favoured exactly the opposite; dogs that passionately want us to control them.

It seems very likely that, in the early stages of domestication, any dog that tried to take control of the human family it lived with would have been rejected in favour of one that was more biddable. Thus, even if there are some wolves that do have this hypothetical drive to dominate their 'pack', and this character trait is heritable, it seems highly unlikely that wolves with this trait would have contributed significantly to the ancestry of the domestic dog.

It has become abundantly clear that the model upon which many people are training, managing and simply interacting with their dogs is fundamentally wrong. The traditional 'lupomorph' model is contradicted both by the current conception of how wolves actually organize their lives and by the logic of the domestication process – and since it does not explain dog–dog social behaviour adequately, it is also highly unlikely to be of any use in explaining relationships between dogs and their owners. Nevertheless, this model is still promulgated by many dog trainers, who use it to justify their methods. These trainers frequently portray owners as misinterpreting their dogs' motivations, and promote the 'dominance' model as the only way to restore healthy relationships. At the very least, this approach saps the joy out of dog ownership; at worst, it is used to justify physical punishment as an unavoidable component of training. Many people now think that these punishment-reliant training methods are unnecessarily stressful for the dog. While they may appear superficially effective, such methods often do not work well in the long term, for reasons that are abundantly clear to those scientists who study how animals learn.

4

Sticks or Carrots? The Science of Dog Training

Currently, dog training has a high profile in the media; evidently it makes for good television, as evidenced by the rise of celebrities like Cesar Millan, the 'Dog Whisperer', and Victoria Stilwell, presenter of *It's Me or the Dog*. But there is tremendous disagreement among dog trainers about the best approach to shaping dog behaviour. A number of high-profile trainers and behaviourists continue to promote the idea that dogs are pack animals and that many can be controlled only through the application of 'dominance' theory and the use of physical punishment. For example, Cesar Millan writes: 'Dogs have an ingrained pack mentality. If you're not asserting leadership over your dog, your dog will try to compensate by showing dominant or unstable behaviour'.[1] Or this from UK 'Expert Dog Trainer and Canine Behaviourist' Colin Tennant: 'Most dogs will strive to dominate any other dogs or humans with whom they come into contact by body language and/or growling, biting or aggressive physical bullying.'[2]

Others, such as Karen Prior, Patricia McConnell and Jean Donaldson, radically disagree with this approach, rejecting the wolf-pack analogy and advocating the training of dogs as if they were any other animal. Furthermore, they emphasize that training should be based around rewards and abhor the unnecessary use of physical punishment. Dr Ian Dunbar, one of the originators of this approach, states that compliance, the goal of all dog training, is most often achieved through positive training methods, specifically the lure-reward methods – using treats and praise – that he pioneered. Dunbar, a veterinarian and dog and puppy trainer with more than twenty-five years' experience, bases his methods soundly on dog psychology, backed up by a doctorate in animal behaviour from the University of California, Berkeley, and a decade of research on communication and behaviour in domestic dogs. The debate between the two camps has at times become heated, even personal. For example, Dunbar has said of Millan: 'He has nice dog skills, but from a scientific point of view, what he says is, well . . . different. Heaven forbid if anyone else tries his methods, because a lot of what he does is not without danger.'[3]

These differences of opinion are not just of interest to the dog trainers involved; they have real effects on the welfare of dogs. Every year, many dogs are abandoned, even euthanized, because they have come to behave in unacceptable ways. In many cases, these behavioural problems are the result of inept or inconsistent training. For this reason, it is essential that we try to understand how dogs really learn, and thus which training methods and philosophies are most effective. Getting training right is essential both to the welfare of dogs and to the peace of mind of their owners.

The notion that dogs are wolves under the skin still pervades much of dog training today, despite having been abandoned by the scientific and veterinary communities and an increasing number of dog trainers. The 'wolf pack' approach promotes two interdependent ideas: that dogs, because of their ingrained 'pack mentality', can be controlled only if their owners adopt the role of pack leader, and that the most reliable way to ensure this outcome is by the use of physical punishment. Both these ideas go back to at least the nineteenth century, but were given added reinforcement, or so it seemed at the time, by the studies of captive wolf packs that were conducted in the middle of the twentieth century. Now that a more accurate picture of wolf society has emerged, based on family ties, the credibility of both ideas has been seriously undermined, yet they are still widely promoted.

The widespread use of punishment-based dog training is usually traced back to Colonel Konrad Most, whose highly influential book *Training Dogs: A Manual* first appeared in 1910 (in German) and was translated into English, thanks to popular demand, in 1944. Most was emphatic that the relationship between man and dog was not only hierarchical – with only one 'winner' – but also could be established only through physical force, by an actual struggle in which the man was instantaneously victorious. The dog had to be convinced of the absolute physical superiority of the man.[4] This approach demands that the owner constantly maintain and reinforce his or her position at the head of the family pack. In this conception the dog perceives the people it lives with as fellow members of its pack, and misbehaviour is construed as being due to a failure of the owners to maintain their dominance over the dog. Training methods are accordingly designed to lower the dog's position in the hierarchy, or 'pecking order' as it is sometimes referred to.

The Monks of New Skete, bestselling authors of dog-training manuals for more than thirty years, are highly influential promoters of this philosophy. They maintain that understanding wolf behaviour will help owners to understand their dogs, and that many books about wolves are often of more use to owners who wish to understand and appreciate their dog's behaviour than dog-training manuals.[5]

The Monks are very specific in turning this principle into practice. For instance, for aggressive dogs, they recommend the 'Alpha-wolf roll-over'. This is a disciplinary technique nicknamed for the way the lead wolf is supposed to punish misbehaving members of the pack,[6] whereby the dog is grasped firmly by the scruff of its neck and vigorously rolled over on to its back. For puppies, they recommend the 'shakedown method', which they claim resembles what the mother does to her pups to keep order in the litter:[7] the puppy is grasped by the loose skin on either side of its neck, lifted off its front feet and shaken.

Those dog trainers, such as Dr Ian Dunbar, who promote reward-based methods regard this 'dominance reduction' as both unnecessarily cruel and based on a complete misconception; they fundamentally reject the assumption that because an animal is misbehaving it must mean that the misbehaviour is motivated by a desire to have high rank. Instead, they rely on much simpler explanations based on the science of animal learning, emphasizing that many of the behaviours performed by animals are performed simply because those behaviours have been rewarded many times in the past.[8] They rarely make special reference to the dog's origins as a wolf, since the effects of reward on behaviour are universal among vertebrate animals.

Some experts go even further, asserting that training techniques derived from the dominance concept can actually harm the dogs they are applied to. Their uppermost concern is that the punishment-based methods, often used in an attempt to cure a supposed 'dominance problem', may initially suppress the behaviour, but can then cause the dog to become depressed and withdrawn.[9] Even worse is what can occur if the 'dominance reduction schedule' does not work: if the misbehaviour continues, the owners may come to think that they are not asserting their position strongly enough, and become more and more aggressive in their attitude. Eventually the dog may become so fearful of them that it bites them in self-defence.[10]

Personally, I am delighted that the most recent scientific evidence backs up an approach to managing dogs that I am comfortable with. As a scientist as well as a dog-lover, I am dedicated to assessing the best evidence available and then deciding on the most logical approach to adopt. If wild wolf packs had turned out to be as fraught with tension as their counterparts in zoos, I would have had to agree that the dominance approach had merit. I would still have been reluctant to adopt punishment rather than reward as my philosophy for training my dog, because for me the whole point of having a dog is the companionship it brings, and for me domination and companionship do not gel. As a dog owner, I was relieved by the discrediting of the wolf-pack idea, since I could then explain to myself and, more importantly, to others why routinely punishing a dog is not only unnecessary but also counterproductive.

Both sides of the debate over proper techniques for dog training claim that their approaches are based on serious science. Dog owners, not surprisingly, have trouble assessing which claims are true and, therefore, how best to train their dogs. The issue of how closely dogs' behaviour aligns with the behaviour of their wolf ancestors turns out to be something of a distraction in this regard, because when it comes to training the most important question is really: how do dogs learn?

First of all, it is important to stress that dogs are learning all the time, not just during formal training. Or, to put it another way, dog owners often do things that train their dogs, without being aware that they are doing them. Dogs learn especially fast while they are growing up; they can modify the so-called 'instinctive' ways in which they communicate with one another and with us, they learn how to get on with other dogs and with the people they meet. From a young dog's perspective, there is not much difference between the training class and its everyday life; the dog will learn all the time. However good the training session may have been, owners need to bear in mind all the opportunities their dogs have for learning, not just those formally labelled as 'training'.

Dogs learn in much the same way that other mammals – including humans – learn. However, all species vary slightly in terms of what they find easiest to learn, and what motivates their learning. One reason that domestic dogs fit into human communities so well is that they find human contact very rewarding and, conversely, become anxious when separated from their human companions, so they are strongly motivated to do things that please their owners, or, if they cannot work out what those are, to at least get their owners' attention.

However, if you want to train any animal to do something, it is easiest to start with behaviour that the animal would do anyway. Obviously, not all animals are equally easy to train, either in general, or to do particular things. Biological heritage does matter. On the one hand, many of the things that we train dogs to do, such as rounding up sheep and retrieving game, make use of pieces of behaviour that evolved millions of years ago as part of their canid ancestors' natural hunting behaviour. On the other hand, as predators, dogs do not naturally run away from things unless they are scared of them, so it is much more difficult to train them to, say, pull a cart than it is to train prey animals such as horses to do so.[11] Nevertheless, there are fundamental disagreements among trainers about how dogs are motivated to learn. Old-school advocates, supported only by tradition, think dogs need to learn their place in the pack; modernists, supported by the scientific evidence, think dogs learn to please their owners.

What, then, does it mean for a dog to learn? We can usually say that a dog has learned something when its typical reaction to a particular situation changes. Short-term changes that can be ascribed to internal processes such as hunger do not count. The more time passes since a dog's last meal, the hungrier it will get, but its interest in food wanes after it has eaten. That is not learning. However, when a dog suddenly gets excited when it hears its food bowl being taken out of the cupboard, and then repeats this behaviour every day, we can be sure that it has learned something.

The simplest kind of learning is *habituation*, defined as the waning of a response to an event that turns out to have no consequences. Most animals have sense organs that pick up far more information about the world than they can possibly attend to, and dogs are no exception to this rule. To avoid wasting time, animals need a mechanism that allows them to avoid responding over and over again to something that their senses are telling them they might want to attend to, but does not actually need to be bothered with. It is a very primitive and universal ability: even animals without nervous systems can do this, or something like it.

Habituation explains, for example, why dogs can rapidly lose interest in a particular toy. If dogs are repeatedly offered a favourite toy – a squashy teddy bear, for example – they will stop playing with it, usually after only five or six presentations. But if the toy is then swapped for one that is only very slightly different – identical in appearance except for a different colour or odour, say – they will start playing with the new toy just as excitedly as they did with the first one. Of course, they quickly get bored with the second toy as well, since there is nothing intrinsically more exciting about it compared to the first toy.[12]

Why do they show this rapid loss of interest? We do not know, but it is tempting to speculate that it is connected to dogs' origins as hunters. Something taken into the mouth and maybe tossed in the air is worth persisting with only if it produces food, or at least starts to break apart and so might eventually yield food[13] – which may be why many dogs love to rip their toys apart. But something that remains unchanged even after repeated chewing is probably not worth bothering with.

Habituation can be useful, for both dogs and their owners, because it reduces a dog's anxiety in reaction to unexpected events. Of course, the technique works only if the trigger for the fear (say, the sound of fireworks) has no actual consequences for the dog (for example, is not actually painful). As a training technique, the stressor has to be presented at a level that is just high enough to be detected by the dog, but not high enough to frighten it. Commercially available recordings of gunfire and firework noises are a very practical way of reducing the anxiety associated with such noises. Once this level has been established, the intensity of the sound can be increased very gradually so that the dog becomes more and more habituated to it, eventually reaching the point where even the 'normal' everyday intensity is no longer important enough to make the dog feel frightened.

Bear in mind that great care has to be taken to avoid raising the intensity of the stimulus to the point where the dog becomes even slightly frightened. If this line is crossed, the process goes back several stages before you can try again.

The opposite process, *sensitization*, occurs when the dog panics because it cannot escape from whatever is scaring it – this is a common cause of so-called 'firework phobia'. Many dogs are frightened of loud noises; some will gradually get used to them, if their initial exposure is not too intense, either by good fortune or because their owner has had the foresight to habituate them deliberately. Others, those that may be intrinsically nervous or whose first exposure is especially intense, on finding that nothing they do makes the noise go away, react more and more intensely on each successive exposure. Once this has happened, even very low levels of the stimulus will trigger the feeling of fear, making habituation almost impossible. The technique known as flooding (exposure to extreme intensities of unavoidable fear-inducing stimuli) can be successful in the treatment of irrational phobias in humans, but when used on dogs and other animals less rational than ourselves it is much more likely to make the fear even more deep-seated.

Both habituation and sensitization are forms of learning; both change the way the dog responds emotionally to situations. Each combination of external events, as recognized by the dog, triggers one emotion – in this case, fear. The specific combination may be important; for example, a dog may lose its sensitivity to loud noises when it is at home, but still become frightened when it is out in the car. The dog may still not like the sound of fireworks, but has learned that nothing bad follows when it is at home. The car introduces a new context, one in which the dog has never previously heard fireworks, and so the fear resurfaces.

The role of context is essential also to understanding much more complicated forms of learning, including *associative learning*. Associative learning occurs when two hitherto unlinked events get connected together in the dog's mind. A dog may learn that 'I get fed soon after my owner gets my bowl from the cupboard', that 'soon after the doorbell rings the door opens and people come through it', that 'there are rabbits in that wood', that 'when my owner says "sit" it's fun to sit down', that 'if I fetch my leash my owner may take me for a walk', and so on. These are all simple associations, either between two sets of information (bowl = food, bell = people, wood = rabbits to chase) or between doing one thing and achieving something (sit = praise from my owner, fetch leash = walk).

In psychologists' jargon, these two types of association occur in what are respectively referred to as *classical* and *operant conditioning*. Classical conditioning is also sometimes referred to as Pavlovian conditioning, after Ivan Pavlov's famous experiments, conducted in the 1900s. Having noted that dogs anticipated the arrival of food by drooling, Pavlov was able to show in these experiments that if the arrival of food was always preceded by a bell, the dogs would start to salivate whenever they heard the bell – whether or not the aroma of food was also present in the air. He helped to establish the fact that animals such as dogs were quickly able to learn the significance of artificial cues that evolution could not have prepared them for. Subsequent studies have demonstrated that something that reliably predicts a mealtime, such as the bowl coming out of the cupboard, does not just make the dog drool (Pavlov used the quantity of drool as his measure of anticipation) but actually conjures up some kind of mental picture of food in the dog's mind. (From my knowledge of dogs, it is probably an olfactory representation rather than an imaginary snapshot of some brown stuff in a bowl.) Thus something that the dog instinctively likes (in this case, the smell of food) gets linked to something arbitrary, something that would otherwise not mean much: the owner getting something out of a cupboard.

Classical conditioning is automatic; it does not involve the dog reflecting on what has just happened. For this reason it usually works well only when the arbitrary stimulus comes immediately – within one or two seconds – before the stimulus that the dog is already programmed to respond to. If the bowl appears and then the owner is distracted, the dog will probably drool until the food eventually arrives. If for some reason owners change their routine and start getting the bowl out long before they fill it, the dog will, after a period of frustration (and drooling) start to unlearn the association, a process referred to as *extinction*. On the other hand, given that food is very important to most dogs, they may become conditioned to another predictor that is present at the same time, perhaps the owner getting the pack of food from the cupboard.

Classical conditioning also works in the opposite direction, if the association is with something the dog does *not* like. If a dog treads on a thorn and hurts its foot, it will immediately associate the pain with the place where it got hurt and avoid it for a while. Such *aversions* are generally quite long-lasting, partly because the dog is not disadvantaged much if it stays away from that place for a while; in biological parlance, it has an alternative strategy available. Dogs also dislike electric shocks, and will rapidly learn to predict when these are going to occur, if they possibly can. This is the concept behind a product for dogs called the 'pet fence', which involves a collar that delivers a mild shock to the dog's neck. The shock is triggered when the dog gets close to a buried wire emitting a radio signal, visually marked out by a line of flags or something similar. The collar also makes a beeping sound just before it is about to deliver the shock; the dog rapidly learns that the beep means the shock is about to happen, and also associates the shock with the location in which it happened. The dog should then be able to learn to turn away whenever it hears the beep, thus avoiding the shock itself. In short, it is given an alternative strategy.

In the context of applying the principles of classical conditioning to dog training, it is crucial to appreciate that dogs live in the here and now to a much greater extent than humans do, and therefore that they may associate any punishment (or reward) with something that we humans may not expect. For example, many owners punish their dogs, verbally or physically, when they come home to find that the dog has done something wrong. They assume that the dog will be able to think back to whatever that deed was, and thereby associate the punishment with it. However, as noted earlier, dogs do not do mental time-travel at all well. What the dog actually does in such instances is to associate the immediate situation – the owner's return – with the owner's angry words, and any physical punishment that follows. The dog associates events that happen immediately one after the other. The mess in the room is highly relevant to the owner, but much less relevant as far as the dog is concerned; the dog is incapable of reflecting on what the owner is angry about. What is different from the 'pet fence' situation is that here the dog has no alternative strategy; it has no means of avoiding punishment, because it does not understand what has precipitated the punishment in the first place, nor has it had any warning that punishment is imminent. Because it does not understand the causation, the dog is unable to predict when its owner is going to come home angry and when not. It is like a rat in a cage, being shocked at random. Researchers have established that rats can become quite tolerant of mild electric shocks, even in situations where they cannot avoid them, if they are given a reliable warning of when they are going to occur. However, a rat receiving exactly the same shocks, but this time without the warnings, becomes progressively more anxious and stressed. The same is true of dogs.

Although almost all learning in dogs takes place between events a second or two apart, there is one major exception, namely, when the 'punishment' takes the form of an upset stomach. An inexperienced young dog may pick up the rotting corpse of some animal on a walk, mistakenly think that it is good to eat, and then feel nauseous and vomit it up an hour or so later. Although these events seem to be much too far apart in time for conventional classical conditioning to work, it would be very useful to that puppy if it could learn not to eat such things again, and indeed this is what happens. There is a special rule for food – connect taste/odour of last meal with painful stomach – but it is confined to food, and does not seem to apply to any other learned associations. This necessary relaxation of the usual rules can have unintended consequences: animals (this applies to humans too) can 'go off' a particular food if they are affected by a gastric virus within a few hours of eating it, even if the food did not actually cause the stomach problems. But this confusion is presumably a price worth paying for learning to avoid genuinely toxic foods.

As we have seen, dogs are continually learning about how the environment they find themselves in works. Domestication has made dogs more attentive to humans than any other animal, wild or domestic, but it cannot have prepared dogs for every eventuality that each one experiences, especially since man-made environments change far too quickly for evolution to keep up. What domestication has given dogs is the capacity to make sense of the world by learning all kinds of associations, some of them between events and sensations that no dog of the previous generation could possibly have met. The first dog to encounter a vacuum cleaner was not specifically pre-adapted to handle the situation, but it did possess the ability to habituate to the unfamiliar sound and vibration.

Such straightforward learning helps dogs to cope with man-made environments in a way that few other species are capable of. However, this is not enough to turn dogs into the kind of model citizens they need to be in order to be accommodated into those environments. For that, they also need to behave in the ways we expect them to, and this rarely happens spontaneously; rather, dogs need to be deliberately trained.

Dog training, as opposed to mere learning, primarily relies on the other major type of associative learning, *instrumental* or *operant conditioning*. This kind of conditioning links together an action that the dog performs and a specific reward. (The reward might also be the avoidance of a punishment.) The action is usually something that the dog would do in other circumstances, but not, until trained, specifically in order to obtain that reward. For example, a dog can be trained to sit down to obtain a morsel of food, even though sitting down is not a normal part of canid hunting or feeding behaviour. Behaviour that does not come naturally is much harder to bring about; for example, it is much easier to train a dog than a horse to retrieve sticks, since the natural model – bringing food back home to feed the young – is an essential part of the canid repertoire, but not that of an animal that grazes grass. Dogs are naturally motivated to perform a diverse range of tasks. For dogs, like all animals, food can be an important reward, but dogs are unusual in that most also regard contact with their owner as rewarding in itself. Some types of dog also find the opportunity to go exploring and/or hunting as rewarding in its own right, independent of any food that might eventually result; this tendency appears to be especially well developed in sled-dogs, for example. Others find play rewarding in itself, over and above the contact with their owner that is often also involved, and thus it is used in some types of sniffer-dog training.

Not all training is deliberate; often a dog will 'train itself', learning by trial and error that when it does one particular thing, something good follows. This is often how the simplest forms of attention-seeking behaviour arise. For example, young dogs will often 'try out' fragments of adult behaviour when playing with their littermates, or with their human family. One of these behaviours is mounting, a component of sexual behaviour that is also routinely seen in play. When, by chance, the puppy attempts to mount the leg of one of the human members of the household, everyone else in the room will laugh in a slightly embarrassed way, and gently push the dog off. In the young dog's rather unsophisticated interpretation of human behaviour, this is just play (that is, rewarding) and so it will repeat the performance, subsequently extending it to visitors, to the even greater embarrassment of the owner. The more entrenched the behaviour becomes, the harder it is to eradicate. Boisterous young dogs may even interpret the owner's smack on the nose as just another part of the game, not the punishment that the owner intended.

Dogs can behave badly – as far as their owners are concerned – not just spontaneously but also due to inadvertent reinforcement: here, too, learning theory can help when attempting to eradicate such unwanted behaviour. Although the association between mounting and praise can be extinguished by simply ignoring it whenever it happens, this can be a difficult tactic in real life, because to begin with the dog may continue trying to obtain the reward by persisting in, and even increasing the intensity of, the unwanted behaviour. Some kind of distraction technique (technically, *omission training*) is usually needed in such instances, the aim being to direct the dog to do something else that is equally rewarding, but more acceptable. For example, a dog that chases cyclists can be rewarded with a game played with the owner whenever a cyclist appears on the horizon. But the game must stop as soon as the dog starts to react to the bicycle; otherwise, the dog could end up interpreting the game as an encouragement to start chasing. We should not be too surprised that some dogs want to chase joggers and cyclists; chasing things that run away is a natural part of hunting behaviour – although this is no excuse for us to refrain from training the dog not to do it.

Dogs being dogs, they will often not make quite the same associations that we would in the same situation. In most real-life examples of training, the action is preceded by a cue that triggers the behaviour, followed by the reward: owner says 'sit', dog sits, dog is praised by owner. However, the 'cue' may not be as simple and straightforward as the owner thinks it is (see box – 'I said, "Sit!"'). Some aspect of the surroundings may be included in the (composite) cue that the dog builds up; consider, for example, the young dog that is obedient in the 'puppy party',[14] where it has been trained consistently under the gaze of the organizer, but is disobedient in other places, where its owner may have been less consistent in delivering rewards.

I SAID, 'SIT!'

As part of his 1994 UK television series Dogs with Dunbar, *well-known American veterinarian and dog behaviour expert Dr Ian Dunbar set up a fascinating demonstration of how dogs can fool us into thinking they've learned one thing, while actually having learned another. Most owners believe that their dogs know the word 'sit'. On camera, he asked several such owners to command their dogs to sit just by saying the word: no body-language, no gestures, just the word. Most of the dogs hadn't a clue as to what they were supposed to be doing. They'd learned the cues that came easiest to them – not the word 'sit', which dogs, with their limited repertoire of vocal signals, must find it difficult to distinguish from other similar-sounding words, but rather the gestures that the owner invariably used to accompany the word 'sit'.*

*Inspired by this demonstration, I set out to find what my Labrador Bruno had actually learned when I had trained him to sit. It turned out that in his case it was a sound – but all he was picking up was the final 't' sound, along with my intonation. If I said 'cricke*t *ba*t*' in the right way, his backside hit the ground instantaneously.*

As with classical conditioning, the timing of the delivery of the reward is crucial. There must be no more than a second or two between the dog performing the desired action and the arrival of the reward. Longer than this, and not only will the learning be slower to establish, but there is also an increased chance that the dog will make unwanted associations with something else. Take the example of an inexperienced owner attempting to teach a young dog the command 'sit'. When the dog does finally sit, the owner is so relieved that he praises the dog over and over again – 'Good dog, good dog, good dog . . .' Meanwhile, the excitable young dog has got up from the sit and is attempting to bounce around. Thus the sound 'good dog', intended as the reward for sitting, instead becomes the cue for this bouncing around, an activity that is highly pleasurable for the dog. The next time the owner says 'good dog', he is surprised to find that the dog instantly increases its activity, ignoring whatever command he is trying to teach at the time.

Delivering a reward is easy when the dog is beside you, but not so easy when it is some distance away – for example when it is chasing after another dog and the owner wants it to learn a command to stop. This problem is especially acute when training aquatic animals – there is usually too much of a delay between the successful performance of a trick presented in the middle of the pool, and the delivery of the rewarding fish by the trainer standing on the edge – and so it was dolphin trainers, rather than dog trainers, who first looked to learning theory for a solution.[15] For dolphins, that solution was a whistle. First the dolphin was taught, at the edge of the pool, that the sound of the whistle was immediately followed by a fish. Subsequently, when it performed a particularly spectacular jump in the middle of the pool, the trainer could, with a quick blast of the whistle, signify that this was the jump she wanted, even before the dolphin hit the water – the delivery of the fish could then follow in slow time. Here, the whistle serves as a *secondary reinforcer*, an initially arbitrary event that, by being reliably and immediately followed by a genuine reward, not only becomes associated with it in the animal's mind – a case of straightforward classical conditioning – but also, somehow, becomes rewarding in its own right.

Whistles were already being used by some dog trainers as cues, so a different arbitrary sound was needed for dogs. Owners can now make use of a commercially available and highly effective secondary reinforcer known as the 'clicker', a tensioned flat metal spring in a plastic case that goes 'click-clack' when pressed and quickly released. Actually any kind of very rapid yet obvious noise will work – including the softer click of a retractable ballpoint pen for a sound-sensitive dog, or a single flash from a bright LED flashlight for a deaf dog. There is nothing magic about any of these; what matters is that they are just both convenient and easily recognized by the dog.

Clicker training

The 'click' is meaningless until it has become linked in the dog's mind to a reward. Many trainers use tiny pieces of something tasty as the reward at first, because there are few dogs which do not respond to food. But as the training advances, it is a good idea to link the click to other kinds of reward as well, such as play with a toy, or petting, otherwise the dog may not respond to the click when it is not hungry. Of course, it is harder to gauge the effectiveness of these alternative rewards. It is easy to see whether or not food is working – dogs reliably enjoy food and will happily eat it – but the effect of the other rewards may be missed. The trainer needs to see the dog's tail wagging, as a check that the dog has registered the reward.

Eventually, the click alone should be enough to secure the dog's attention, and thereby function as a reward in its own right. For instance, in the early stages of training a dog to come back to the owner, the click can be used on its own as an instant reward as soon as the dog responds to the owner's preferred recall signal ('Fido, come!'), by moving in the right direction. The advantage is that the click can be given while the dog is still some distance away, and then repeated, closely followed by the treat when it reaches the owner. The important principle is that once the clicker has become rewarding in its own right, it does not always have to be followed immediately by the treat, although if it is never followed by the treat (the primary reinforcer), its value will eventually dwindle to nothing.

In real life, the dog does not just learn the sound of the click; it also learns a lot about the circumstances in which it hears it. This was brought home to me forcibly the first time I witnessed mass clicker-training, in the kennels at the Waltham Centre for Pet Nutrition in Leicestershire. These are the dogs that check the efficacy of all Pedigree® foods, and they are all looked after like pet dogs, with plenty of exercise and contact with people. Clickers are used all the time, sometimes with several dogs simultaneously, yet it is rare for any dog to respond to the wrong clicker. On the rare occasions that it does, of course it does not get rewarded – the dog quickly learns whose clicker is the one that is rewarding, and whose is not. Since the clickers have all come from the same manufacturer, they probably sound identical, even to a dog, so what's most likely is that the dog has also memorized who is carrying 'its' clicker.

Provided they can all be linked to the delivery of a real reward at the end, there is no reason why a dog should not learn several secondary reinforcers. Professional trainers can use this basic principle to teach dogs complex tricks and tasks such as assisting a blind owner to avoid obstacles, adding complexity by joining several learned associations together. The final stage is usually rewarded first, and then once that has been established the earlier stages can be added one at a time, as performance of each stage becomes rewarding in its own right. This *forward chaining* is easier than backward chaining, because the final reward is always linked to the same action, rather than being delayed every time a new element is added to the chain. A dog that not only comes to its owner when called but also always sits down beside him or her has learned a behaviour chain.

Widely employed in more advanced training is a technique known as *shaping*. Here, the first step is to reward the dog whenever it spontaneously behaves in a way that approximates to part of the task that needs to be taught – in the case of the guide dog, this would probably be a simple turn away from an obstacle. Once this connection is established, the dog gets rewarded only if it starts to walk around the obstacle, and finally only if it turns, walks round the obstacle and then returns to the original path. In this way, a series of actions that would rarely happen spontaneously, and would therefore be difficult to train in one step, can be progressively built up from any spontaneous behaviour that approximates, however loosely, to the desired result.

Shaping is an extraordinarily powerful technique, one that can be used even to alter completely the dog's body-language, which is supposedly 'instinctive' (according to the supporters of lupomorphism). Gwen Bailey, who pioneered the use of behaviour modification in the United Kingdom to help rescued dogs become fulfilling pets, originally convinced the rehoming charity she worked for that this was possible, by rehabilitating an aggressive dog, Beau. With a history of biting people, dogs and cats, Beau had been abandoned by his owners, but Gwen was able to rebuild his confidence and remove the fears and anxieties that were causing him to bite. Indeed, by the time a television company wanted to make a documentary about this achievement (an extraordinary one for its time), Beau was far too well adjusted to even snap at anyone, let alone bite. So Gwen set about training Beau to snap (in the air) on a very specific cue, using standard shaping techniques, just so that his original snappy disposition could be faked for the documentary. In this way she was able to change what had been a species-typical 'innate' signal of aggression into a meaningless response to an arbitrary cue that she produced only when she wanted it to happen.

Shaping is not, however, the exclusive preserve of the expert trainer – in fact, far from it, since dogs spontaneously, if unconsciously, 'shape' their own behaviour. If my own experience is anything to go by, there are plenty of dog owners who have shaped their dogs without even knowing it. For instance, I have encountered several dogs that use growling and snapping as (relatively) harmless ways of getting their owners to make a fuss of them. What has probably happened in such cases is that the dog once used this display for real, when it was irritated about something, but the owner accidentally reinforced it, perhaps by simply laughing aloud, and then making a fuss of the dog. Dogs are always looking for ways to get affection from their owners, so when they are presented with such an opportunity, they can switch the 'meaning' of this display into this new context. Growling has become a signal for 'Play with me!' – which is almost a reversal of its original meaning as a warning. (This is not to say, however, that the same dog will not still use growling and snapping as a prelude to real aggression as well. Indeed, unintentional shaping of this kind can set up the possibility that the owner will, perhaps when a child is nearby, misunderstand what is going on, and unwittingly put the child in danger.)

It is thus possible to get dogs to do most of the things we want by rewarding them. Such techniques are especially easy with dogs because there are several types of reward available – food, attention, play. It is also possible to use rewards to reorganize much unwanted behaviour, especially if that consists of natural behaviour occurring in what we humans consider the wrong context. A straightforward set of training methods has been devised from the science of reward-based learning, itself established on the basis of thousands of experiments done on rats, mice, pigeons and many other animals, including dogs, training methods that eliminate the need to strike a dog, even once. Unfortunately, however, our relationship with dogs predates the science of learning theory by many thousands of years, and so they come with much historical baggage attached, including the mistaken idea that training can best be achieved by physical punishment.

So far, I have mainly discussed how dogs learn based on things they like to do – eating, playing, getting praise from their owners. Dogs must have learned in this way ever since they were domesticated, and indeed the most modern training methods are largely based on setting up associations between rewards and things that the owner wants the dog to do. However, as we have seen, dogs also learn to avoid things that they do not like. Until recently this was the main principle behind the craft of dog training, which was largely based on the selective application of physical punishment.

Confusion can arise from the difference between the everyday use of the word 'punishment' and the psychologists' use of the term. Punishment-based dog training implies the everyday meaning, 'rough physical treatment', which refers to actions that can produce pain or discomfort, such as choking the dog's windpipe, pinching its ear, beating it with a stick, giving it electric shocks and so on. Psychologists use the term 'punishment' to describe all of these, but they also include other sensations that the dog does not like – indeed, any that lead to negative emotion such as fear or anxiety. (For a sensitive dog, this could be something as slight and momentary as its owner's raised eyebrow.) However, most of the arguments about what is and is not acceptable in dog training revolve around physical punishment.

Learning that occurs as a result of physical pain or discomfort is classified by psychologists as *positive punishment*. The commonplace 'choke chain' is a good example of a positive punisher; the discomfort of being choked is intended to reduce the dog's desire to pull on the leash. Dogs have sensitive necks, and so the neck is an obvious target for inflicting pain. The traditional 'choke chain', also known as a 'slip-collar' or 'check chain', and its hardcore variant the 'prong-collar', are designed to inflict momentary pain on the dog's neck when it pulls on the leash. The dog should then learn, via positive punishment, to avoid the pain by not pulling on the lead. But this kind of training is ultimately ineffective: most dogs whose owners require them to wear such a collar do continue to pull, whenever their motivation to move towards something outweighs the pain. They may also habituate to the discomfort of the collar. In the case of the 'citronella spray collar', which is designed to suppress barking by dispensing an aversive odour whenever the dog vocalizes, a study has revealed that although it is effective for a week or so, dogs then habituate to the odour, and after two or three weeks, bark almost as often as they did before the collar was fitted.[16]

Slip- and prong-collars can be effective only when the dog is on-leash, and close to the owner (who could therefore just as easily be training the dog using positive reinforcement). Collars that deliver electric shocks allow the pain to be delivered remotely, by radio control. Either the controller can be held by the trainer and the shock timed to immediately follow the undesired behaviour – livestock-chasing is a commonly cited example – or it can take the form of an 'invisible fence', a buried wire encircling an area that the dog is to be confined within; if the dog approaches the 'fence', the shock is delivered.

There is a long tradition in animal psychology of using mild electric shocks to study the effects of punishment on behaviour, and no doubt under controlled laboratory conditions they do alter an animal's tendency to behave in a particular way. Dog training is not, however, carried out under controlled laboratory conditions, and so what the dog learns is often not entirely what was intended. For example, research has shown that German shepherd dogs trained to be guard dogs using shock collars were more frightened of their ('expert') handlers, even when they were not wearing their collars, than were dogs trained conventionally (using a mixture of reward and punishment).[17] It seems very likely that these dogs were associating the shocks with their handlers, as well as with the mistakes the dogs had made that triggered the shocks.

When the shock is not timed properly, the dog's fear and anxiety may become even worse than this. Owners who believe that dogs can 'know what they've done wrong' may go on applying the shock even after the dog has stopped performing the undesired behaviour. Even under controlled laboratory conditions, unpredictable electric shock makes animals much more likely to react aggressively, so it is a real possibility that owners who use shock collars without proper technique are setting up their dog for an attack that will condemn it to euthanasia. Cases have been documented in which shocks received from invisible fences apparently caused dogs to launch unprovoked and serious attacks on people.[18]

The pain from the shock itself has a significant effect on the dog's welfare, ranging from slight to considerable. This depends on whether the shock is used appropriately or not. Because dogs can habituate to aversive events, for the collar to be effective it is essential to get the level of shock right first time; too weak, and the dog may habituate to the pain, requiring the trainer to increase the shock level in an attempt to get the dog to respond. There is a temptation to apply the maximum available shock right from the start, even though the pain felt by the dog will vary widely, depending on the thickness of its coat, the electrical resistance of its skin and whether its coat is wet or dry. At worst, this can result in immediate discomfort, and then anxiety if the dog cannot predict when the next violent pain to its neck is likely to arrive.

Repeated delivery of electric shocks is likely to lead to serious fear and anxiety. It is unarguable that the shocks must be momentarily painful, otherwise they would not have any effect on behaviour. A single shock delivered at exactly the right moment to suppress undesired behaviour may have only a transitory effect on the dog's welfare, and, therefore, may be preferable to other, less effective, punishments that have to be delivered repeatedly. However, if the dog receives several shocks and is unable to work out why, its heart rate goes up and its stress hormones increase dramatically; both are indicators that its welfare is being impaired. In the hands of inept operators who do not understand the principles behind their use, or, worse still, are using the collar as an outlet for their own anger that the dog is not doing what it is supposed to, electric shocks may not only upset the dog, but undermine the relationship between the dog and its owner.

Physical punishment can also be used in another way, in which the dog learns to do something that enables it to avoid a painful sensation – as opposed to not doing something to avoid pain, as in the examples so far. The technical term for this is *negative reinforcement*. Negative reinforcement is the principle underlying training methods that teach the dog to perform a behaviour in order to eliminate pain that is being inflicted by the trainer. One example is a traditional method of teaching young gundogs to retrieve, in which the dog learns to associate the removal of pain with opening its mouth and picking something up. The trainer presents a suitable object – usually a cloth-covered 'dummy' – a few inches in front of the dog's nose while at the same time pinching the dog's earflap tightly. The dog cries out in pain, opening its mouth and allowing the trainer to insert the dummy into the dog's open mouth.

Force-fetch training. The trainer simultaneously pinches the dog's ear and beats it with a stick until it opens its mouth above the 'dummy'.

At that instant, the aversive stimulus (the pain from the pinch) is abruptly stopped. The dog is supposed to learn that picking up the dummy results in the cessation of pain (this is an example of negative reinforcement). In the 'force-fetch' method, the dog is additionally beaten with a stick while the ear pinch is being applied – in this case, both are abruptly terminated when the dog performs the desired action.

There is no doubt that both positive punishment and negative reinforcement, if performed skilfully, can be highly effective in the very short term – if we put any ethical considerations to one side, that is, and ignore any long-term damage to the dog–human relationship. Things go wrong, for both dog and owner, when the way that punishment works is not properly understood, or, worse, when punishment is applied as an outlet for the owner's anger, frustration or embarrassment.

The most serious problem with physical punishment is that it is easily misapplied. As with other kinds of learning, a dog will almost always associate any sudden pain or fear with the event that immediately preceded it. Almost every day, I see owners beating or remonstrating with their dogs for being slow to come back to them. This action usually follows some mildly embarrassing incident that the dog has been involved in, and seems to be, in part, an emotional response from the owners, and in part a sign to anyone watching that they are dissociating themselves from their dog's behaviour. What are the dogs learning from such incidents? That coming back is (sometimes) a bad idea. Is this going to make them more, or less, attached to their owners? More likely to come back when called the next time, or less? Dogs do not think, 'I was naughty a minute ago, so I deserve to be punished when I get back to my owner.' If anything, they think, 'Sometimes my owner makes a fuss of me when I go back, but sometimes I get hit; I don't understand.'

In short, punishment is often misused by owners who do not understand how dogs learn. But even if punishment is applied with the correct timing, it is difficult to predict in advance what the dog will associate the punishment with. Will it be the intended event, or will it be the person administering it, or the place in which the punishment happened? One of my colleagues recently found his neighbour's small terrier wandering in the road. He picked it up and carried it back to the neighbour's house. As he approached she appeared at the door, repeatedly pressing the control for the electric shock collar that the dog was wearing and shouting, 'Bad dog, bad dog.' The dog jerked violently every time the shock was applied, growling and snapping in fear. From that day on, the terrier growled whenever anyone it did not know came near – it had learned that unfamiliar people mean inescapable pain.

It is also difficult to get the severity of the punishment right. Typically, owners will gradually escalate the degree of punishment that they use, until they achieve the desired result. Unfortunately, the dog will at the same time be habituating to the punishment, such that the intensity that eventually works (if at all) is much higher than would have been needed if it had been applied correctly in the first place. Contrast this with the use of positive rewards in dog training: if the owner mistakenly gives too much of the reward each time, the value of the reward will merely be somewhat diminished; for example, too big a food reward will just make the dog less hungry. But if a punishment is more intense than necessary, the dog will suffer unnecessarily – and if it is not sufficiently intense to begin with (due to the owner, understandably, erring on the side of caution) it can lead to escalation and therefore also eventually result in too much being applied.

In fact, a growing body of evidence indicates that in inexpert hands physical punishment is not only likely to harm the dog but is ineffective as well. Two separate surveys of dog owners have revealed that dogs trained with punishment tend to be less obedient and more fearful than those trained with reward. In the first of these, conducted in the United Kingdom,[19] 364 owners were asked about the training methods that they used for training seven basic tasks, including house-training, coming when called and giving up an object upon command. Vocal punishment was reported by 66 per cent of the respondents, and physical punishment by 12 per cent. Rewards were also commonly used: 60 per cent used verbal praise and 51 per cent used food treats. The owners using rewards reported much greater obedience from their dogs than those using punishment predominantly, whereas those using mainly punishment reported a larger number of behavioural problems, such as barking at people and dogs, fearful behaviour and separation disorders. The other survey, conducted in Austria, has also concluded that frequent use of punishment is associated with high levels of aggression, especially in small dogs.[20]

Not all punishment is physical, however, even in dog training. Training almost inevitably involves subtler forms of punishment that most owners would not even identify as such. In addition to the physical punishments discussed so far, psychologists also identify a category that they call *negative punishment*, which involves the removal of some reward that the dog has come to expect will occur under a particular set of circumstances. For example, one way to stop a dog jumping up at people is to always ignore it when it does so. No pain or fear is involved; however, the dog presumably becomes mildly anxious when it finds that its strategy for getting interaction with its owner suddenly no longer works. Some trainers in the United Kingdom regard even this emotional shift as unethical, but, given that even experimental psychologists cannot always determine whether learning is mainly due to negative punishment (brief anxiety that the anticipated reward will not arrive) or to positive reinforcement (joy when it does), it is probably difficult to avoid all occurrences of negative punishment even during everyday interaction with a dog. Perhaps the best compromise is never to use negative punishment on its own, but always to offer the dog a rewarded alternative. In any event, withdrawal of reward, as with all forms of punishment, actually works faster when the dog is given an alternative, positively rewarded, strategy. Such a strategy, for example in cases involving jumping up, might involve making a fuss of the dog only when it is calm.

It is also possible to transfer the negative punishment to a *secondary punisher*, which is analogous to a secondary reinforcer. In the context of dog training, an arbitrary yet distinctive sound can be used. For this purpose, owners can purchase so-called 'training discs',[21] but a distinctively uttered word can be just as effective. First, an association is built up between the cue (for example, dropping the training discs on the ground) and a mildly frustrating event (perhaps temporarily removing the dog's food mid-meal, or offering and then withholding a treat). The cue itself then becomes a secondary punisher, and can be used under other circumstances as well, such as getting the dog to stop barking. As with all punishers, including negative reinforcers, the desired response, such as sitting and not barking, should be rewarded as well (that is, by positive reinforcement).

Punishment, in the psychological sense, is an inescapable component of the dog owner's armoury of training methods. Today's most knowledgeable trainers agree that it is in fact impossible to avoid at least some negative punishment (the withholding of a reward that the dog is anticipating) when training a dog. And few would argue that it is unethical to make a dog feel slightly uncomfortable by delaying somewhat a reward it was expecting. (Indeed, in real life this may be virtually unavoidable. Each time owners give a dog a food treat or other reward, they set up expectations that the same reward will appear again when the situation is repeated. If the situation recurs and there is no treat, then the dogs are, technically speaking, being punished.) Many trainers who avoid physical punishment nevertheless use the withholding of reward as a way of modifying behaviour, clearly a very good way of getting and holding a dog's attention,[22] once reward-based training has begun.

It is the use of physical punishment that remains controversial. Traditions die hard, and 'traditional' training methods based on physical punishment are still widely employed. One recent US survey of clients at a veterinary behaviour clinic found large numbers of owners using confrontational methods, including 'hit or kick dog for undesirable behaviour' (43 per cent), 'physically force the release of an item from a dog's mouth' (39 per cent), 'alpha roll' (31 per cent), 'stare at or stare [dog] down' (30 per cent), 'dominance down' (29 per cent), and 'grab dog by jowls and shake' (26 per cent). All of these actions had elicited an aggressive response from at least a quarter of the dogs on which they had been used, indicating that none of them could be regarded as safe.[23]

The reason for the widespread occurrence of physical punishment was unclear from the research, since few owners in the survey indicated that these techniques had been recommended by dog trainers (although television was the most frequently reported source for the practice of abruptly jabbing the dog in the neck). However, much of the advice reported to have come from trainers did involve the punitive use of collars and leashes, such as prong-collars and forcing-down, which also caused aggressive responses. The survey found no link between aggression and the use of training methods that did not involve physical punishment. Although the majority of the dogs had been brought to the clinic for problems involving aggression, none of the non-aversive, neutral and reward-based interventions that their owners had used produced aggressive responses in more than a tiny fraction of the dogs they had been used on, in stark contrast to the aggression triggered by physical punishments.

Why, therefore, do television companies seem to prefer to publicize methods based on confrontation and punishment? Perhaps because conflict and its dramatic resolution make for compelling entertainment.[24] Reward-based methods are slower, if surer, and much less dramatic. If dog-training programmes were regarded as mere entertainment, then none of this would matter very much. But if the use of physical punishment and other techniques that supposedly reduce 'dominance' are adopted in good faith by dog owners, problematic behaviours can easily be exacerbated. When such techniques do not work as quickly and effortlessly as the television version seems to promise, there is a risk that owners will escalate the punishment, in the belief that they have not got through to the dog. The result can then be a dog that resorts to aggression because it finds this is the only tactic that gets it noticed. Inept use of reward, by contrast, is only likely to result in an overweight or over-dependent dog, both conditions that, while not exactly desirable, can at least be readily resolved.

Given all the scientific evidence that is piling up against the use of physical punishment in training, the question has to be asked why such methods still remain so popular with owners. The main issue seems to be that dog training originated as a craft, and hence has no clear route for integrating scientific understanding of dogs into its methods. Neither dog training nor the treatment of behavioural disorders in dogs are regulated professions, and so keeping up to date with the latest developments, or indeed getting some kind of formal education in the field, is not legally required. Television companies seem not to value presenters with formal qualifications – for example, neither Cesar Millan nor Victoria Stilwell (whose approaches, it must be said, are very different) mention any academic qualifications on their websites. Increasingly, however, there are moves on both sides of the Atlantic to introduce self-regulation at all levels. The biennial International Veterinary Behavior meetings and the *Journal of Veterinary Behavior* (neither, despite their names, restricted to veterinarians) are just two of the forums in which new ideas and research are being exchanged internationally.

As a result of such exchanges, there is a growing feeling that the dog's supposed drive to 'dominate' is, in fact, just a convenient myth for those who wish to continue physically punishing dogs, even though it has been demolished by studies of both wolves and dogs. The wolf's natural social behaviour is now known to be based on harmonious family loyalties, not on an overwhelming and incessant desire to take control. Could such a desire for control conceivably have been induced in dogs during the process of domestication? It seems much more likely that precisely the opposite must have happened, since dogs that showed a tendency to control their human hosts would have been selected against, deliberately or accidentally. Yet despite all the accumulating evidence, old habits are proving remarkably slow to die, in terms of both training and the perception of dog as wolf.[25] Thankfully, there are now some signs that the tide is beginning to turn; for example, some rapport seems to be developing between the old-school and reward-based trainers: Cesar Millan has even asked Ian Dunbar to contribute to his book *Cesar's Rules*.[26] The hope is that dogs will soon be universally portrayed as the utterly domesticated animals that they are, not as superficially cute animals disguising demons that lurk within.

5

How Puppies Become Pets

Dogs are not born friendly to humans. No, that's not a misprint. Dogs are born to *become* friendly towards people, but this happens only if they meet friendly people while they are still tiny puppies. Scientists have known this for half a century, but the implications are still not universally applied or even widely appreciated. Today, many puppies are still raised for the pet market under impoverished conditions, conditions that predispose them to a life blighted by fear and anxiety, and causing behaviour that will not endear them to their owners or indeed anyone else they come across. Yet all this is entirely preventable.

Domestication has not adapted dogs to human environments; it has merely given them the means to adapt. Exposure to both people and man-made environments must occur, in a gentle and gradual way, to enable them to learn how to cope. This process starts in about the fourth week of their life and goes on for several months. If the exposure is either deficient or defective, the dog will develop deep-seated fears or anxieties that can be very difficult to eradicate later. Although some details of precisely how this happens have not yet been scientifically explored, the overall process of this 'socialization' is well charted, and it is a tragedy that so many puppies do not receive enough experience of everyday life to allow them to cope adequately with their life among humans.

In 1961, a short paper appeared in *Science* that completely revolutionized our thinking about the bond between man and dog.[1] In order to study when puppies are most sensitive to exposure to people, the researchers raised five litters of cocker spaniels and three litters of beagles in fields surrounded by a high fence, so that they never saw people – food and water were provided through holes in the fence. Then every other week from the time the puppies were two weeks old until they were two months old, a few of them were taken out to live indoors for a week's 'holiday', receiving an hour and a half of intensive contact with people each day. At the end of their week's socialization, they were put back in their field with their mother and littermates.

The timing of the 'holiday' was absolutely crucial to how the puppies reacted to being handled. At two weeks old, they were too immature and sleepy to interact much, but the puppies taken out at three weeks were instantly attracted to the person looking after them. They would paw and mouth the researcher and play with the hem of his lab coat. Five-week-old puppies were wary for a few minutes, but soon started boisterously playing with the person. Seven-week-old puppies needed two *days* of coaxing before they could be persuaded to play, and nine-week-old puppies took even longer, only becoming friendly in the second half of their week's holiday.

The timing of their first introduction to human contact was absolutely crucial to how the puppies reacted to people later on. All the puppies in the experiment were taken out of the field when they were fourteen weeks old, and at that point began to live with people like normal dogs. The five puppies that had spent all of their lives in the field never learned to trust people, even after months of intensive handling. The six that had been taken on 'holiday' when they were only two weeks old, and were then returned to the field for eleven weeks, fared better: though they were initially quite wary of people, they became somewhat friendly after a couple more weeks of gentle attention. All the other puppies were instantly friendly – remarkable, given that some had last seen a human over half their lifetime ago. The six that had not seen a person for ten weeks were initially difficult to leash-train, but training the others was straightforward.

Overall, the results indicated that puppies need some (but not very much) contact with people if they are to react in a friendly way towards them. There also seems to be an optimum age for this contact to be effective. Two weeks old appears to be too early. Twelve weeks old is definitely too late; by this age the puppies observed in the study had become fearful of anything they had never been exposed to when they were younger. This implies a window of opportunity between about three weeks and ten or eleven weeks of age – what the scientists referred to as their 'critical period'.

The idea of a 'critical period' derives from a 1930s study by Nobel Prize-winning biologist Konrad Lorenz. Suspecting that some animals have to learn their mother's identity, rather than knowing it instinctively, Lorenz hand-raised a clutch of goslings. His prediction proved to be correct: having never seen their mother, they adopted him as their 'parent', following him around like a pack of faithful hounds, and paying no attention to their biological mother.

What Lorenz had discovered was the process now known as *filial imprinting*, whereby young animals learn the characteristics of their parents.[2] Geese will imprint on to the first moving object of about the right size that they encounter between twelve and sixteen hours after hatching. In the wild, this is so likely to be the mother goose that the chances of anything going wrong are remote. It is essential to their survival that goslings know what their mothers look like, otherwise they could easily stray away from the nest and perish. But why do they need to learn this? Would it not be more sensible if they hatched with the mother's image already burned into their brains? Biologists have no definitive answer to such questions, but perhaps learning is simply easier; three-dimensional images are probably difficult to encode in DNA. In fact, studies show that young birds are born with some inbuilt guidelines for what to look out for: something that moves, makes bird-type noises, and has a head and neck. (But not much more than this: for example, if they are prevented from seeing their mother, domestic chicks will readily imprint on to a stuffed ferret.)

Lorenz originally conceptualized his 'critical period' as a rigid timetable of events. In the gosling example this enables a young bird that is mobile within a few short hours of hatching, and unlikely to survive for long on its own, to quickly latch on to its mother. It is now known that there is more flexibility in this type of learning than was first thought: subsequent research has shown, for instance, that a gosling hatched in an incubator and kept away from its mother until it is thirty-six hours old can nonetheless bond to her immediately. Thus the timetable is not quite as rigid as Lorenz originally thought, and for this reason these windows of opportunity for learning are nowadays usually referred to as 'sensitive periods'. They seem to be modifiable according to circumstances, rather than coming to an abrupt end when a clock in the brain says they should. Nevertheless, it is true that eventually, after a few days, imprinting cannot be reactivated. The young bird's brain does not wait indefinitely for the mother bird to show up; that door does eventually close as its brain matures.

Once the young bird has finished learning, persuading it to change its attachment to its mother is almost impossible. It will usually flee from other animals – a very sensible thing to do, considering that some might want to catch and eat it. The blocking that prevents the young bird from accidentally forgetting its mother and latching on to something else is called 'competitive exclusion': once a complete picture of the mother has built up, the imprinting process terminates automatically, preventing the bird from accidentally attaching itself to another goose if its mother is temporarily absent.

This 'sensitive period' concept explains the behaviour of many young animals. For example, it can explain why hand-raised rhesus monkeys, taken from their own mothers soon after birth, prefer to be with their surrogate 'mother' rather than with real monkeys, even when the surrogate is only a cloth-covered, unresponsive dummy.

Dogs do this too: they imprint on to their mothers, and vice versa, and they do this using their number one sense, olfaction. In one set of experiments, researchers collected scents from two-year-old dogs by placing cloths in their beds for three consecutive nights. The dogs had all been separated from their mothers since they were twelve weeks old or even younger. Nonetheless, when their mothers were presented with a selection of these cloths, they were much more interested in their offspring's scent than in the scent of unrelated but otherwise similar dogs. Likewise, the young dogs' behaviour showed that they recognized their mothers' scents. A second experiment done at the same time showed that the two-year-old dogs were able to recognize their littermates by odour alone, but only if they were currently living with another member of the same litter.[3] This suggests the existence of a 'family odour' that reminded each dog of the brother or sister it was currently living with, even though the odour was coming from a dog living in a completely different household. Similar tests given to four–five-week-old puppies showed that, even at that young age, they had already learned their litter odour. Unexpected abilities such as these serve to remind us that we still have a great deal to learn about how much information dogs get from odours, especially those that are completely imperceptible to us.

However, the 'competitive exclusion' principle does not seem to apply to imprinting in the domestic dog. Puppies 'imprint' not only on to their own mothers and littermates, but also on to people. (Strictly speaking, this phenomenon is slightly different from true imprinting in that it does not seem to be restricted to one individual person, even at the start.) In fact, puppies can also 'imprint' on to other animals that they have friendly encounters with during their sensitive period, such as cats. One of the beauties of the capacity for multiple socialization among dogs and cats is that they only become fearful of one another if they first meet in adulthood. I have usually kept both dogs and cats at home, and if they are introduced to one another, carefully, when they are young, they can become great friends. The accompanying picture shows one of my cats, Splodge, performing a tail-up rub, a sign of social bonding, on my Labrador retriever Bruno, while he is wagging his tail in greeting (although I suspect neither understood much of what the other was saying).

Inter-species socialization expressed as species-typical greeting behaviour

Some traditional uses of dogs exploit this flexibility. The sheep-guarding breeds, such as the Great Pyrenees and the Anatolian karabash, if raised with sheep, grow up to behave as if the flock is their family, although of course they behave like dogs rather than like sheep. I say 'of course', because the dog's capacity to bond to two or even more species at the same time is so obvious that we take it for granted. Such a capability is, however, highly unusual in the animal kingdom as a whole. Most animals are programmed by evolution to learn about just their own species, and no other. Indeed, hand-raised animals often have great difficulty adjusting to living with their own kind, as zookeepers once found, to their dismay, when first trying to breed many endangered species of carnivores, especially some of the wild cats.

Sheep-guarding dog with its flock

Domestic dogs do not appear to lose their species identity, even as they form attachments to humans. Not only do they learn about how to interact with other species, but there is no evidence to suggest that this in any way disadvantages them in terms of how they interact with other dogs. The capacity to adopt multiple identities is unusual, but its origins must lie in regular biological processes. Likewise, since the capacity for interaction with humans cannot have sprung from nowhere, its antecedents must lie in the social behaviour of the wolf. While I am highly critical of the old 'lupomorph' model when it is applied to social structures, as a biologist my instinct is to look for something pre-existing for evolution to work on. Since dogs are neotenized wolves, it is logical to look for the answer in the behaviour of wolf cubs and juveniles, rather than in that of adult wolves.

When wolf cubs are born, they are looked after by other wolves. They learn the characteristics of those individuals, based on the eminently reasonable assumption that they must be their parents, or, in a large pack with existing helpers, their close relatives.[4] When puppies are born, they are usually looked after by both their mother and their owner. Their mother's characteristics are slotted into the 'parent' category, simply because she is there and looking after them. This learning will be retained throughout life, forming the basis for one set of social preferences – namely, for members of their own species (as happens in both wolves and feral dogs). Their owners' characteristics, since they do not match this first category, will be slotted into a second category, generated spontaneously, because they are there and are also caring for them. Apart from this parallel recognition arrangement, there is no reason why everything else about these early social preferences should not be based on the same model: that of parent and offspring. Indeed, it is hard to imagine what an alternative model might be.

Put another way, we humans hijack dogs' normal kin recognition mechanisms. The domestic dog puppy's unusual capacity for multiple socialization is the mechanism whereby we can insert ourselves into their social milieu and substitute ourselves into a role that in the wild would be served by their parents. Until weaning is complete, the bond with the human owner is probably weaker than with the mother, but after that, attachment to humans is reinforced every day, when we feed our dogs, play games with them, and reward them during training. There are fewer opportunities for pet dogs to reinforce attachments to one another. Even in a multi-dog household, it is the humans that act as the parental figures, providing food, controlling where the dogs are at any given time of day, and so on. (There are of course a few intentional exceptions to this scenario, such as hunting dogs housed in packs, and sled dogs, where leadership from one dog is essential to the co-ordination of the team.)

Is this really imprinting? Dogs certainly imprint on to their mothers but science has yet to address whether they also imprint on to their first owners. Imprinting, in the narrow sense of a bond formed to a primary carer, cannot account for the generally outgoing nature of dogs and, more specifically, how easy it is for many dogs to change their allegiance from one owner to another. During the early stages of their lives, most mammals learn both the general identity of their species, and the specific identities of the individuals around them, especially those that look after them. Normally, the latter characteristic leads to the more powerful attachment – but not so in the dog, which shows a much greater flexibility, presumably as a consequence of domestication. However, imprinting, or something very like it, does play a strong role in directing the dog's preferences for whom to approach, and whom to avoid. These preferences are set up early on in the dog's life – specifically, during the socialization period.

Even though dogs can possess several 'friendly' categories simultaneously (a capacity unusual among mammals), each category has its boundaries. This is well exemplified by some dogs' distrust of children. How do dogs know that children are little humans and not another species entirely? The answer appears to be that they do not. Children are distinctly different from adult humans in a number of respects, in the way they move, the sounds they make, and – probably of particular significance to dogs – in the way they smell. Dogs that were never exposed to children during puppyhood can be very wary of them when they first meet them as adults, although being dogs they can easily be trained to overcome this initial reluctance. On the other hand, if their first encounter with a child involves the pulling of their tail and ears, such dogs can easily become irritable and snappy with other children. The dog generalizes between children, treating them as a category rather than as individuals. In the same way, during socialization puppies must generalize between one adult human and another. Although puppies undoubtedly come to recognize some people as individuals, unfamiliar people are presumably categorized as 'friendly', based on their similarity to the first handful of people that the puppy has met.

This is why it is so important to (gently) introduce puppies to as wide a selection of people as possible; men as well as women, people wearing different kinds of clothes, men with beards as well as clean shaven, and so on.[5] This process serves to expand the boundaries of what the dog categorizes as 'adult human'. If the template is left too narrow, perhaps because the puppy meets only one or two kennel-maids during the whole of its sensitive period, then later on the appearance of men, in that instance, will trigger fear and anxiety. This is one of the several reasons why owners have difficulties with dogs from puppy farms and pet shops; such puppies' concept of what the human race looks like is often too narrow, and they default to fearful avoidance of every other two-legged animal they meet.

As we have seen, the organization of the dog's social brain is different from that of most other mammals. It can form multiple, on-demand, representational spaces for each of the species that the puppy encounters during the socialization period.[6] The change in the dog's social brain may have been a product of domestication; alternatively, it may even have arisen as a pre-adaptation to domestication, in certain wolves that no longer exist in the wild today. Regardless, any dog that only meets other dogs until it is fourteen weeks old develops only one such space, defined initially by its littermates and mother, because they are all that is available, but potentially extendable to all types of dog a little later on in its life. The evidence suggests that a dog born in a human household develops two such spaces, one for dogs and one for humans (again, each with the capacity to accommodate other types of dog, and other types of human, that do not respectively look/sound/smell like the owner's family). A dog born into a human household also containing a dog-friendly cat may develop three such spaces. And it is possible that dogs born into households with small children develop yet another space to cover the children – or perhaps they learn to generalize between adult and infant humans, and thus essentially conceive of them as part of the same continuum of two-legged animals.

In short, dogs therefore have very unusual brains, which allow them to construct several social milieux simultaneously. It is this capacity that enables them to be so useful to us; to cite just two examples, hunting dogs can run in a pack, and sled-dogs can run in a race, while remaining under the control of their human handlers. Dogs are born with the potential to develop multiple identities, but all the detail and context has to be provided by experience. One might argue that this is the only way that domestication could have been made to work. Evolution does not possess foresight, so it could not have provided built-in knowledge of what humans are and how they function in advance; the best that natural selection is likely to be able to provide is the machinery to acquire this knowledge. Socialization to other dogs, on the other hand, is most likely based upon mechanisms set up in the early evolution of the carnivores, millions of years before domestication, and may therefore involve some additional processes.

Dogs have to learn about species that are not their own, including humans. But do they also have to learn how to be dogs? In the 1961 experiment described at the beginning of the chapter, all of the puppies developed normal dog-to-dog social behaviour, because they were brought up by their mother, the normal circumstance for a wild animal, or indeed a feral dog. It was their dog-to-human social behaviour that depended on their being exposed to people when they were between three and nine or ten weeks of age. They were still dogs, despite the fact that the ability of some of them to interact with our species had been compromised.

The extent to which dogs learn how to be dogs can be tested only if they never meet another dog from the minute they are born. In a series of experiments conducted in the 1960s, researchers demonstrated that puppies hand-raised from less than eight weeks old, and kept away from other dogs from then on, tended to be aggressive towards other dogs, presumably because they had forgotten, or had never learned, how to interact with members of their own species.[7] However, this was not a surprising result: hand- or machine-raised animals of many species show all kinds of abnormalities due to their restricted early experience (for example, they have very restricted opportunities for play, which affects the development of their brains as well as their physical co-ordination).

A few years later a remarkably simple yet elegant study avoided these abnormalities, giving puppies as normal an upbringing as possible short of actually leaving them in their own litter.[8] Rather than raising puppies in isolation again, the scientists reasoned that a small enough dog could have a relatively normal life if brought up with a litter of kittens – normal, of course, apart from what they were testing, which was the opportunity to interact with others of its own species. The researchers worked with four litters of Chihuahuas. From each litter, two puppies were chosen to be raised in the normal fashion by their biological mothers. Another puppy from each litter, however, was instead introduced into a litter of kittens, beginning when the puppies were three and a half weeks old, at the beginning of the 'sensitive period'. From then on until they were sixteen weeks old, that is, after the 'sensitive period' had ended, each puppy had only kittens as playmates. The stoical mother cats apparently adopted them without any fuss.[9]

Chihuahua puppy fostered by a cat

Cat-raised puppy shying away from dog-raised puppies

When the behaviour of the two types of puppies was compared at sixteen weeks of age, the differences were remarkable. Each pup was presented with a mirror. This was a very exciting experience for the pups that had been raised by their own mother; they barked over and over again at their reflections, jumped up at the mirror and pawed, scratched and dug around it, presumably to get at the puppy they thought was on the other side. The cat-raised pups either ignored their reflections, or acted as if they were something alien, gingerly approaching with their tails tucked between their legs. Presumably they had no mental image of what a dog looked like, having not seen one since their eyes began to work fully. When the two types of litters met, one dog-raised, the other cat-raised, the cat-raised puppies huddled together with the kittens and seemed not to know how to play with the dog-raised pups. If they interacted at all, they behaved just as they had done when presented with their reflection, keeping silent and tucking their tails away.

This is conclusive evidence that puppies do indeed have to learn how to be dogs – they are born with a basic repertoire of responses but need experience of other dogs before these can be properly expressed. However, the experiment also showed that even at sixteen weeks, when the window for socialization to people is coming to a close, dogs can rapidly adjust to living with their own species. After the initial experiments at sixteen weeks, all the puppies were put together. Within two weeks the cat-raised pups were playing like dogs; they were also reacting to their reflections as if they were other dogs.

This finding suggests that the 'sensitive period' during which puppies learn how to socialize with other dogs is actually longer than the 'sensitive period' for socialization to humans. However, since such research has never, as far as I know, been repeated or extended, a number of alternative explanations present themselves. For instance, it is possible that Chihuahuas develop their social preferences more gradually than the spaniels and beagles used in the earlier experiments. It is usually assumed that dogs have a single sensitive period during which they simultaneously learn about the other species they meet, but this possibility has never been examined scientifically, hence we do not know whether different types of dog have sensitive periods of different durations. We can be sure, however, that socialization to dogs and people is still far from complete at eight weeks of age, the time when most puppies are transferred to their pet homes.

It is remarkable, given how unformed a puppy's personality is at eight weeks old, that breeders rely so heavily on puppy behaviour as a way of predicting the grown-up dog's eventual character. 'Puppy tests' carried out at seven or eight weeks of age, before the puppy leaves its breeder, are still widely believed to have this predictive potential. Yet this is the precise age at which the puppy's behaviour is at its most malleable. Numerous scientific studies have failed to find any validity in 'puppy testing' as a predictor of future character. Most such tests also set out to predict characteristics that are probably erroneous, such as a direct correspondence between aggression and 'dominance'. The only personality trait that seems to be resistant to change after seven weeks is extreme (genetically based) fearfulness, which is very rare; such a trait is so effective at inhibiting learning about new situations that it is virtually self-perpetuating. Puppy tests may, however, be useful to prospective owners by indicating deficiencies in the breeder's socialization of the puppies that they will need to address. For example, the test could reveal whether a puppy is fearful of men or children due to lack of exposure – though breeders are hardly likely to promote them for this purpose!

The sensitive period in today's wolves is much shorter than it is in dogs, indicating a fundamental change that must have arisen prior to or early on in domestication. Wolf cubs usually stay in the den with their mother until they are about three weeks old, and only then emerge to meet the other members of the pack. Within a few days, they start to become fearful of all new animals that they meet, and this 'fear reaction' is what marks the end of their sensitive period. At this age, dogs are just starting their sensitive period, which will continue for another ten weeks or so. This extension of the socialization 'window' must be a consequence of domestication. It is possible that the wolves that selected themselves for domestication had a longer socialization period than do the wild wolves that survive today, smoothing the initial transition from wolf to proto-dog, but it is also likely that the proto-dogs with longer socialization periods were more able to thrive in human environments. So over a period of time, progressively longer and longer socialization periods were selected for, becoming fixed when no significant further advantage could be gained.

Today's wild wolves can become attached to people, but they are far more restricted than dogs in the number of attachments they can form. Wolves, like dogs, probably learn a 'family odour' while they are in the den, and are thus able to bond with the rest of the pack once they emerge into the daylight and can learn what the others look and sound like. If they are extensively handled by people during this period, they can become friendly towards them, but they usually restrict this behaviour to the people who did the handling, rather than generalizing to all similar people, as dogs seem to do. They also usually prefer wolf company to human company, however well acquainted with people they are. Imprinting in wolves is more like imprinting in birds than socialization in dogs.

Nevertheless, what we see now in dogs must presumably have evolved from imprinting in wolves. The key changes are therefore likely to have been (*a*) the delay of the beginning of the 'fear reaction', and (*b*) the extension of learning about the characteristics of close 'family' (whether biological or not) to other similar individuals. It is quite possible that some of these differences between dogs and modern wolves were already present in their common ancestor, making domestication easier; as I have already emphasized, we can only guess at what the behaviour of this common ancestor was like. Presumably, domestication would have been very difficult if this ancestor had been as resistant to socialization as modern wolves are, so it is tempting to speculate that the onset of the fear reaction may have been somewhat later in (some) wolves then, as compared to wolves today.

The first three to four months are arguably the most important time in a dog's life. Born with a powerful urge to learn about the world around them, dogs adjust during this period to whatever type of environment they find themselves born into, from the back streets of a village in the Punjab to a Victorian terrace in London. As with most animals, their default reaction to the unknown is fear. But for dogs, unlike most other animals, that fearful reaction is easily nullified by the right kind of experience. To be readily acquired, this experience has to be presented in a way that does not in itself instil fear. Puppies brought up in a chaotic, unpredictable environment can fail to assimilate the information with which they are being bombarded, and develop into generally anxious dogs. Too much stimulation can be as damaging as too little. But everyday experience tells us that the

BROTHERS AND SISTERS

Most puppies are separated from their littermates when they're about eight weeks old, the typical age at which they go to their new homes. The evidence suggests that, even at this age, they have only just begun to recognize one another as individuals (hence 'dominance hierarchies' are even more unlikely than in groups of adults), and that their 'personalities' are not yet fully formed. Two students of mine tested these ideas by following the development of puppies in two litters, one of French bulldogs and one of border collies. They took siblings out of their litter two at a time and let them play together with a tug-toy for one minute. They also observed the whole litter playing together, noting which puppies seemed to 'win' when they were play-fighting. At six weeks old, who 'won', whether in the pairs or the whole litter, changed from day to day, and each puppy seemed to begin each interaction afresh, as if it had no memory of which other puppy it was competing with. At this stage, puppies can tell their littermates apart from other puppies by their characteristic 'litter odour', but they may not be able to tell their brothers and sisters apart from each other. At eight weeks, who 'won' had begun to settle into a pattern, and the puppies showed signs of investigating each other before and during the competitions, presumably trying to establish which puppy it was that they were playing with. However, even then there was no indication of anything resembling a 'dominance hierarchy' within the litter. A puppy that had just 'won' possession of a toy and was then put back into the litter was as likely as not to 'lose' in a play-fight, even with the puppy it had just been paired with. At this age, puppies' personalities are still being formed, and they seem to be using their playing to try out all the personas available to them – giving in, holding back but then pouncing, trying to push every other puppy out of the way in quick succession, and so on. All this goes on under the watchful eye of their mother, and no one gets seriously hurt; indeed, it's at this stage that, by listening to feedback from the squeals of their 'victims' (human as well as canine), puppies begin to learn to inhibit their bites.

It wasn't until the litters were about eleven weeks old that their relationships became consistent, with the smaller, less active puppies tending to give way to their heavier, more active littermates. Even then, there was no indication that the puppies had any concept of their 'status' in the litter; rather, they were simply beginning to use their memories of previous encounters with their littermates to help them decide how best to interact with them.

majority of puppies do get roughly the right degree of experience, simply by being brought up in normal human households – precisely the environment that dogs have, of course, evolved to live within.

The sensitive period is when dogs begin to learn about people, not when that learning ends. Rather, as the sensitive period ends, a second phase begins. In the first phase, the 'socialization period', the puppy learns who it can trust, but once it is about twelve weeks old, it will start avoiding animals or types of people, even objects, that it has never met before. Individual relationships with other dogs also begin to appear at eleven to twelve weeks (see box – 'Brothers and Sisters'). For many weeks after the socialization period is over, the young dog will greedily continue to gather information about its companions and the physical environment they live in, guided by the 'friend or possible foe' categories established during the socialization period.

In this *juvenile period*, which is generally assumed to extend from the onset of the fear reaction until puberty at about one year of age, the young dog's character is still very malleable. The experiences it has during this time can have a profound effect on its personality for the rest of its life. In fact, there is some evidence that the month or so immediately after the socialization period, between twelve weeks and sixteen weeks of age, is almost as important to the development of the dog's adult personality as the socialization period itself, but surprisingly little research has been done on the effects of the environment on a dog's behaviour at this age. For example, few studies have examined the benefits of 'puppy parties', which, as already noted, are structured socialization sessions for puppies in their juvenile period (see box – 'Puppy Parties'). Among those that have, researchers found only weak effects on, for example, obedience, even though regular socialization sessions for puppies are widely believed to be an essential part of dog ownership.

In contrast to the sensitive period, there is no evidence for anything special about the processes whereby puppies in the juvenile period adjust their behaviour to their surroundings; the normal processes of learning are quite adequate to account for this. It is simply that as the dog gets older and more set in its ways, its capacity to deal with change gradually diminishes. The learning that takes place during the juvenile period is often loosely referred to as 'socialization', but this term really ought to be reserved for what happens during the sensitive period. What seems to happen in the juvenile period is that the young dog, now vaccinated and able to go out and encounter the world, learns more about what the world is like, how to deal with it and what strategies work best when coping with the unexpected. The first two

PUPPY PARTIES

Modern lifestyles and the nuclear family mean that young dogs do not have the same opportunities as many of their forebears did for meeting other dogs, and people other than their owners. The 'puppy party' can be a way of filling this gap, giving the puppy the range of experiences that it needs in order to cope with adult life. Although their name implies a free-for-all, to be effective these sessions need to be expertly run and comprehensively structured. Although it was traditionally believed that dogs could not be trained until they were over six months old, it is now well established that puppies can learn basic commands much younger than this, and so puppy parties incorporate short sessions of training, exclusively using rewards. Punishment, which could instantly cause the puppy to develop an aversion to the whole business of getting on with people and dogs, should never be used. Controlled play with other puppies helps to continue the process, which started in the litter, whereby the puppy learns to control and inhibit its own behaviour. Having people other than the owners handle each puppy, in the right way, extends each puppy's concept of the human race as good to be with.

For advice on how to choose a puppy party, see Further Reading at the end of this book.

can be likened to an inventory of things that the dog recognizes and has a suitable reaction for; the last, to a toolkit of default responses when the usual rules-of-thumb do not work. For example, research has shown that hearing fireworks during either the socialization period or the first few weeks of the juvenile period protects puppies against becoming fearful of loud bangs. Puppies that do not hear loud noises until later on are more likely to develop noise phobias. In general, dogs that fail to develop both knowledge and coping skills become especially vulnerable to developing rather non-specific anxieties, and will tend to adopt strategies based on avoidance, or even aggression, when they are confronted with something unfamiliar that they feel they cannot deal with.

'Problem' dogs – dogs whose owners have actively sought help for their pets because of behavioural issues – reveal a great deal about the importance of early-life experience. A decade ago I did an analysis of clinical records with leading British behaviourist David Appleby, looking for factors that might predispose dogs to show fearful aggression or avoidance.[10] Specifically, we were looking for dogs that had been bred in kennels and never brought into the house, and then gone to homes where they had been largely kept away from people other than their owners: due to their restricted early experience, such dogs should find it much harder to cope with novel experiences than the average dog. None of these dogs was 'wild'; they had all received some contact with people during their 'sensitive period', or it would have been very unlikely that they would ever have become pets.

In certain ways, these dogs functioned normally. They were no more likely than the average dog to be aggressive towards their owners, with whom they had had every opportunity to develop a normal relationship. Nor were the dogs bred in kennels predisposed to become aggressive towards other dogs; after all, they had had a typical amount of exposure to their own species. But they were different in one crucial way: they were often aggressive towards people they did not know, or tried to avoid them when they met. I found an anticipated exception in the small number of dogs that had left the kennels where they had been born at seven weeks of age rather than the usual eight weeks, and then happened to have gone to a busy urban family environment. Puppies taken out of kennels at a young enough age seemed to be able to compensate for their restricted early experience.

The great majority of these dogs had been homed at eight weeks, which is standard because it is when puppies can be fully weaned. However, this age is also right in the middle of the 'sensitive period' for socialization, so it has been suggested that a sudden change of environment at eight weeks may be particularly stressful for the puppy. There have been few other studies of this kind that could test this idea, and none in which the age at homing has been varied systematically. We therefore cannot yet be sure what is the optimum age for building up dogs' experience of the world, although we do know that to be most effective it should start before seven weeks, and should go on for several months after that. There is also some evidence that taking puppies out of their litters before eight weeks of age predisposes them to become fearful of other dogs, so ideally the whole litter should be kept together until eight weeks, while at the same time beginning to introduce them to a wide variety of humans.

The process that leads to the bond between dog and owner is

therefore set in motion when the puppy is about three weeks old. The behavioural strategies established during the sensitive period channel the puppy's behaviour and set the ground rules for the subsequent formation of close relationships with individual human beings. Puppies that are given only very limited experience of the man-made world are likely to fail to adapt to that world when they meet it. Specifically, although they should be able to form well-balanced relationships with their owners, they may react fearfully towards other people because of their impoverished experience of the human race in all its diversity. Their default strategy for dealing with anything unknown may be to try to flee from it, rather than adopting the cautious curiosity that is the default strategy of the well-balanced dog.

All of this presupposes that a dog's formative experience begins at three weeks of age. However, the dog has already existed for twelve weeks before this – nine as a foetus, and three as an apparently helpless puppy. When the original research into the dog's sensitive period was conducted fifty or sixty years ago, it was thought that foetuses and helpless newborn animals were incapable of learning very much, and would grow along a predetermined path unless some catastrophe occurred. Reinforcing this idea was the anthropocentric view that newborn puppies, being blind and deaf, were incapable of learning much about their environment. Their sense of smell was largely forgotten about, although we now know that puppies can learn to distinguish between odours even before they are born as well as during their first three weeks. In short, this research largely overlooked the possibility that the twelve weeks following conception may be a time when reactions to the world are significantly influenced by outside events.

Although dogs have not been studied directly with regard to external influences during the time from conception to birth, other research indicates that this period may be particularly critical to the development of behaviour. We now know, from studies of other species, including our own, that the environment experienced by the mother can have profound effects on the character of her offspring. Research on rats, mice, monkeys and humans has shown that the development of the foetal brain can be powerfully influenced by the mother's experiences during her pregnancy. There is no reason to suppose that the same does not apply to dogs. Most of the research on brain development in the foetus has focused on severe stress experienced by the mother. In our own species, it is now well established that maternal stress can be linked to a whole range of mental disorders in children, including chronic anxiety, attention deficit hyperactivity disorder (ADHD) and inadequate social behaviour. Longer-term problems can result, including poor intellectual and language skills, lack of emotional control, and even schizophrenia. Studies of rats have shown that these problems almost certainly stem from the effects of stress hormones produced by the mother that cross over the placenta into the foetus itself. There, they change the way that the brain is developing, resulting later, after birth, in reduced activity of some neurohormones (such as dopamine and serotonin) and a hyperactive stress-response system. Although the details vary slightly depending upon the stage of pregnancy during which the stress occurs, the young animal can then exhibit impaired learning, poor play skills, and a weakened ability to cope with challenges.

Luckily, these deficits appear to be reversible if the infant animal receives additional maternal care after birth,[11] but they can also be made worse if the young animal is taken away from its mother prematurely, or if her maternal skills are deficient. Surprisingly little attention has been paid to this phenomenon in domesticated animals, despite the potential lessons to be learned about how best to look after them. One study has shown, however, that domestic sows kept in unstable social groups not only become stressed, but their female offspring are, in turn, more than usually aggressive to their own piglets, implying a profound and long-lasting effect on the development of their brains.[12]

Are these effects all pathologies, or do some of them actually prepare the young animal to cope with a changing world? Because much of this research has been done in an effort to substantiate factors affecting mental illness in humans, less thought has gone into trying to understand why evolution has allowed stress experienced by the mother to affect her offspring so profoundly. Indeed, the general assumption has been that these are indeed pathologies, beyond the reach of natural selection. Nevertheless, research on guinea pigs (and birds) suggests that it may sometimes be helpful for offspring to be pre-programmed in this way. Female guinea pigs that give birth in overcrowded social groups tend to produce female pups that behave more aggressively than normal. Their male offspring, on the other hand, become 'infantilized', for example continuing to play-fight at an age when their normal counterparts are competing with other males for real. These changes may actually prepare the young guinea pigs for the environment in which they will live; in order to find food and space to breed in a crowd, females need to be pushy, whereas young males need to keep their natural competitive nature in check until they are big and strong enough to win against the most experienced males.

It is quite possible that some of the changes in the brain wrought by maternal stress are, at least to some extent, adaptive, in the sense that they prepare the offspring for an uncertain world. However, this is more likely to be the case with wild animals than with domestic animals such as dogs; any response to stress that evolved in the wild ancestor, the wolf, is unlikely to still be adaptive in the man-made environment of today.

All these findings strongly suggest that dog breeders should place great emphasis on the psychological well-being of their breeding bitches. They should neither induce the stress of separation by isolating them for long periods, nor allow the bitches to be intimidated by other dogs. Some of the deficits that we found in dogs born in non-domestic environments were quite possibly due as much to stress induced in their mother as to impoverished experience during the first eight weeks of their lives. (The owners who brought their dogs in for treatment were simply unable to give us this much detail about the environment where their dogs had been born.) Purchasers of puppies would therefore do well to examine the conditions under which breeders keep their bitches, as well as the environment experienced by the puppies themselves. Of course, owners also have a duty to ensure that their new puppy gets the right kind of experiences during its first few months, but however good these are, there is a risk that they may not be sufficient to completely reverse the consequences of having had a chronically stressed mother, or an impoverished environment during its first eight weeks.

Overall, it is clear that a puppy's experiences, from soon after conception to when it is roughly four months old, play a crucial role in affecting its character. A dog that gets the wrong start in life can grow up to be overly fearful or anxious. This is not absolutely inevitable, as nature has built in a capacity, up to a point, to compensate for setbacks early on and return development to a balanced trajectory. Nevertheless, there is much we still do not know about why some dogs develop behavioural problems and others do not.

For example, why do some dogs find it relatively easy to cope with being left on their own, while many others find it difficult? At the present time, research has not been able to shed much light on this matter. One possibility, however, is that dogs have been so heavily selected to form strong attachments to humans that they all have the potential to develop separation problems – but the lucky ones have owners who, whether accidentally or knowingly, teach them that being left alone is not a catastrophe.

Most dogs seem to become more distressed when they are separated from their owners than when they are separated from other dogs. So the question arises, do dogs love people more than they love other dogs? This does not sound like a particularly scientific sort of question, but it could be a test of just how domesticated dogs have become. Few scientists have ever considered this a question worthy of an answer, but there is one study that conclusively shows that dogs are indeed prone to bonding more strongly with people than with other dogs.[13] The subjects of the study were eight seven-to-nine-year-old mongrels that had been living as littermate pairs in kennels since they were eight weeks old; all had been fully socialized to people, and they were being looked after by one carer who was, as far as they were concerned, equivalent to their 'owner'. When the experiment began, the kennel-mates had not been apart even for a minute during the previous two years, and hardly ever during their whole lifetimes. However, when one of each pair was taken out of earshot for four hours, the remaining dog's behaviour did not alter appreciably. Puppies separated from their littermates will usually yelp until they are reunited, but these adult dogs barely even barked. Moreover, the level of the stress hormone cortisol in their blood did not change as a result of the separation, provided the dogs had been left in their familiar pen. Overall, therefore, there was no indication that any of these dogs was upset, this despite the fact that, since they had virtually no history of being left alone, they would not have been sure that they would be back with their pen-mate in a few hours' time.

In contrast, when the dogs were taken to an unfamiliar kennel, they did become upset. They were visibly agitated, and their levels of stress hormone went up by over 50 per cent. Remarkably, this proved true whether they were on their own or with their kennelmate. When the two were together, they did not interact with one another any more frequently than usual; whatever the bond between them, it was not sufficiently comforting or confidence-building to help them cope with being somewhere new, outside their familiar territory. However, if their carer sat quietly with each dog in the novel kennel, it would stay near him and pester him for contact (which he responded to by brief episodes of stroking). This was apparently enough to alleviate the dogs' stress completely, because if the carer was there, their cortisol levels stayed close to normal.[14]

These dogs, although they had kept the company of another dog for their whole lives, behaved as if they were much more attached to their carer than to their brother or sister. While they had not led quite the same kind of life as a pet does, everyday experience suggests that the same is probably true of pet dogs. Dogs do have territories, in the sense that they feel most calm when they are in familiar places, but, like the wolf, they can comfortably go to new places if they are with their 'pack', the difference being that in this case the key 'pack' member is almost always a human (namely, the owner), and not a member of their own species. For many dogs, the owner will be a constant feature of their lives from the middle of the socialization period onwards. However, others will be forced, through changes in circumstances, to alter their primary attachments on several occasions during their lifetime. So in addition to the capacity to accept both humans as well as dogs as social partners, domestication has given dogs sufficient social flexibility to form new 'familial' ties at almost any time in their lives.

Since the need for a human attachment figure seems to be unusually powerful in the domestic dog, dogs that are abandoned by their owners and end up in rehoming centres must feel this very acutely. Research has shown that just a few minutes of friendly attention from one person on two consecutive days is enough to make some of these unowned dogs desperate to stay with that person; when left on their own, these dogs will howl, scratch at the door that the person has left through, or jump up at the window to try to see where she has gone. For many dogs, this perception of humans as potential attachment figures may last their whole lives; luckily for many of them, one individual or one family will satisfy this need from eight weeks of age for the rest of their lives. This craving certainly explains why so many dogs develop separation disorders at some point in their lives.

Even though most of the evidence for these strong and rapidly forming attachments comes from the behaviour of dogs that are distressed by separation, the strength of such attachments suggests that they should also be expressed in pet dogs' normal behaviour. Unfortunately, however, very few biologists have studied the everyday interactions between pet dogs and the families they live in. There are probably a variety of reasons for this: such studies are time-consuming; they use techniques more commonly employed by anthropologists, who are rarely interested in animals; the data they generate are complex and not straightforward to analyse; and there is the real risk that the mere presence of an observer would change the way that family members behave towards their pet. For example, some people may feel inhibited, while others might use the opportunity to 'show off'. Nevertheless, such studies are a very useful counterpart to the much more structured investigations of, for example, dogs' cognitive abilities.

One of the earliest, and still one of the best, of these ethnographic studies shows just how people-focused most pet dogs are. Ten middle-class dog-owning families living in the suburbs of Philadelphia were observed for a total of twenty to thirty hours, usually in the late afternoon and early evening when the children were at home. The researcher noted that the dogs paid much more attention to the human members of the household than vice versa. They watched, approached or followed one or more household members. When they rested, they often faced people in the same or the next room. When they happened to be looking elsewhere, such as out of a window, they were evidently still aware of where the people were, often turning towards them and approaching. Conversely, however, the family members rarely interrupted what they were doing to seek out the dog when the dog was in another room.[15]

The apparently single-minded vigilance on the part of the dog was not uniformly directed, however. Dogs are very good at sensing who in the family likes them best. In the three families where the husband was not attached to or interested in the dog, the dog seldom watched or followed him. In this way, the dogs showed that they had learned who had been most responsive to them in the past. The implication is that dogs, once they have an attachment figure, are not indiscriminate in terms of who else they become attached to, presumably relying on their experiences of people to guide them in how they should best react.

The 'lupomorph' or 'pack' model, while flawed in many respects, is therefore correct in one: dogs do behave towards us using a set of rules and behaviour patterns that are ultimately derived from those of the wolf and more distant canid ancestors. However, these are not the rules of 'Dominate or be dominated, crush or be crushed'. They are the rules of the family, the rules of 'Those who raise you are those who are most likely to continue to cherish you throughout your life'. Our pet dogs' behaviour clearly shows us that they see us as attachment figures, based on a parent–offspring framework. Indeed, the dog owner who tells her friends 'I'm Fido's mum' is really not far wrong.

Dogs are fundamentally different from all other animals in this respect. We take it for granted that we can exercise them off-lead, and that, once trained, they will return to us for no more immediate reward than being reunited with us. The mechanisms involved are essentially developmental; domestication has imbued the dog with the capacity to achieve this unique social behaviour, but it is only through the learning environment we give them that dogs come to understand how to behave towards people.

6

Does Your Dog Love You?

Dogs are obviously attached to their owners – in the sense of their behaviour, in the sense that they follow them around. But does your dog actually love you? Of course it does! It tells you, every time you come home, by the way it greets you. Your dog may be 'just' a household pet, but I would be very surprised if most owners could not bring themselves to say that they loved their dog, and that their dog loved them in return. Anything less, and the relationship is probably in trouble.

Emotions are not easy to pin down, scientifically speaking. As a scientist, I can investigate how much you love your dog, and, as a human, I can be reasonably sure that what you describe to me as 'love' is much the same emotion that I have felt for my own dogs. We can both articulate this, first because we are members of the same species and therefore are likely to have similar emotional repertoires and, second, because we can communicate our feelings to each other through language.

However, the love that flows in the other direction, dog to owner, is much harder to pin down. First of all, dogs cannot tell us how they feel, so we have to deduce it from their behaviour. Can we be sure that we always get this right? Second, because we belong to different species, we cannot simply assume that dogs experience the same array of emotions that we do. In fact, I would go so far as to say that it is unethical to make that assumption. Scientists have a responsibility to convey as much as they know about the reality of canine emotions, guiding owners to a proper perception of what their dogs can and cannot feel.

I am convinced that giving proper consideration to the emotional life of dogs is not just an academic exercise; it has real and practical implications for their welfare and their relationships with people. But not all scientists agree that dog emotion is even a proper subject for investigation. Some behavioural scientists think that every attempt should be made to explain the behaviour of other species without referring to emotions at all, because emotions are, ultimately, subjective and therefore not completely accessible to scientific investigation.[1] Others think it is acceptable to ascribe emotions to our nearest relatives – perhaps just the apes, or maybe the higher primates – but are more inclined to restrict themselves to more mechanistic explanations of behaviour in less closely related species, including dogs. Of course, most pet owners would find this degree of scepticism absurd – they firmly believe in the emotional lives of their pets. These points of view are so divergent that many scientists have simply come to regard owners as deluded, while dog owners dismiss science as too out of touch with the realities of dog ownership.

But in fact the human mind is sufficiently sophisticated to comprehend both views simultaneously. Subjective and objective perspectives of emotion can exist side by side even within the same person. Scientists will casually talk about their own pets as if they have complex internal emotional lives, but if pressed will admit that there is little direct evidence that the animal is actually experiencing precisely those emotions.[2] Does this mean that they are living in a fantasy world at home, in which they have fallen into the trap of behaving 'as if' animals have emotions, but then return to objective reality at work, and deny that such emotions exist at all? Although this seeming contradiction may appear paradoxical, I do not see it that way. Rather, I consider it a natural expression of the complexity of human thought and consciousness.

It is well established that the human mind loves to project emotions and intentions on to everything, especially things that it cannot control. Anthropomorphism, the attribution of human characteristics to non-human creatures – to phenomena such as the weather, and even inanimate objects like rivers and mountains – is an intrinsic part of human nature.[3] So are zoomorphism and totemism, the complementary processes by which humans ascribe the characteristics of animals to other humans. We talk about dogs as being 'little people', and we may refer to a person as 'a dog' (though what we might mean by that will vary from culture to culture and possibly with the gender of the target!). Does that mean we do not know that dogs and people are different, not only in outward appearance, but also in their inner characteristics? We may blur the distinction from time to time, but mostly these attributions are metaphors, and we use them with full awareness of that fact.

As humans, we have the ability to stand back from a situation, detaching ourselves from its emotional component and making logical decisions on what to do next. Parents can simultaneously experience an emotional bond to their children while objectively analysing their transgressions and the motivations behind them. Our capacity to detach ourselves from our automatic emotional reaction to something they have done, in order to work out the most effective response, does not mean that the emotional response is in any way demeaned or diminished. Equally, why should we not express ourselves in anthropomorphic terms as animal-lovers, while being simultaneously aware that such projections may be the product of our imaginations? I cannot see any dissonance – as psychologists call it – in such behaviour.

Without an emotional bond, there would be no pets – and yet this bond can sometimes create problems for dogs and humans alike. The emotional bond between owner and pet is often, perhaps to some degree always, bound up in anthropomorphic projections.[4] Many people appear unthinkingly to treat their animals as if they were little people. Yet most pet owners are also capable of conceiving of their animals' behaviour in a logical way, especially when decisions have to be made that affect the well-being of that animal. It is perfectly possible to hold a logical view on the 'otherness' of animals, without interfering one iota with the emotional aspects of the relationship. It is when these two approaches become blurred that the relationship is destined for problems and potential breakdown. For example, owners who treat their dog as if it were a person may project responsibilities on to it that the dog is not even aware of, let alone capable of responding appropriately to. And consequently owners may feel justified in punishing the dog for something they mistakenly think the dog 'knows it has done'.

Even owners who treat their dogs quite rationally can fall into the trap of presuming that they know more than they actually do about how their dog is feeling. In one study conducted in Switzerland,[5] the investigators showed sixty-four Swiss dog owners, and sixty-four otherwise similar people with little or no experience of dogs, still photos and short video clips of dogs interacting with one another as well as with people. Both groups were able to correctly associate dogs' facial expressions with obvious emotions and behavioural states such as fear and inquisitiveness. But this was not the case with other emotions, such as anger and jealousy; moreover, the dog owners tended to be more anthropomorphic in their descriptions than the non-owners. The closeness of their relationship was evidently affecting their judgement.

Dog owners may think they can interpret canine communication, but in actuality they are often misled by their anthropomorphism. In the second part of the same study, the dog owners were shown a video clip of an owner getting her dog ready for a walk – putting on her coat, putting the dog on the leash – and then immediately removing the leash, taking off her coat and ignoring the dog for a few minutes. The dog followed her to the door, then went back to where she kept her coat, and finally sat down watching her while she directed her attention elsewhere. Shown the whole sequence, almost all the participants identified the dog's emotion while it was being ignored as 'disappointment'. But of those who were shown only the last part of the scene, the part after the owner had left the picture, very few people identified the dog's emotional state in this way. Clearly, those who had seen the whole clip were projecting on to the dog's body-language their own sense of how they would feel under those particular circumstances. The dog's actual behaviour was almost irrelevant. The implication, of course, is that even the most well-meaning and rational of owners may know significantly less than they think they do about their dogs' inner lives. Those owners who regard their dog as a 'little person' may even unconsciously prefer explanations for their dog's behaviour that rely more on projections of what they guess the dog is feeling than on what its body-language is telling them.

A better understanding among pet owners of the emotional life of dogs would improve their relationships with their pets. It would enable them to deal with their dog's behaviour in a reasoned and informed way, ultimately enhancing rather than diminishing the emotional depth of the relationship. Some dog owners may treat their dogs as little people, attributing mental and emotional capabilities to them that they do not actually have, simply because it has never been pointed out to them that there is a more rational basis for understanding why their dogs behave the way they do. This more rational perspective, in turn, can allow them to make sensible decisions about how to resolve any problems that arise.

In order to understand the emotional lives of dogs, we first have to come to grips with what emotions actually are. Unfortunately, psychologists are still not in total agreement about what emotions consist of or, indeed, precisely how they should be discussed. One key issue is the role that emotions play in guiding behaviour. Some philosophers have suggested that, even in man, the brain controls behaviour directly, and that what we experience as emotion is merely our consciousness commenting on what is going on. In this view, full consciousness is required for emotions to exist at all. Since dogs do not appear to have the same degree of consciousness that we have, this seems to suggest that they cannot experience emotions either, or at least not in a way that would be intelligible to us.

However, we no longer have to think about emotional states in such an abstract way. New techniques now available to neuroscientists have enabled a fuller understanding of how emotions are generated; specifically, through an interplay between hormones, the brain and the rest of the nervous system. For example, MRI scanning can show what is going on in the brains of fully conscious humans (and one day soon, it is to be hoped, dogs too), helping to pinpoint where in the brain emotions are generated.

It is now generally agreed that what we experience as emotions are an important part of the machinery that allows us to lead our everyday lives, and not just a side effect of consciousness. They are thought to act as essential filters, enabling us to make appropriate decisions at the right moment, without waiting for our brains to come up with all the possible courses of action and attempt to choose logically between them. In this conception, emotions exist for the purpose of providing a rough-and-ready indicator of where we are in relation to where we ought to be. If I see a figure approaching me at dead of night out of a dark alley, fear will instantly propel me in the opposite direction. If someone breaks into my house while I am at home, anger will take over and make me aggressive towards the intruder. The first of these responses is probably as effective today as it was for my hunter-gatherer ancestors 100,000 years ago. The second was probably more appropriate then than it is now, and I shall have to keep my anger in check if I want to remain within the limits of reasonable force that the law allows in deterring intruders. Nevertheless, anger does channel my brain towards the immediate threat (the intruder) rather than wasting its time on less urgent tasks that can wait (such as working out how I am going to get the newly broken lock on the door repaired, or trying to remember where I wrote down the phone number of my insurance company).

If emotions are indeed survival mechanisms, then they most likely evolved to fulfil specific functions. And those functions – avoiding danger, counteracting threats, forming pair-bonds that enhance the survival of offspring – are not unique to man. They apply just as much to wolves as to our own human ancestors. Indeed, since both wolves and humans are mammals, and our brains and hormone systems are based on the same biological pattern, it is highly likely that both our emotional systems evolved from those possessed by our common mammalian ancestor. It therefore stands to reason that our emotional lives, and those of dogs, are similar. However, because millions of years of evolution separate us, it is also highly likely that they are far from identical.

In order to investigate further these similarities and differences, I am going to take it as read that emotions, far from being a luxury that only humans can appreciate, are a fundamental part of the biological systems that regulate behaviour. I am also going to assume that, like any other biological system, emotions have been selected for, and subsequently refined by, the process of evolution. The model I will adopt divides emotions into three components.[6] The most primitive level involves responses of the autonomic nervous system (the part that we are unaware of but which keeps the various parts of our bodies functioning for us), acting in concert with the hormones that are associated with arousal, fear, stress and affection and so on – Emotion I in the accompanying diagram. As humans, we are not always aware of these autonomic responses (exceptions include the pounding heartbeat and sweaty palms triggered by fear) but thanks to the techniques of modern physiology they can all be measured and understood. Emotion II is the corresponding behaviour; the postures, displays and signals (and in the case of dogs, these most likely include odour signals that are imperceptible to us humans). Emotion III is what we are most interested in here, the feelings that we, as human beings, experience subjectively.

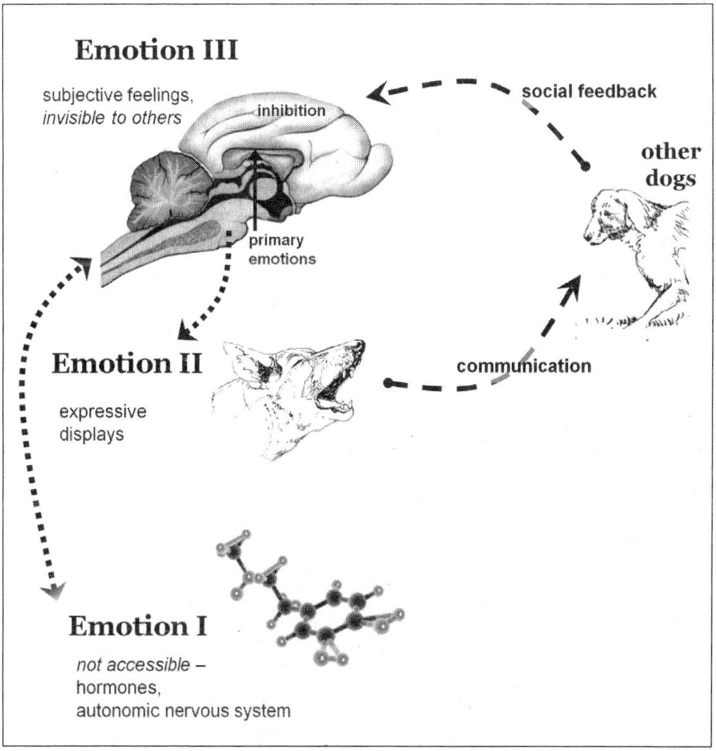

The three components of emotion. Emotion I is the sum of changes in hormone levels and in the nervous system. Emotion II is the outward expression of emotion, for example in body-language and vocalizations. These can be detected by other dogs (and people), whose reactions can be perceived and may subsequently modify how emotions are felt and reacted to. Emotion III is the subjective experience of the emotion itself, for example, 'fear'. Arrows indicate interactions.

They are what we refer to in everyday terms as emotions and moods, as in 'I feel anxious', or 'I'm happy today', or indeed 'I love my dog'.

What is the point, then, in also labelling both the underlying physiology and the associated behaviour as 'emotion'? In the context of improving our understanding of dogs, this model emphasizes that if we can measure a change in the underlying physiology (for example, a sudden increase in the stress hormone adrenalin), and at the same time observe the corresponding behaviour (the animal runs away), we can be reasonably sure that the dog is also experiencing the matching emotion (fear). Quite what that experience is like for the dog, we can never entirely know – just as we cannot even know precisely how another human being is feeling. Feelings are private, but that does not mean that we cannot and do not take them into account. When dealing with other people, we just make a best guess and proceed accordingly – and if our first guess is wrong, there is a good chance that the other person will let us know. Dogs, however, may be less good at letting us know when we misjudge them, or perhaps we are not as clever as we should be at decoding their signals. Either way, what is important is trying our hardest to understand their emotional lives.

My second reason for considering this three-level conceptualization of emotion to be helpful is that it proposes that emotions are useful to the animal: they act as special-purpose information-processing systems, alongside the general systems of learning and cognition (to which humans have added symbolic language). Emotions are an essential aid to survival, and if dogs possess the two 'lower' levels (and without a doubt they do), then it is difficult to maintain that they do not also experience the third level, the emotional reactions.

My third reason is that this conceptualization emphasizes an evolutionary continuum. It posits that human emotions, while possibly unique in some respects, have evolved from those of mammals, which in turn have evolved from those of reptiles, and so on. Unless one subscribes to the view that human-type consciousness and self-awareness are absolutely essential to the experience of all emotion, it is very difficult to deny – even from such an apparently dry, purely scientific viewpoint – that dogs must experience at least some form of emotion.

Alongside the many advantages of this model, however, there is one major disadvantage: the implicit assumption that subjective emotion

(Emotion III) always emerges as overt behaviour (Emotion II). In humans, most emotions are also linked to facial expressions that vary little from culture to culture, thus serving as a near-universal language of feelings. However, we can all think of situations in which we try to hide our feelings, or project emotions that are different from those we are actually feeling. Dogs, too, have expressive faces – and bodies – that give away much, but possibly not all, of what they are feeling.

It is worth briefly considering why dogs have evolved such expressive faces. Cats have not. Cats suffer in silence. Cats can communicate extreme fear, or extreme anger, but what about anxiety, or joy?[7] This striking difference between cats and dogs stems from their evolutionary histories. Domestic cats are descended from solitary hunters, an 'every man for himself' culture: two male (or female) cats are essentially lifelong competitors in the business of passing on their genes to the next generation. A gene that made one cat likely to look pleased with itself when it had just returned from an especially successful hunting trip would die out, because it would contribute to its rival's success at finding food, not its own. The absence of a connection between communication (Emotion II in the model) and the physiological and subjective components of emotion (Emotion I and Emotion III) can thus sometimes be in the animal's own interest.

In fact, across the animal kingdom as a whole, the honest display of emotions is favoured only in certain quite specific circumstances – namely, when co-operation is the desired result. Humans are among the most co-operative species alive, and indeed many of these special factors apply to us. As a species we evolved in the context of extended-family groups, and so, according to the theory of kin selection, we should tend to be honest with one another. Also, we are extremely good at recognizing other individuals of our own species and recalling our previous encounters with them. Accordingly, we have highly sophisticated cognitive mechanisms for detecting deception among those familiar to us. In other words, most of us are very good at detecting when someone we know is hiding his or her true feelings.

It is worth detouring briefly to look at the evolution of human body-language – to see why the connection between facial expression and some emotions should be so transparent in our own species – before going on to speculate on whether the same might apply to dogs.

The human face is particularly expressive. And our facial expressions for the more primitive emotions – such as fear, joy and anger – seem to be the same the world over. Human expression is clearly a species-typical, evolved trait. The idea underlying this trait was first proposed by Charles Darwin, who attempted to apply the same principle to dogs (see box, pp. 158–9 – 'Darwin's Dogs'). Indeed, scientists have recently discovered that the facial muscles used to generate these particular expressions are common to virtually all humans, whereas other facial muscles vary widely between races and between individuals. As a species, we cannot function socially without facial expressions – facial paralysis leads almost inevitably to isolation and depression.

Our facial expressions are directly connected to our emotions. Just watch someone's face when she is talking to a friend on the phone: she will smile, frown and so on, just as though the other person can see her. One of the functions of our facial expressions – perhaps even their primary function – is to let people know what we are feeling, not only while we are talking to them, but also while we are listening to them. Especially when listening, we often express the emotions that we think we should be feeling, even if we're not actually experiencing them. The intention in such instances is to convince the speaker not only that we are paying attention to her, but also that we are on her emotional wavelength. Overall, our unconscious facial expressions tend to reassure those around us that we are trustworthy.

We also consciously use or suppress many of these same facial expressions to modify the behaviour of others, to our own benefit. There is a direct connection between Emotion III (feelings) and Emotion II (facial expression) but it is under at least some degree of conscious control: indeed, we use our expressions to manipulate those around us. Certain expressions of emotion, such as blushing when we are embarrassed, are almost impossible to fake or suppress, but some people can produce an apparently sincere smile at will. (Others can only manage a fake smile, technically referred to as a non-Duchenne smile, in which the mouth smiles but the eyes do not.) We also try to cover up our emotions when it is socially advantageous to do so: for example, after winning some prize, many people will attempt to block their spontaneous smile by locking their facial muscles, or hiding their faces behind their hands, so as to avoid the appearance of gloating.

Most of us are adept at detecting false expressions of emotion in others, even though we may not be able to describe precisely how we have detected an insincerity. Masking emotion totally requires considerable practice, as evidence by the comparatively few individuals who can achieve a 'poker face'. Evolution has evidently given us a highly tuned lie-detection system – again presumably because the success of hunter-gatherer groups depended upon it.

Are dogs equally manipulative? Dogs do sometimes appear to be 'lying' to each other, especially when there is some conflict of interest involved, although as far as I know no one has studied this systematically. My Labrador retriever Bruno loved people, but was always a bit wary of other dogs, especially other males. When he encountered people he did not know, he would wiggle his way up to them, half-crouched, his tail twirling round and round like a demented helicopter. When he saw another male dog, he would stand as tall as he could, and up would go the hackles on his back. In both instances, Bruno was trying to ensure that the meeting would go the way he wanted it to. In the case of the person, he always wanted to make friends, so he used the wolf-cub greeting. He was trying to make himself look smaller than he really was (which rarely succeeded, considering that he was a rather portly Labrador). Towards another male dog, he did the opposite: he tried to make himself look bigger than he really was. Actually, he was bluffing: if the other dog persisted, he would quickly change tack – he was not very brave – and back away with his tail tucked down. In other words, he appeared to be trying to mislead the other dog. I do not mean that he was deliberately and consciously setting out to deceive; it is doubtful that dogs have this degree of intelligence. Nevertheless, attempting to make an impression on a potential rival, most dogs do try to make themselves look bigger than they really are, hoping to scare the other dog off without risking getting hurt in a tussle. However, for this to work every time, the other dog would have to be stupid enough to be taken in by this rather obvious attempt at browbeating. And that seems unlikely.

So why is it that both dogs do not simply signal that they have no intention of fighting? In fact, dogs appear to have no way of negotiating such a climb-down. The first few individuals that adopted the tactic of hackle-raising probably gained an advantage from doing this, because their rivals would have been taken in by it. Once most individuals have adopted the habit of raising their hackles, they will expect their rivals to do the same. Any dog that does not raise its hackles will therefore be perceived as smaller than it really is, increasing the probability that it will be attacked. So this piece of behaviour became fixed in the repertoire; almost all dogs will display it from time to time, even if they have little or no intention of actually fighting. Bear in mind, however,

DARWIN'S DOGS

In his book The Expression of the Emotions in Man and Animals, *Charles Darwin used the domestic dog extensively to illustrate his ideas on the interpretation of animals' postures and expressions. One of his central precepts was the 'principle of antithesis', the idea that opposing emotions induced exactly opposite postures, which thereby conveyed precise information about the animal's state of mind and intentions. He contrasted the 'attacking' dog that stands tall, leans forward with tail and hackles raised, growls and bares its teeth, with the 'friendly, submissive' dog that crouches low to the ground, with tail held down. Although Darwin's 'principle of antithesis' is rarely referred to today, his interpretation of the dogs' emotional states is still considered sound.*

Darwin's 'attacking' dog

Darwin's 'submissive' dog

that although their body-language suggests that they are bluffing, we have no evidence that dogs are actually aware of this deception – they are simply doing what evolution and their own experiences have told them will achieve the result they want.

A more complex version of this process probably gave rise to the 'bared teeth' signal that many dogs use as the next stage after hackles are raised. Scientists hypothesize that this strategy originated because actual biting of another dog has to be preceded by pulling the jowls out of the way, to protect them. The 'bared teeth' signal is useful for the other dog as well, because it gives a fraction of a second's warning that the first dog is about to bite. Presumably, the baring of teeth was often sufficient to forestall conflict; by raising its top lip well before it bit, a potential attacker could force an inexperienced opponent to recoil without having to submit to the risk of an actual fight. But was this really a sensible bluff? The receiver can now see his opponent's teeth, well in advance of the actual bite. If they are broken or missing, then he can be confident that the resulting bite may not be particularly painful. Thus both parties gain an advantage from the signal: the attacker shows that he may be about to bite, and the target can check how damaging this threat is likely to be if carried out. And so this signal, too, gets fixed in the repertoire. Such signals are especially stable, as far as evolution is concerned, because they contain a kernel of honesty in addition to an element of bluff. The attacker is really ready to bite, and the intended victim can really get an idea of what the bite will feel like.

Bared teeth – an honest signal of fighting potential

The fact that evolution favours a certain degree of bluffing when two animals are in conflict accounts for why animals' emotional states may sometimes be difficult to gauge. But dogs, as highly social animals, evidently have more open communication than many other species do. If early dogs (and wolves) were really in a continual struggle for dominance, then evolution should have favoured a great deal more dishonest signalling and a complete masking of emotion – not a good starting point for domestication. By contrast, co-operation, in dogs as well as in humans, tends to favour transparency. For their ancestor the wolf, sustaining the family unit is essential to survival, so it benefits everyone to know how everyone else is feeling. This principle applied equally well to our own hunter-gatherer ancestors. Hence both *Homo sapiens* and *Canis lupus* alike usually show their emotions openly, although wolves (and dogs) use their whole bodies, not just their faces, to communicate their emotional state. This happy coincidence must have been one of the factors that smoothed the path of domestication, enabling each species to learn to read the other's minds.

An even greater degree of emotional transparency may have been selected for during domestication, with humans favouring dogs whose body-language was easy to 'read' over those that were more inscrutable (that is, until our penchant for unusual features and 'baby-faces' started to drive selection in the opposite direction). By implication, those dog owners who are prepared to take the time to learn the signs will find their pets very easy to read.

Although observing dogs' behaviour and physiological states can offer clues about dogs' emotions, the connection between physiology and emotion is sometimes murky. A dog's body-language and, more particularly, its attempts to communicate provide one strand of information as to what it is feeling at any given moment (Emotion II). A second strand comes from its hormones and the activity in its brain (Emotion I): is the dog internally stressed, elated or in a state of anticipation? These physiological changes are invisible to owners and are also not yet well studied by scientists, at least not in the dog. Moreover, what is known indicates that such changes often do not correspond one-to-one with a particular behaviour or a single emotional state. For example, stress hormones such as adrenaline and cortisol can rise not only when the dog is in a situation it finds uncomfortable but also when it is approaching a potential mating partner. The hormones are preparing the body for activity, not directly reflecting any one emotion. Likewise, most emotions are not simply associated with individual chemicals in the brain. For example, we know that opioid neurochemicals are connected to emotional states, because of the effects on emotion brought about by the narcotics, such as heroin, that mimic them. However, the latter also reduce the perception of pain (as when morphine is used as an analgesic), so their effects are not simply emotional in nature. Natural opioids – endorphins – are produced in the mammalian brain during social bonding activities such as play and mutual physical contact; the fact that their levels are especially low when the animal is distressed by social separation suggests links to several different emotional states.

The complexity of these relationships seems to have arisen as the mammalian emotional repertoire evolved piecemeal from that of ancient reptiles, which have much simpler emotional lives (or even, some scientists argue, none at all). As a consequence, each emotion is not located in its own unique part of the mammalian brain. Rather, most emotions appear to arise in various parts of the midbrain, which is connected to the spinal cord through the hindbrain, and, in mammals, is almost completely encased inside the much larger forebrain, the 'thinking' part of the brain. Two structures in the midbrain that are key to the generation of many emotions are the hypothalamus and the amygdalae, but these structures are also engaged in other functions, such as hunger, thirst, the sleep/wake cycle and learning.

Despite this complexity, it is clear that emotions do have a physical presence in the brain, and that they are associated with changes in hormones circulated around the body; in short, they have predictable physical manifestations. Thus a combination of the two aforementioned approaches – the physiological or Emotion I, and the behavioural or Emotion II – can be used to investigate which emotions dogs almost certainly possess, and which they almost certainly do not.

Emotions can be placed in a rough hierarchy, from the most primitive (that is, those that are thought to have appeared first in the evolution of the vertebrates) to the most complex. Since dogs are mammals like us, but have less complex brains than our own, it is logical to conclude that we share the simpler emotions, but also that the most complex emotions experienced by humans are likely to be ours alone.

The most basic emotions, such as hunger, thirst, pain and sexual desire, are perhaps better described as 'feelings' than as 'emotions'. They are primarily processed by the most primitive parts of the brain – the brainstem, the midbrain and the hypothalamus. The hypothalamus also processes information relating to reward and punishment; it is therefore crucial to the way that dogs learn.

The simplest of the true emotions – fear, anger, anxiety and happiness – are often referred to as 'primes'. These are 'instinctive' in that they do not have to be learned: no one has to learn how to be frightened, it just happens. They are also 'basic' in the sense that they are generated by the most primitive parts of the mammalian brain, the limbic system, which appeared very early in the evolution of the vertebrates, perhaps as far back as 500 million years ago. It is therefore almost inconceivable that dogs should not possess these emotions, although it is difficult to gauge precisely what their subjective experience is like.

Fear, anger, anxiety and happiness all evolved as ways of responding to significant threats or opportunities. One way of looking at them is to see them as providing 'short-cuts'. For example, an animal does not have to scan its memory for the specific threat it is encountering and then devise a response; rather it is prompted by its emotional reaction (fear) to run away quickly, after which it can determine from a safe distance what the threat actually was. This is not to say, of course, that learning does not play a part in categorizing such threats more accurately, based on accumulated experience; nevertheless, the underlying emotion will almost always stay the same from one such experience to another.

Fear may be the most primitive emotion of them all. As for the other simple emotions, the amygdalae, paired almond-shaped structures buried deep in the centre of the brain, play a central role in both forming and retrieving memories of frightening events and also in generating the response. The posterior part of the hypothalamus is another key structure, relaying information to and from the brain and out to other hormone-producing structures, such as the adrenal glands that produce the fight-or-flight hormone adrenaline.

The expression of fear in dogs follows a pattern that is recognizably similar to the expression of fear in man. It usually begins with the dog becoming suddenly alert and then freezing, rooted to the spot while the amygdalae furiously signal to the cortex, the 'thinking' part of the brain, for the correct response to the situation. Meanwhile the dog holds itself tensely, possibly shaking visibly, with eyes wide and teeth bared, as a general preparation for all things dangerous. Beneath the skin, the heart rate and breathing both speed up.

If the situation is unprecedented, there may be nothing helpful in the memory bank. This can lead to behaviour that may seem downright bizarre to us more logical humans. For example, a dog that has never seen a large cardboard box before in its life may fail to identify it as a harmless inanimate object, and by default go into a full-blown fear response.[8] Fear is a short-cut for categorizing events, and what falls into the 'scary' category depends upon what the dog has experienced before, and what it has not, especially during the first six months of its life. The 'scary' category will consist of two sorts of things: those that have frightened the dog in the past, and those the dog has had no experience of whatsoever.

The dog's response to the scary situation will depend on what it has found to work best in the past. Some dogs will almost always freeze; others will usually run away. Still others, especially if their escape route has been blocked on previous occasions, may resort to aggression almost immediately. Indeed, many clinicians will tell you that most of the cases of aggression that they see are motivated by fear, not by anger or any need to 'dominate'. Fear also lies at the heart of many other behavioural disorders, and is arguably the most powerful of the emotions that dogs possess.

Fear is also a powerful trigger of learning. Dogs that are suddenly frightened by something unfamiliar, such as a cardboard box, are not only likely to continue to be frightened by similar boxes, but may also show palpable signs of apprehension when they revisit the place where the original fright occurred, even though the scary object is no longer there. This is one way that dogs can develop what appear to us to be 'irrational' fears, although they presumably make perfect sense to the dog, which is recalling the whole event, not just the 'obvious' unfamiliar stimulus.

Anxiety is sometimes confused with fear, in that it shares some of the same manifestations. But anxiety is about the anticipation of fear; it is triggered not by an actual object or event that is intrinsically frightening but, rather, by predictors of a frightening event that may occur at some indeterminate time in the future. My first two dogs, Alexis and Ivan, both Labrador/terrier crosses (Jack Russell and Airedale respectively), were self-confident to the extent that I doubt they ever felt much anxiety. My third, Bruno, was a purebred Labrador, and an altogether more emotionally dependent animal – not easily frightened, but very reliant on the humans around him. When he arrived at our house as an eight-week-old puppy, nearly thirty years ago, I had never heard of 'separation anxiety' – nor had many veterinary surgeons, ours included.

Fifteen years later, I started a research programme that revealed, among other things, that half the young Labradors in the UK hate being left alone, but in those days I do not think anyone even suspected that this was the case.

Bruno could not hide the anxiety he felt whenever he realized that we were about to go out. Locating of car keys, putting on coats, collecting children from the four corners of the house – these actions triggered an expression of absolute misery on his face, and he slunk off to his bed, the place he felt most secure. The 'experts' at the time told us that this was only a game he was playing to stop us going out, that gundogs were bred to be left in kennels for hours at a time and were perfectly happy doing so. As soon as we were gone, we were told, he would settle down and sleep until we returned. Wrong: his ongoing anxiety was obvious from the chewed-up bed, furniture, even wallpaper, that we found when we returned home.

These are all signs of anxiety. Retrievers are very mouth-focused, and chewing seems to be their favourite way of relieving tension; if Bruno had been a different type of dog, he might have barked, paced, scratched at the walls, or urinated or defecated on the floor. When we tried to put him in boarding kennels, where the opportunities for chewing were limited, he turned to howling – for hours at a time. In the end we accepted that he was just a very attached dog, and tried to make sure that he was always with someone he knew. He was not frightened of our going out, but he knew that he hated being left alone, so the signs that told him that he was about to be left made him anxious. He was probably also anxious that we would never return; dogs' concept of time is not fully understood, but seems less precise than our own, so it is difficult to know how much they can anticipate things that might or might not happen at some indeterminate time in the future.

Anger is not the same as fear. Both can lead to aggression, which is why the two emotions are often confused. But in fact they are readily distinguishable, based on the dog's body-language.

Fear arises when the dog's brain identifies potentially damaging situations that are outside its control; anger occurs when the dog's expectations of the world are threatened. For example, dogs that are very attached to what they perceive as their territory will become angry when another dog (especially one of the same sex) intrudes into that territory. An angry dog, much like a fearful dog, will probably growl and bare its teeth, but these are primarily signals of intent and only secondarily expressions of emotion. It is easy to tell the difference between a fearful dog and an angry dog. The fearful dog will obviously be trying to escape, with everything from its ears to the corners of its mouth pulled backwards, and, if given the opportunity, it will most likely actually run away. The angry dog will be stiffened and poised to move forwards to counter the threat.

Anger, like all emotions, is an evolved survival mechanism, but also one that has been radically altered by domestication. A wolf that never defended its food or resting space from other wolves would not live for very long in the wild. However, the capacity to feel and express anger is less of an asset to domestic dogs, whose survival is crucially dependent on their owners' goodwill, rather than on competition with others of their own kind. Indeed, domestication has raised the dog's threshold for anger to the point where most dogs rarely become angry.

Dog trainers who still regard dominance as the key motivator for dog behaviour tend to explain most aggressive behaviour as driven by anger, specifically anger arising from the dog's perception that its 'status' in the household has been challenged. This notion is almost certainly based upon a misinterpretation of what actually motivates most dogs. However, it would be irresponsible to insist that dogs never become angry, that they never try to assert themselves over other dogs, or challenge people who they think are trying to deny them something they value highly. For example, some dogs are highly territorial and will bark when their territory is invaded to show that they are angry at the intrusion. Among wild animals, ignoring such a threat would lead to actual aggression; the combined effects of domestication and training make this much less likely to occur in domestic dogs.

Although dogs are much less reactive than wolves, they still need to be taught emotional control, so that they can coexist peacefully alongside people and other dogs. In the wild, one of the crucial lessons mothers teach their offspring is to inhibit their bite: puppies' teeth cannot do much damage, but it is essential that they learn to control the amount of force they apply when biting, so that they do not hurt their littermates while playing. Otherwise a full-scale fight could ensue.

Moreover, once they have their adult teeth, uninhibited biting can cause serious injury. In the same way that they can learn to control their biting, an expression of anger, so dogs can learn to control anger itself. A dog that is never taught the consequences of its expressions of anger has the potential to become at least a nuisance, and at worst a danger to society and to itself. Dogs need to be taught boundaries, and by this I mean emotional even more than physical boundaries; permissiveness, allowing the dog to do as it pleases, is not humane. In nature, such behaviour would quickly be met by either aggression or avoidance, neither of which promotes survival in a social species. In human society, dogs cannot afford such trial and error, which ultimately leads to the pound or to euthanasia.

There is a very small minority of dogs that occasionally become aggressive without displaying any signs of fear or anger. It is often unclear whether such dogs are true 'psychopaths', whose emotions are abnormal, or whether they are simply able to inhibit the normal signals that would otherwise disclose their intentions. Such dogs are valued in the small sections of society where dogs are primarily used as weapons, but they are otherwise unsuited to life alongside humanity. (This is not to say that all 'fighting dogs' are psychopaths; many have been trained to become instantly aggressive on command, behaviour that is therefore potentially reversible.)

Such unannounced aggressive tendencies should not be confused with the so-called 'aggression' that, in the wolf, is an essential component of predatory behaviour. A dog that kills a sheep may casually be referred to as 'aggressive', but it is highly unlikely that the dog was frightened of the sheep or perceived it as a rival; rather, it was simply, if unacceptably, obeying the instinct to hunt. Motivationally, predatory 'aggression' is quite distinct from aggression driven by anger or fear – for example, it is controlled by a completely different part of the hypothalamus, and if it has an emotional component, this is more likely to be positive than negative (predators should be motivated to find hunting 'fun', to ensure that they keep doing it).

The range of dogs' negative emotions is thus largely dominated by anxiety and fear, with anger appearing more sporadically. Individual dogs vary greatly in terms of both how intensely they feel each of these emotions and, to an even greater extent, in what external events trigger them. All, especially fear, are powerful promoters of learning, and so if a situation provokes a particular emotion once, it is likely to do so again if repeated. Fear and anxiety are associated with obvious body-language, although the precise form in which this appears varies from dog to dog: some dogs have learned that the best way to reduce their emotional discomfort is to move away from the source, while others may in the past have been given little choice other than to confront the problem directly. Thus aggression (aggressive behaviour) may be associated with either fear or anger – or indeed with no emotion at all, as in predatory 'aggression'.

The physiological basis for positive emotions is less well understood than for fear, anxiety and anger (mainly because in human medicine it is much more important to characterize and treat the latter emotions, which are involved in many psychiatric disorders). Nevertheless, research suggests that the limbic system (including the amygdalae and the hypothalamus) is again among the key structures, and that the neurohormone dopamine is also crucially involved. One brain region that is especially important for positive emotions is the nucleus accumbens, the brain's 'pleasure centre', which is situated quite close to the amygdalae.

Happiness – joy – seems to radiate from the majority of dogs, much of the time. Happy dogs have relaxed, open faces, and bodies that wiggle from the shoulders backwards, including the tail, of course. (But note that the tail may also be wagged when the dog is unsure and in conflict.) A cynic might say that dogs are conning us, that they merely behave as if they were happy, because happy-looking dogs are more likely to be well looked after than grumpy dogs. But scientists now firmly believe that mammals such as dogs do experience happiness.

There are good evolutionary arguments for the existence of happiness as a modulator and stimulator of beneficial behaviour. At its most basic level, learning theory postulates that all behaviour needs to be rewarded if it is to be repeated. Hunger causes an animal to seek out food, and once it is found and eaten, hormones released from the gut reinforce the behaviour, making it more likely that the dog will seek out and eat that food again. However, if there is something wrong with the food, and it makes the dog sick, then other hormone systems trigger an aversion. The dog will be unlikely to eat that particular food again for a long time – and may even avoid the place where it found the food.[9]

These straightforward examples posit the presence of immediate reward or punishment to trigger learning. However, other equally important types of behaviour are not associated with any immediate reward, and therefore must be performed simply because they make the animal feel good – in other words, happy. In the autumn, squirrels bury nuts in the ground rather than eat them so that they will have stored food for the winter. It is unlikely that a squirrel in its first year of life has the foresight to know that (*a*) bad weather is coming, (*b*) there won't be much food available then, and (*c*) if it buries food that is abundant now, that food will still be nutritious in a few months' time. More likely, evolution has shaped the squirrel, once it has satisfied its immediate hunger, to find burying food and memorizing its location rewarding in itself. In other words, this activity makes the squirrel happy. Likewise, biologists used to have trouble understanding what motivates play behaviour. In wild animals, play must promote survival; otherwise, evolution would select against it – a young animal that is playing out in the open is much more obvious to a predator than one sleeping in its den. However, the benefits of play do not usually become apparent until months later, when they emerge in the form of better social integration or more sophisticated hunting techniques (to name but two, which vary from one species to another). Again, the simplest explanation is that play is self-rewarding; in other words – it is fun! Not just fun to watch, play actually generates happiness in the participants. Indeed, play and happiness seem inextricably linked in dogs, consistent with the idea that they are wolves which never grew up. It can take very little to bring about happiness in a well-cared-for dog; for example, when a dog catches sight of a favourite toy and starts playing with it spontaneously, that impromptu activity will have been generated by the feeling of happiness that the dog recalls from the last time it played with that toy. Dogs are also presumably happy when they are with their owners, but the overriding emotion in this case will be love.

Love – that which biologists, nervous about being misunderstood, call 'attachment' – fuels the bond between dog and master or mistress. For a young wolf, a strong attachment to its parents is crucial to its survival. The parents have all the skills necessary to protect and nurture the young cub – while it is growing up the cub can pick up those skills for itself, simply by observing and imitating its parents, rather than having to learn each one by trial and error. If it leaves the family group too early, the chances of surviving long enough to become a parent are significantly reduced. It is difficult to see how such a strong and essential attachment could not be emotionally based, given the underlying physiological machinery. If we accept the probability that dogs derive much of their typical behaviour from the repertoire of the juvenile wolf, then it is logical that their emotions should be similarly derived. In short, there is a sound biological reason for supposing that dogs do actually love us, rather than just appearing to do so.

At the physiological level, love is distinct from other positive emotions in that it specifically involves the hormone oxytocin. Originally this hormone was believed to be solely a trigger for care of newborns by their mothers (that is, nurturant behaviour), but it is now thought to be involved in all kinds of attachment. In fact, dogs experience a surge of oxytocin during friendly interactions with people. It is widely believed that interaction with dogs is a good stress-buster for humans. The reverse is probably also true. In one study, researchers set up a series of friendly interactions between dogs and people, consisting of stroking and gentle play.[10] In the course of playing, the dogs' blood pressure dropped slightly, as expected, and the circulating levels of several hormones increased dramatically (specifically, oxytocin levels quintupled, and endorphins and dopamine doubled). Similar, though less dramatic, changes occurred in the people.

The remarkable thing about this strong physiological response is that it is triggered by contact with *Homo sapiens*, a different species. As noted earlier, dogs' attachment to people is often more intense than attachment to individuals of their own species; dogs that become very upset when their owners go out are rarely comforted by the presence of other dogs. It is tempting to speculate that 'one-man dogs' may lack oxytocin, but so far no one has looked into this possibility. What is clear is that all dogs have been programmed by domestication to have intense emotional reactions towards people. This lies at the root of the 'unconditional love' that many owners describe and treasure in their dogs. Such intense feelings are not easily turned off, as attested by the high proportion of dogs that hate being left alone (as many as one in five, according to one of my surveys).

Dogs really do miss their owners when separated from them. Many dogs also seem to become much more emotionally fragile under these circumstances; for example, they react much more negatively to sudden shocks, such as the noise of fireworks going off. In this sense, the capacity for love that makes dogs such rewarding companions has a flipside: they find it difficult to cope without us. Since we humans have programmed in this vulnerability, it is our responsibility to ensure that our dogs do not suffer as a result.

Without love, the dog–owner bond would not function. Yet as we have seen it is such a powerful emotion in dogs that many become anxious whenever they guess that they are about to be parted from their owner, and then remain anxious until they are reunited. This frequently leads to behaviour that the owner finds unacceptable. In the past, such problematic behaviour was often dismissed as 'wickedness' on the dog's part, but we now know that it is actually deeply seated in the emotions of love and anxiety.

Dogs often leave all too visible signs that they hate being left alone, although these can be misinterpreted by owners who do not appreciate just how attached to them their dogs really are. The veterinary profession usually refers to cases of dogs that misbehave when alone as *separation anxiety*, but since it is not clear that all such cases are primarily due to the emotional state of anxiety (some are due to the dog panicking when it has been startled by some external event), I prefer to use the term *separation distress* when describing the symptoms.

Separation distress can take a variety of forms, depending on the dog's breed and personality. Manifestations include destructiveness (biting, chewing and scratching of furniture or other materials, often close to the place where its owner has most recently left the premises, and in some cases involving items bearing the owner's scent), vocalization (barking, whining or howling) and elimination (urinating, defecating or vomiting). Rarer symptoms include such signs of chronic and unbearable stress as self-mutilation and repetitive pacing.

Separation distress

I first started researching separation problems more than a decade and a half ago in response to an ill-conceived study purporting to show that dogs that had been through rescue and rehoming were very likely to develop separation distress. This conclusion placed the responsibility for separation problems firmly at the door of the rehoming charities, leading to the suggestion that every dog that was rehomed should be given a course of anxiolytics (anti-anxiety drugs) to tide it over during its first few weeks in its new home. There was very little research to support this assertion at the time, apart from one investigation that showed that mongrels were more likely than dogs with pedigrees to have separation problems. Animal charities rehome far more mongrels than purebreds, so logically it must be their fault! In fact, subsequent research I did with colleagues including Emily Blackwell, Rachel Casey and Justine McPherson has detected that rehomed dogs do have a slightly increased risk of developing separation distress, but this can probably be accounted for by the large number of dogs that are relinquished by their owners because they cannot be left alone.

Indeed, pedigree dogs are far from immune to separation distress, as our first longitudinal study showed.[11] We followed the development of seven litters of Labrador retrievers and five of border collies, forty puppies in all, from the time when they were eight weeks old (and still with their breeders) to eighteen months of age. I was expecting that a few of these dogs might dislike being left alone. To our surprise and amazement, well over half of the Labradors, and almost half the collies, showed some kind of separation distress lasting for more than a month, peaking at about one year of age.

Our survey opened our eyes to the real scope of the problem. Based on 676 interviews with dog owners, we found that 17 per cent of their dogs were currently showing signs of separation-induced distress, and that a further 18 per cent had done so in the past but had recovered, mostly without their owners seeking any specialist help. But many other dogs suffer from separation distress that is unrecognized by their owners. In another study, Emily Blackwell recruited twenty owners who were certain that their dogs were happy to be left in the house while they went to work. She then filmed each dog when it was left alone. Three showed signs of separation distress (pacing, panting or whining) that their owners were completely unaware of. One case was so severe that we recommended an immediate clinical consultation. Since separation distress is, by definition, something that happens when no one is there, with hindsight it is not surprising that only its more obvious manifestations – chewing, elimination, barking or howling that is loud enough for the neighbours to object to – tend to come to the attention of owners. While the sample taken in this study was tiny, it does suggest that research solely based on the self-reporting of owners considerably underestimates of the real scope of the problem.

If we assume that approximately 20 per cent of dogs suffer from separation distress, then the implications across the entire dog population are truly staggering. Of an estimated 8 million dogs in the UK, our figures indicate that at any one time, more than one and a half million of these dogs are suffering in this way.[12] And of the 70 million or more dogs in the United States it is possible that well over 10 million may be experiencing separation distress.[13] This is happening now, today. Such numbers suggest a real and ongoing crisis for dogs – and a totally preventable one. Separation distress could be virtually eliminated if every young dog, before it is left alone for any length of time, were trained to expect that departures lead to reunions (see box – 'Home Alone: Can Dogs Be Trained to Cope?'). Once established, it is much more difficult to cure.

Why are so many dogs prone to this problem? My take on this is that it is not a 'disorder' at all, but perfectly natural behaviour. After all, we do not say that human children have a 'separation disorder' when they cry for their mothers. We have selected dogs to be highly dependent on us, so that they can easily be made obedient and useful; why is it so surprising that they do not like being left alone?

There is still a great deal of debate about how many different kinds of separation disorders exist, but two in particular have been verified. In one category are the over-attached dogs that cannot bear even to be shut in a different room from their owners.[14] If they are destructive, these dogs tend to target their destruction to the area around the door that the owner has just left through.

In the second category are dogs which seem quite confident most of the time, but have a phobia – often of loud noises – that sends them into a panic if their owner is not present to provide reassurance. These dogs typically do not show signs of separation distress every time they are left alone, because the trigger, whatever it is, does not always coincide with the owner's absence. Such dogs sometimes leave clues of their panic, such as a ripped-up sofa cushion that they have tried to bury their head beneath.

As noted earlier, separation disorders can be difficult to cure once they have become an established habit, in direct contrast to the ease with which they can be prevented. Such disorders constitute as many as one in three of clinical behaviourists' caseloads, yet it is often only as a last resort that owners seek expert help – after the dog has been performing the behaviour for years, at which point some change in their circumstances forces them to take action. By then, the behaviour may have become habitual, divorced from its original cause (rather like the stereotypic pacing behaviour of big cats, or the weaving behaviour of bears confined in small, boring enclosures), and it will often continue even after the original cause has long since been removed.

HOME ALONE: CAN DOGS BE TRAINED TO COPE?

This book is not an instruction manual, but so many dogs seem to suffer when left alone, and prevention is so straightforward, that I have included the following summary of how to teach a dog to be on its own. More detailed advice, prepared by my colleagues Emily Blackwell and Rachel Casey at Bristol University, for the Royal Society for the Prevention of Cruelty to Animals, can be found on their website at http://www.rspca.org.uk/allaboutanimals/pets/dogs/company.

Most owners equate training with obedience – sit, stay and so on. However, this is only one role for training in responsible pet ownership. Dogs learn all kinds of connections quite spontaneously, and sometimes these need to be directed for the dog's own well-being. Many dogs learn that when their owner picks up the car keys, an indeterminate period of loneliness follows. The trick is to link such cues to good outcomes – affection, and the owner's return – before they can become associated with the negative outcome of separation. Thus: pick up keys, praise dog (or feed titbit if this is what motivates your particular dog). Pick up keys, go to door, praise dog. Pick up keys, go through door, come straight back inside, praise dog. Pick up keys, go out, wait a few seconds (then a minute, then a few minutes, and so on), come back inside, praise dog. After any sign of anxiety from the dog: don't reward, but go back a stage. The dog learns that these events predict the owner's return (good outcome), not departure (bad outcome). Result – a dog that doesn't get anxious when its owner goes out.

Many dogs, even those who are not particularly emotionally affected by their owners' absence, also get bored when left alone for long periods, and may end up destroying valued possessions simply for something to do. Such dogs, especially those that love to use their mouths, can be diverted by a meat-flavoured 'chew', or a puzzle-feeder filled with a favourite food.

Because dogs rely so heavily on the scents in their environment, they can sometimes be comforted by having a piece of clothing that smells of their owner in the room where they are left.

Finally, do not punish your dog when you get home to find he's done something you'd rather he hadn't. It will make him more anxious, not less.

As well as being useful for prevention of separation distress, these tips may also work to calm a dog that has just started to become distressed when left alone. However, if they do not work within a week or two, my recommendation is to seek advice from a qualified clinical behaviourist.

Although separation distress is far more widespread, the behavioural disorder that grabs all the headlines is, of course, aggression. What they have in common is that their emotional basis is often misrepresented. Dogs that chew up the house when their owners are out are labelled 'naughty'; dogs that bite are labelled 'dominant' or 'aggressive', and motivated by anger. Neither label is valid, and neither diagnosis is helpful in finding a humane solution.

Although canine aggression does not occur on anything like the scale of separation distress, it is not uncommon. Pet dogs very rarely kill other dogs, or people (although when they do, a media frenzy often follows). Pet dogs do, however, bite their owners and members of their owners' families quite frequently. According to one recent estimate, 4.5 million people are bitten each year in the United States. Although most of these incidents are relatively minor, nearly a million require medical attention, and children are more at risk than adults. Because a dog that bites, especially one that bites children, is socially unacceptable, such cases form the greatest proportion of behaviour consultants' caseloads. Dogs that have bitten are often euthanized. A great number of dogs would benefit if we could understand better why they bite, and, even more important, what can be done to stop aggression towards people before it gets to the stage of biting.

Twenty years ago, the explanation seemed obvious. Dogs were believed to bite when they felt that their status in the household was being threatened, and so most cases in which owners or members of their families (as opposed to unfamiliar people) were bitten were described as due to 'dominance aggression'. The majority of dog behaviour specialists now regret ever having used this term. Why have most of the experts recently changed their minds?

One review suggests three answers to this question.[15] First, owners' accounts of the behaviour of their dogs around the time of the attacks are not consistent with the idea that they were trying to assert their 'status'. Rather, the dogs had exhibited body postures more accurately associated with fear and anxiety, with only a tinge of anger; for example, they were often noted to have been trembling immediately before they bit. Immediately after the bite, many had engaged in appeasement and affiliative behaviour, such as crouching, tucking their tail between their legs and licking their lips. Second, most dogs that bite start biting before they are one year old, much younger than they logically should be if they were ready to 'take over the pack'. Third, and perhaps most telling, those dogs that lived with other dogs were not especially confident with them and thus were certainly not behaving as the 'dominant dog' ought to.

Although every case is different, a logical explanation for a typical dog bite often goes something like this. While they are puppies, dogs try out a number of strategies for dealing with situations that they find threatening – in other words for dealing with fear. Take the example of a dog that, to its owner's embarrassment, launches into an unprovoked attack whenever it sees dogs of a particular kind – say, small white ones. This dog is unlikely to be a psychopath; rather, it was probably attacked by a small white dog in the past, and as a result is initially fearful of all dogs of similar appearance. Over the course of several such encounters, it will have found that the best way of quelling its fear is to threaten to attack – and the more successful this strategy is, the more likely the dog is to repeat it. This will become especially likely if the dog has not been trained properly, since its owner will be unable to intervene with a command, and by the time the dog has been dragged away its aggressive strategy will already have been reinforced. Similarly, puppies inevitably nip their owners as part of play. If they discover that nipping gets them what they want, and if their owner happens to ignore all their attempts to communicate by signalling rather than through physical contact, then biting may become their default strategy for dealing with frightening or even just unfamiliar situations.

If biting works better than anything else, dogs will gradually become more confident about using aggression. They will use it whenever they feel threatened, not just in the context where they originally learned it. It has been noted that people who have highly distorted, anthropomorphic relationships with their dogs are more likely to get bitten, probably because they are very inconsistent in interpreting their dog's body-language (and potentially explaining why it is little dogs – those most likely to be anthropomorphized, because of their size – not big ones, that bite their owners most). Furthermore, puppies that have a serious illness during their socialization period, and therefore do not have as many opportunities to work out how to deal with challenging situations, are also more likely to bite later in life than dogs that had the full range of opportunities for learning before the fear reaction set in.

A word of caution: training techniques that suppress aggression using punishment do little to resolve the underlying problem in such cases, although they are often superficially successful in the short term. Fear of a beating will temporarily inhibit the dog from performing its preferred, if unacceptable, way of resolving conflicts. However, it may become even more unpredictably aggressive, when it subsequently encounters circumstances that do not match those under which it has learned that aggression is followed by punishment, for example when the trainer who originally beat it is no longer nearby. Alternatively, it may find an outlet for its misery in some other behaviour, for example, one of the so-called 'obsessive-compulsive'[16] disorders, such as tail-chasing.

Fear is also the underlying emotion behind some dogs' threatening behaviour towards unfamiliar people, so-called territorial aggression. A dog that barks and bares its teeth, apparently confidently, when it sees someone passing by on the street will often be the same dog that adopts a much more ambiguous posture if that person stops by the gate. It may then begin to cower, albeit still barking loudly, when the same person actually enters the property – hence the truth in the old saying 'His bark is worse than his bite'. That dog will have learned that barking is a good way of keeping people it is not sure about at a distance. Only if cornered may it resort to an actual attack.

Fear is also the motivation behind aggression in dogs that have been specifically trained, using punishment, to attack intruders. In their case the fear is triggered by the memory of the handler's beating, and they attack the intruder in order to alleviate that fear. In the case of the unruly pet dog the fear stems not from any threat posed by the owner, but from the imagined threat of an unfamiliar person. Nevertheless, from the dog's perspective there is an underlying similarity: it is pursuing a learned course of action that enables it to avoid a negative emotion, fear.

As far as we can tell, dogs experience the same range of basic emotions that we do, both positive and negative. Much of their behaviour, both that which we cherish and that which we do not, is driven by those emotions: joy, love, fear, anxiety, anger. The idea that animals act like robots, acting without feeling, self-evidently cannot be true of the dog (and therefore is equally unlikely to be true of other mammals); we simply find dogs to be more expressive than other animals, so their emotions are there for all to see. These emotions are part of the biological systems that regulate and guide dogs' behaviour, and as such are essential to the capacity for learning that allows dogs to adapt to the world that they find themselves in today.

However, dogs and humans may experience even these basic emotions in subtly different ways. One of the paradoxes of human behaviour is that we actively seek out and apparently enjoy some self-evidently negative emotions such as fear, sadness and anger: how else to explain the popularity of horror films, thrillers and tearjerkers? But there is nothing to indicate that dogs ever do this, suggesting that consciousness has given humans a unique capacity to evaluate, and then attempt to distance themselves from, such emotions. Conversely, dogs may experience fear, anger, joy and love more intensely and in more nuanced ways than we do, precisely because they are less able to reflect on and damp down those feelings by rationalizing them. The difference in intelligence between our two species may in turn be reflected in different subjective worlds. While acknowledging the basic similarities in our experiences of emotions, we therefore need to be careful when projecting all our own awareness of emotion on to our dogs.

7

Canine Brainpower

Some people treat their dogs as if they are as smart as humans, others, as if they were particularly dimwitted children. They are neither! Dogs are as intelligent as dogs need to be – which means that their intelligence is not like ours. Canids evolved in environments different from those that shaped the human race, so it should hardly be surprising that they do not think in exactly the same way we do. That said, there are some similarities; for example, their associative learning capacities, as well as the emotions that drive them, follow the general mammalian pattern and are therefore the same as ours. Like us, dogs try to avoid situations that have scared them in the past and repeat experiences that they have found rewarding. It is their more complex cognitive abilities that are likely to be qualitatively different from ours, since these will have been selected to match the canid lifestyle. For example, the usefulness of guide dogs depends upon their ability to 'think outside the box' – to use their canid brain to predict what is going to happen next in the ever-changing environment with which their owners are interacting[1] – a skill that may be derived from the wild canids' ability to predict their prey's next move.

After decades of neglecting the topic, scientists have recently begun to probe the ways dogs 'think'. Biologists and psychologists interested in canine intelligence are now examining the more complex things that dogs' brains can do – and, indeed, what they apparently cannot do. What is becoming clear is how domestication may have affected their 'intelligence', and also why it seems to mesh so well with our own. Recently, primatologists have come to realize that domestic dogs can outperform even chimpanzees in some very specific ways (although there seems little doubt that overall chimps are more 'intelligent', however that is defined, than dogs). Some researchers in the field have even proposed that dogs have a special brand of intelligence, unique in the animal kingdom, which they 'co-evolved' with us humans, as part of the process of domestication.[2]

Other scientists make direct comparisons between the cognitive abilities of dogs and those of human children, but these are not necessarily helpful. For example, in one study dogs' word-learning abilities were claimed to be comparable to those of a two-year-old; their ability to understand goal-directed behaviour to that of an infant between three and twelve months old; and so on. Such attempts to anchor the dog's abilities to a particular stage of human development may be illuminating in some respects, but, inasmuch as they are entirely anthropocentric, must also underestimate the dog's capacity to just be a dog. How, for example, can one use this approach to quantify the dog's ability to detect bombs by their odour alone – something an adult human, let alone a child, could never do unaided? In any case, it is not clear to me what this approach tells us about how dogs perceive people; it seems unlikely that this aspect of canine intelligence could ever be encapsulated in a simple statement like 'Dogs think of their owners in the way a three-year-old child thinks of his parents'. Dogs are much more complex than such a statement implies, and, as already noted, their intelligence is unique, shaped by evolution (when they were wolves) and then by domestication. Moreover, it seems but a short step from comparing their intelligence with that of children to regarding them as children, albeit four-legged ones, and treating them as 'little people' rather than as the dogs they actually are.

Analysing canine intelligence is not straightforward. Just as we can never be sure precisely what the inner world of canine emotion is really like, we shall probably never be certain whether dogs think the same way we do. Science has so far been unable to tell us how self-aware dogs are, much less whether they have anything like our conscious thoughts. This is not surprising, since neither scientists nor philosophers can agree about what human consciousness consists of, let alone that of animals. However, it is possible to examine scientifically whether dogs can or cannot do various things, and then to infer the kinds of thoughts they might have, bearing in mind that, as dogs, they may not have the same priorities that we (or other animals) have in the same situation.

I have a good reason for delving into the dog's actual intellectual capabilities, rather than assuming, as many owners and even some scientists seem to, that their abilities are simply marginally inferior to ours. If we overestimate their ability to reason, we are led into the trap of making them accountable for their actions in situations where they are actually unaware of what they are doing. If a dog could really work out what its owner was thinking when he or she arrived home to find a cushion in tatters, then punishment for that 'crime' would work: the dog would be able to reason that it was being punished for something it had done a while ago, rather than what it was doing when it heard the sound of the key in the door. As soon as we start treating dogs as little people, rather than the dogs they are, our actions become incomprehensible or misleading. Indeed, our actions are of such importance to dogs (as confirmed by every piece of research done on their cognitive abilities) that they cannot but become confused and distressed when unable to understand us.

The simpler forms of learning both enable dogs to piece the world together, and allow us to train them to behave the way we want them to. But dogs can also think for themselves: they do not just have feelings about the world, but also, in their own way, have knowledge about their physical environment and the other animals around them (including humans, of course). The formal study of canine intelligence dates back to the earliest years of the twentieth century, and the puzzle-boxes of Edward Thorndike. Thorndike's approach to studying how animals learn was different from Pavlov's; he was more interested in how they solve problems. Many of his experiments involved placing animals, usually domestic dogs or young cats, into puzzle-boxes of his own devising. These could be opened from the inside when the animal performed some kind of action. For example, in the box illustrated, the door was attached to a weight that would pull it out of the way once the dog had unlatched it. The latch could be one of the wooden toggles on either side of the door, which the dog could paw upright by pushing its foot through the gap between the slats. Or it could be a bolt at the top of the door, connected by a rope to a loop hanging from the roof that the dog could pull on with its teeth. Or it could be a treadle in the middle of the floor, which the dog had to press

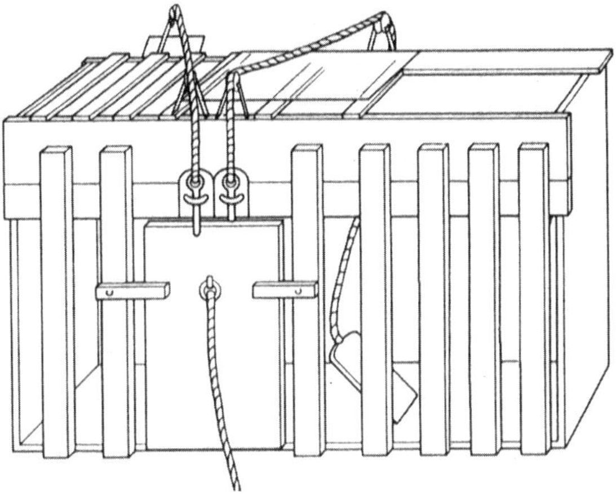

Thorndike's puzzle-box

with its paw in order to release the door (all three are shown in the drawing).

Thorndike was interested in finding out how the dogs solved the problem of getting out of the box, and also whether they subsequently remembered how they had done it. At the time, many people believed that animals like cats and dogs were capable of considerable insight – that they could, as it were, sit down and think things out. Thorndike, however, believed that a much simpler explanation would suffice. He considered the possibility that simple associative learning, coupled with the dog's natural inquisitiveness, might actually explain such apparently intelligent behaviour. He found that his dogs would initially scrabble around the puzzle-box until they blundered on the mechanism that would let them out. He then fed them, as a reward, and put them straight back into the box to see if they could now escape any faster. If the dogs had insight into what they had done, they would have immediately returned to the lever or pedal that had previously let them out. But in fact the dogs rarely did this. However, after repeated sessions in the box, they did take less and less time to escape, and eventually, after several repetitions, did start going immediately to the releasing mechanism.

Largely on the basis of these experiments, Thorndike came up with the concept of *trial-and-error* learning. Animals faced with a problem to solve will try out a variety of tactics that they would normally use in such a situation (in this case, being trapped). When one of these tactics happens to work, it produces rewards (in this case, being let out and then fed). The next time they are in a similar situation they will be more likely to perform the action that got them out last time, or to focus on the area where they had been when the door had opened on previous occasions. Both are explainable by simple operant conditioning: either repeat whatever action preceded the previous escape, or go to the place where you were immediately before the door opened (or both). This behaviour requires no insight – no problem-solving skills – on the part of the dog. Based on Thorndike's experiments, and others like them, most scientists now believe that dogs have rather limited powers of reasoning, certainly inferior to those of chimpanzees (and even a few birds).

The point here is not that dogs are stupid, but rather that their brand of intelligence differs from the primate model. Though Thorndike's dogs showed little evidence of problem-solving skills, they excelled when it came to recalling the correct escape method. In fact, they retained this memory for several months, even without any further exposure to the puzzle-box. (Dogs' retention of skills they have acquired is generally very good, but they find it much harder to remember for more than a few seconds things they have merely observed.) Memories of events, as opposed to memories of their own actions, may not be of great value to canids; indeed, they may be confusing. Canids, especially foxes, are known to be capable of remembering where they buried food, for days or even weeks afterwards. Since the ability to retrieve food in this way is clearly adaptive, it is believed that they evolved the ability to recall where they buried the food. Conversely, canids are also often faced with the problem of what to do when the prey they are chasing disappears. This is not something that it is useful for them to remember for very long, because prey is unlikely to remain in one place for more than a short time without leaving some other clue. If the prey is not where it vanished from, and its scent is fading fast, then it has probably long gone; better to move on to another hunting site than to hang around hoping that it is stupid enough to return to the very place it had just been chased away from. Thus evolution seems not to have selected for retention of such information for more than a few seconds.

Dogs' short-term memory has been investigated experimentally. Using a method called *visual displacement*, scientists have tested how long dogs can remember where something has disappeared from.[3] Initially, each dog is taught that its favourite toy is hidden behind one of four identical boxes: it first watches the experimenter hiding the toy, and is then allowed to retrieve it. Once it reliably goes to just the box it has seen the toy disappear behind, and is no longer searching the boxes at random, the dog can be tested to see how long it remembers where the toy has been hidden. In this second phase of the experiment, a screen is placed between the dog and the boxes immediately after the toy has been hidden, so that the dog has to remember which box its toy is behind. Then when the screen is removed, it has to recall that memory in order to locate the correct box. If it cannot, it will go back to searching the boxes at random. If the screen is kept in place for only a few seconds, most dogs will go straight to the correct box, showing that they are indeed capable of both memorizing and recalling the location, provided the interruption is only brief. However, just a thirty-second delay is enough to induce mistakes. (Although dogs make even more mistakes after a minute's delay, they do not get significantly worse if the screen is left in place for four minutes, at which point many are still performing better than chance.) Subsequent experiments have shown that dogs are better at remembering where things have disappeared from in relation to their own positions ('to my left') than in relation to landmarks ('under the box that has boxes on either side'). Overall, many dogs' short-term memories of single events appear to be rather fallible, perhaps because they are much more interested in working out what people want them to do here and now than in recalling precisely what happened a few minutes ago. That is not to say, however, that they pay no attention to the more fixed features of their surroundings, otherwise they (or their evolutionary forebears) would quickly get lost.

Although most pet dogs do not have to memorize the features of the environment where they live (because most of the time we humans decide where they can or cannot go), they nevertheless retain their wild ancestors' ability to find their way around, and can use it if they need to. Indeed, dogs have very good memories for places, as might be expected from the descendants of animals that roamed widely in search of food. They have a variety of cognitive methods at their disposal for this purpose, such as the ability to memorize landmarks, but also more complex skills such as constructing mental maps of how those landmarks are distributed. Landmark-learning does not require a complex brain – it is how many insects find their way around – but it is useful nonetheless and, indeed, an essential part of more complex skills. Just as humans do, dogs effortlessly and continuously memorize the features of their surroundings; unlike us, however, they rely heavily on what things smell like. We might recall turning left around a dark green shrub; a dog would remember that shrub as smelling of orange with grassy top-notes. Yet despite these differences, dogs continually store (and then, presumably, gradually forget) information about features of the environment that they have recently encountered.

The dog's propensity for memorizing landmarks can actually impede training. Younger dogs are so good at learning locations that they often spontaneously memorize their surroundings as part of the set of cues that tells them to do something. For example, puppies taught the verbal command 'sit' in a training class may appear to have forgotten it as soon as they get home – because, in addition to the command, they have spontaneously memorized as the relevant cue some feature of the room where the class was held and, in different surroundings, do not recognize the command. Many dog trainers therefore repeat a training exercise in a variety of places, in order to break such associations and isolate the intended cue, in this case, the verbal command alone.

Dogs, as the descendants of hunters that roamed far and wide in search of prey, ought to have more refined navigational abilities than simple landmark-learning, and, indeed, it has been shown that they simultaneously construct maps inside their heads. The standard way of investigating mental maps is to see whether animals can work out short-cuts for themselves. In one experiment, animal psychologists examined the mapping abilities of half-grown German shepherd dogs by showing them two caches of food hidden in the undergrowth in a large overgrown field (they chose young dogs because older ones might already have learned something similar to the task they were about to test them with, and they wanted to investigate the dog's natural abilities).[4] Starting at point C on the diagram shown here, one of the experimenters walked the dog to the first cache of food, at A, walked it back to C, and then walked it out and back to the second cache at B. Each dog, still on-leash, was then allowed to take the experimenters wherever it wanted to go. If the dogs had been using landmarks to find the food, they should have retraced the paths they had already been taken on. But in fact they invariably took a short-cut. Often this was a direct path from A to B, but not always; sometimes a dog went to B first and then used the short-cut in reverse to get back to A. This suggests that some dogs, perhaps especially young ones, may spontaneously look for new solutions to a problem once they are comfortable that their first way of solving it works – and can then go back to that solution once they are sure that the new method is not an improvement on the original one.

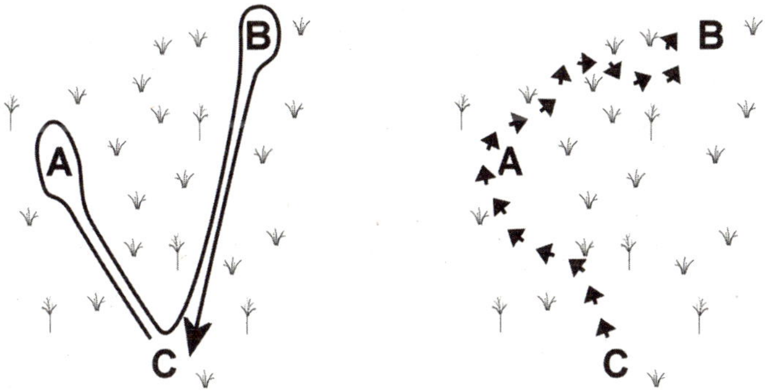

Bird's-eye view of an experiment demonstrating dogs' abilities to take short-cuts. (Left) The dog was first led from C to A, where it was allowed to find hidden food, then back to C, then to and from B, where it also found food. Lines of sight between A, B and C were blocked by vegetation. (Right) A typical track taken by the dog after release from C.

The fact that some dogs seem to be able to use mental maps more flexibly than others suggests that this ability approaches one limit of the dog's cognitive abilities; specifically, older dogs, or dogs that have been under stress for a long time, seem to lose some of their ability to orientate themselves. In one experiment, my colleague Elly Hiby investigated spatial ability by allowing gundogs to search a square grid of sixteen buckets, placed four feet apart. A few of the buckets always contained food, which the dogs were allowed to eat once they had found it, but most buckets only smelled of food (in this way, she prevented the dogs from simply finding the buckets with food by their smell).[5] Once they had had one opportunity to search the buckets, it was possible for the dogs to make two different kinds of mistakes: on subsequent searches, they might either visit buckets where there had never been food, or revisit buckets that they should have known they had already emptied. In the second phase of the experiment, she made the task harder, by releasing the dogs from the corner of the grid opposite to the one they were used to starting from; to succeed, they would then have to effectively turn their mental maps upside down in order to know which buckets contained food. The younger dogs learned the task quickly, and made few mistakes, even when released from the 'wrong' corner. By contrast, older dogs, and those whose hormones suggested they had been stressed for a long time, made the most mistakes; they were especially confused when the release point was changed, suggesting that some part of their spatial memory had become impaired.

As we would expect from their evolutionary past as wide-ranging hunters, dogs appear to memorize their surroundings continuously and effortlessly, and also to cross-reference different memories to construct mental 'maps' that enable them to navigate efficiently. However, they are less skilled than we are at re-orienting themselves when viewing familiar landmarks from an unexpected direction; the 'maps' themselves are probably accurate enough, it is the ability to think about the maps that they appear to lack.

When they are finding their way around, dogs probably use their acute sense of smell in preference to relying on what things look like, as we do. Their memories, too, are probably based as much on odour as on visual appearance, or even more so: dogs can remember a particular odour – say, that of a previous owner or a dog they have lived with before – for many years, possibly as many as ten.

Even scientists sometimes overlook the dog's preference for focusing on smell, and consequently think that they have demonstrated complex abilities in dogs that are in fact more probably merely evidence of how well dogs detect odours. In one experiment, dogs were outfitted in blindfolds and ear defenders and taken on a short walk. They were nonetheless able to retrace their footsteps. The scientists took this to mean that the dogs had memorized each turn, left or right, and how many steps they had taken in between, much as you or I might under these circumstances. But crucially the scientists who performed this research did not allow for the dog's acute sense of smell. In short, they failed to account for the possibility that the dogs could have retraced their steps either by following the odour of their own footprints, or by using olfactory 'landmarks' that they had memorized while their vision and hearing were blocked.

Another experiment that illustrates the dog's ability to pick out subtle differences in smell that mean little or nothing to us – though again not designed for this purpose – involved a border collie called Rico, living in an apartment in Leipzig, who had been trained to retrieve his toys based on their 'names'. As far as the dog was concerned, these were probably not literally the names of the toys but just commands, one for each toy (thus in his mind 'sock' was not an abstract label for a sock, but actually meant 'Fetch your sock'). The experimenters laid out some of Rico's own toys, adding one that they had brought with them, different from any of those in the apartment. When Rico's owner then called out a word that Rico had never heard before, the dog often retrieved the novel object. Although the experimenters claimed that this was evidence for linguistic skills in this dog,[6] and therefore by extrapolation in dogs in general, a simpler explanation is that Rico retrieved the novel objects because he found them fascinating, since they smelled different to everything else in the apartment (having never been handled by his owner). In other words, he was able to categorize toys as 'mine' and 'not mine', an interesting cognitive ability in itself, but apart from that all his behaviour was explainable by simple associative learning.[7]

In sum, dogs find their way around by a combination of abilities that overlap with, but are distinct from, our own. They have a good memory for locations, and a capacity for integrating these memories into 'maps' that they carry in their heads, so their intuitive skill at finding their way around is probably rather similar to ours. As in our species, old age and chronic stress impair these functions, eventually to the point that the dog may appear confused when it loses its usual terms of reference. However, the features on dogs' cognitive 'maps' are at least as likely to be olfactory as visual, whereas the representations of the environment that we carry in our heads are almost entirely visual.

Dogs' ability to construct mental maps suggests that they understand how things are connected together in the physical world, in the same way that we do, but, when tested experimentally, this hypothesis has been found not to be true. Their intuitive understanding of the ways in which objects connect together, their 'folk physics', is quite different from ours; they remember connections between actions and consequences, but without necessarily understanding how those consequences come about. One of the standard ways that psychologists use to test the ability to comprehend physical connections is the *means–end* test. For dogs, this involves animals retrieving inaccessible food by pulling on a string. In the simplest form of the test, one piece of food is attached by a single string to a wooden block. The food is made detectable but inaccessible (for example, under a mesh cover) whereas the block is left accessible. Most dogs can learn by trial and error that pulling on the block results in the food at the other end of the string coming out from under the cover, and can then repeat this whenever they are asked. A casual observer would conclude that the dog had understood the reason for what it had achieved; specifically, that the food was connected to the block by the string. However, if the task is made a little less straightforward, dogs are soon flummoxed. If there are two strings that cross one another, and only one has food on the end, then the dogs should, if they understood the physics, choose the one connected to the food. But they do not. Some pull on the block nearest to the food. Others just give up and try to dig the food out from underneath the wire mesh (some find even one string a problem, if it goes under the mesh at an angle).[8] The implication is that when dogs do learn to get the food, they do so through straightforward operant learning, and not through understanding that the food and the string are physically connected together. What they learn seems to be simply this: pulling on a wooden block near the smell of food produces food. Other 'intelligent' animals, such as monkeys, parrots and crows, perform much better at this task, but does this mean that dogs are stupid? More likely, the experiment in question is just not a suitable test of their intelligence. The canids' hunting lifestyle does not require a detailed understanding of precisely how things work, unlike the more opportunistic foraging strategies of monkeys, parrots and crows.

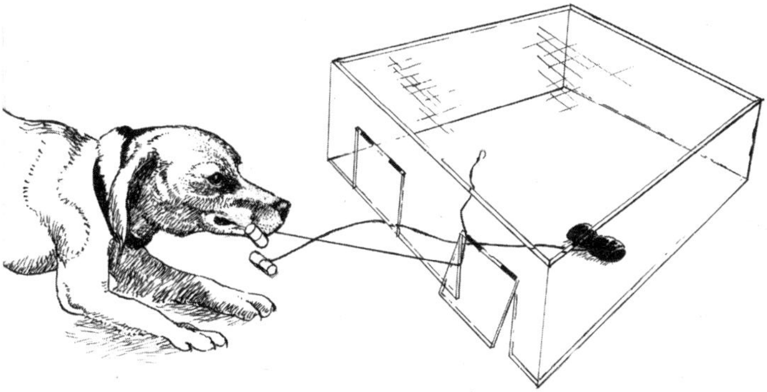

In the means–end test, most dogs pull on the string that is nearest to the food, not the one actually connected to it

Dogs do better in another aspect of 'folk physics', the ability to count. Because this ability is regarded as an indicator of intelligence, scientists have examined it in a wide variety of animals, including dogs. It is clear that dogs can tell the difference between a half-full bowl of biscuits and one that is a quarter full, but do they actually count the biscuits or simply judge the size of the pile? Researchers have attempted to answer this question using a technique first developed for the study of human infants.[9] When babies as young as five months are shown first one doll, and then a second, and then, after a brief gap, three dolls in the place where logically there ought to be two, they look at the three dolls for longer than expected – they seem surprised that the third doll has apparently come from nowhere. Their reaction suggests that they had added together one doll plus one doll, and were therefore expecting only two. It seems logical that dogs should also be able to do this; a bitch that sees two of her puppies go momentarily out of sight should presumably be surprised (and get up to investigate) if, say, three, or only one, reappears.

To test dogs' ability to count, the researchers in this study used food treats rather than dolls. The dogs were shown first one treat being placed in front of them, and then a second. Next, a screen was placed between them and the treats. When the screen was removed and either one treat or three treats were revealed, they stared at the treats for a long time, as if in disbelief. If there were two, as there should have been, they glanced at them only briefly.

In summary, although rather few studies have been conducted, it seems that dogs have little intuitive grasp of how the world around them works. This was Thorndike's conclusion from his puzzle-box experiments, and one that has been confirmed by all subsequent experiments. Of course, dogs can easily learn how to manipulate some specific aspect of their surroundings in order to get what they want, but they do not appear to understand why the manipulation works, just that it does.

Dogs, as the descendants of social animals, are likely to be much more attuned to one another than they are to the physics of their surroundings. Accumulated experience evidently plays a big part in enabling canids such as dogs to exploit their environment and find enough to eat; indeed, it would seem inefficient if each animal had to learn everything from scratch. Evolution should favour the transfer of skills from parent to offspring, and the longer the young are dependent on the parents, as in the canid 'family pack', the more frequent are the opportunities for this to occur. Thus there is good reason to conclude that dogs should have inherited some potential for learning from one another.

This is not to say that one dog deliberately teaches another in the way that we teach our children. Biologists who study how one animal learns from another usually try to use simple explanations rather than those that require a capacity for complex mental processes. Start digging your garden, and your dog may try to 'help' by digging alongside you. Is the dog really imitating what you are doing? If so, why does not it try to pick the spade up in its paws? More probably, your digging has simply drawn its attention to the soft earth, and digging is a normal thing for a dog to do in soft earth. Biologists refer to this as *stimulus enhancement*: it is sensible for one animal to keep an eye on what other animals are up to, in case it sees something useful. But the observant animal's subsequent behaviour is more likely to be dictated by what it would normally do than by an urge to imitate the other's actions precisely.

Some studies have found no evidence for copying. Thorndike himself researched the question of whether his dogs could learn to escape from his puzzle-boxes by watching other dogs that had already learned the trick, but he concluded that there was no evidence that they learned anything from observing the behaviour of the other dogs. In another study, pet dogs watched through a transparent gate as a trained German shepherd cross called Mora performed one of two tricks: lying down on her belly, or 'playing dead'.[10] Both are tricks that many dogs can do, and indeed might have already been trained to do. The twist was that the trainers issuing the commands to Mora used arbitrary words as the cues (their own names), which the observer dogs had presumably never heard before: 'tennie' for lying on the belly, and 'josep' for playing dead. Each observer dog was allowed to watch (and hear) the demonstration going on five times. The researchers then tested to see if the observer dogs had learned the commands from watching Mora. Apparently not; when they were tested with the commands, none seemed to know what to do. A few lay down on their bellies, but not in response to 'tennie', and none 'played dead', with or without the 'josep' command. Children gain the ability to learn by imitation at about eighteen months, so the dogs did not do very well at this task, if judged by human standards.

However, other research has shown not only that dogs can copy other dogs, but also that they are selective and logical about what they copy.[11] In one study, dogs between twelve months and twelve years old were trained to obtain food from a box that opened when a wooden handle was pulled down. Most dogs would naturally do this by grabbing the handle in their teeth and pulling it, but these particular dogs were trained to pull it down with their paws, as shown in the picture below. Next, other dogs were allowed to watch the dogs performing their new trick. If all the trick did was draw attention to the handle and the food, then most of the dogs should simply have pulled the handle using their mouths. But some of the dogs started using their paws, as the demonstrator dogs had, suggesting that they were copying the action itself.

A dog demonstrating pulling a handle with its paw, while holding a ball in its mouth

The experimenters then added a twist to this test that seems to show why the dogs sometimes copied the action of the demonstrator. The dogs that were demonstrating the handle-pawing action had been trained to hold a ball in their mouth while doing so. When actually demonstrating, they were sometimes given the ball to hold, at other times not. When the demonstrator was holding a ball (as in the picture), the other dogs often used their mouths; it was as though they were thinking, 'That dog is using its paw only because its mouth is full – I'll use my mouth, it's easier.' In contrast, when the demonstrator was not holding a ball in its mouth, most of the observers used their paws, as if thinking: 'That dog is using its paw, not its mouth, so that must be the only way to get the food.' This experiment, if understood correctly, suggests that dogs are capable of quite sophisticated reasoning (although human children can make deductions of this type as young as fourteen months). Experiments like this one may in the future lead to more insight into what dogs are capable of thinking. Perhaps we shall find out that dogs are better at imitating when they are trying to get hold of something they can see than when doing something simply to please their owners, such as lying on their bellies or playing dead.

In any case, dogs' abilities to solve problems and to learn from observing other dogs should not be explained glibly in terms of the emergence of similar abilities during the development of human infants. Dogs develop skills and insights that are appropriate for their own species; we do likewise. For example, human infants begin to acquire language skills at an early age, something dogs never achieve, but children are older than dogs when they acquire the ability to imitate selectively. Dogs, in turn, have inherited a set of learning skills from their canid ancestors that evolved over millions of years to allow co-operative hunting and rearing of young. Hunting as a pack can be only as efficient as the least experienced member of the pack, since it will be the weakest link that allows the prey to escape. Young canids must therefore pick up skills from their parents as quickly as possible if they are not to jeopardize the hunting success of the pack. Biologists are only just beginning to understand dogs' ability to learn from each other: the necessary experiments are difficult to design and the results are often open to more than one interpretation.

Unlike the other canids, domestic dogs also have the opportunity to learn from people. Indeed, the close co-operation that can occur between man and dog suggests that domestication is likely to have enhanced this aspect of the dog's intelligence. Most of the abilities discussed so far in this chapter are probably held in common with wolves and other canids; it is simply that we know more about domestic dogs because they are easier to study. Yet the fact remains that dogs are domesticated and other canids are not, so the question arises: is there anything about the dog's intelligence that is a unique product of the domestication process, one that has enabled dogs to interact with us at a level of sophistication no other animal can match? In proportion to body size, the dog's brain is somewhat smaller than that of its ancestor, the wolf, so it is unlikely that dogs are simply smarter than wolves. Nevertheless, dogs can outperform even chimpanzees, probably the most intelligent mammals apart from man, in certain selected tasks. Nowadays biologists tend to think of animals not in terms of whether they are more or less intelligent than one another but rather in terms of how their mental processes match the demands of their lifestyles. The dog's lifestyle is so intimately connected with our own that it is reasonable to look for special intellectual capacities that they may have gained during the long process of their domestication.

One area in which dogs especially outdo chimpanzees is in their ability to extract information from what humans are doing, in particular their ability to read human faces and gestures. Even hand-reared chimpanzees take a long time to learn this. And they can become confused when, for example, the person who first trained them is replaced, even if that person does his or her best to behave in exactly the same way as the original person. In contrast, dogs trained by one person can quickly learn another person's version of the same commands. Dogs are particularly good at following pointing gestures, outperforming even chimpanzees. There is currently some argument among scientists about whether or not this ability is a unique product of domestication, but it seems most likely that it was present to begin with, pre-domestication, and has been refined and developed since (though what its function might have been for wild wolves is unclear).

Dogs' ability to follow pointing gestures (and, by inference, other human gestures as well) is not quite what we would expect intuitively. Like humans, dogs can follow pointing not only with the arm nearest to the target (in the tests, usually a pot covering a food treat) but also cross-pointing, with the opposite arm (as shown). They prefer to follow a pointing arm even when the person pointing is nearer to, or moving towards, the 'wrong' target. However, dogs do have their limitations.

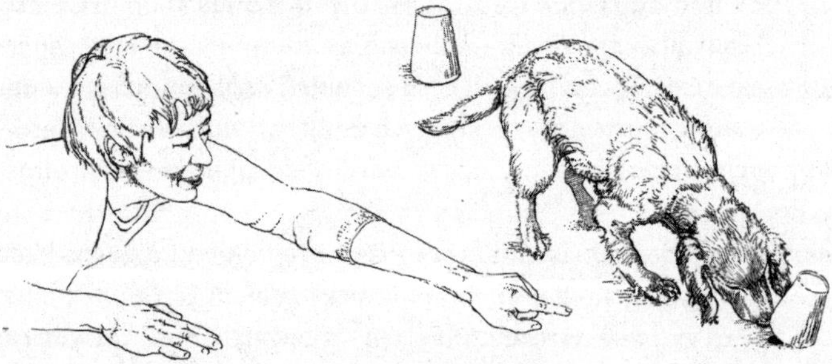

Following a cross-point

They take much less notice of a pointing finger than a pointing arm (children are happy with either) – but they do follow a pointing leg! The rule seems to be: 'Take the direction indicated by whatever whole limb is obviously pointing somewhere.'

There is also some argument about whether dogs are born with the ability to follow pointing gestures, or, conversely, have to learn it. Six-week-old puppies seem to know what pointing means, but are less good at following it than adult dogs are – puppies may just be too easily distracted. There is little doubt that this ability can be refined by training; for example, gundogs that are highly attentive to their handlers test better than other types of dog. It is also possible that domestication has prepared dogs to learn the significance of pointing very quickly, without giving them an instinctive ability that they can use the very first time they need it. But the response to pointing is clearly not universal: in some studies of pet dogs, over half do not respond spontaneously to pointing. Clearly, a strong component of learning is involved. Some dogs seem to find it difficult to learn to follow pointing even when rewarded for doing so, but many of these are dogs from shelters, and may have become fearful of outstretched hands due to physical punishment that they have received in the past. The unanswered questions are (*a*) whether the underlying ability is universal, but some dogs learn not to respond to hands because they deliver punishment, or (*b*) whether all dogs have to learn the significance of pointing, and some simply find the task easier than others.

Although pointing has become the scientists' favourite experimental tool, it is by no means the only activity to which dogs are particularly attentive. They also follow gestures such as nodding and hand movements much more attentively than most animals do. In addition, dogs seem fascinated by people's eyes and faces: they will follow the direction of their owner's gaze almost as reliably as they will follow pointing.

Domestication's main effect on dogs seems to be that it has rendered humans their most relevant source of information. For example, most dogs faced with the impossible problem of getting a tasty food treat out of a locked box turn to the nearest person for help within a few seconds, whereas even hand-raised wolves just keep scrabbling at the box. However, wolves outscore dogs when quick decisions have to be made, whereas dogs will tend to repeat what they have learned from people, even when it is obviously the wrong thing to do.

In one experiment that supports the idea that dogs are hyper-dependent on people, a comparison was made between the abilities of dogs, ten-month-old human infants, and wolves, in following the progress of a ball between two screens.[12] The experimenter first hid the ball behind one of the screens four times, each time talking to and maintaining eye contact with the dogs. Each time, the dogs were then allowed to retrieve the ball from behind the screen and play with it. Next, the experimenter walked behind the first screen, but quite obviously left the ball behind the other screen, finally showing the dogs her empty hands. The dogs nonetheless continued to look for the ball behind the first screen, even though they had seen it disappear behind the second one. Clearly, the attention they had received from the experimenter on the first four occasions had marked the first screen as the best place to try first. The ten-month-old infants made exactly the same mistake, again apparently prioritizing social cues. The wolves, however, believed their eyes and went straight to the second screen. Giving a low priority to cues given by humans, they instead relied on their interpretation of the physical world, in this case presumably a skill that would enable them to guess where a prey animal was most likely to be hiding.

Interestingly, however, the dogs were not incapable of understanding where the ball had gone. They did get the right answer when the ball was moved from one screen to another by an invisible string rather than by a person. Evidently their first priority was always to do what a human had encouraged them to do in the past. Even hand-raised wolves maintain a sufficient degree of independence from people to keep their minds on the problem as presented to them; dogs are too easily distracted, too eager to please a human. Just because they can follow a human's gaze or hand gesture does not necessarily mean that dogs understand what that person is thinking. They might simply be using the person's eyes as a convenient but otherwise arbitrary pointer as to what they should attend to next. Two remarkable studies done in France have exposed some of the dog's limitations.[13] Detailed comparisons were made between guide dogs, owned by blind people for several years, and ordinary pet dogs living with sighted owners. First, the researcher studied how the dogs tried to get food from their owners. They all used the standard doggie routine of looking forlornly at their owner, then at their bowl, and then back again: the guide dogs gave no indication that they knew their owners were blind. The only difference was that the guide dogs made louder slurping noises, which their blind owners could and did attend to. This tactic can be accounted for by simple associative learning – the dogs had learned that food followed when they made the noises – and does not prove that the dogs understood anything about blindness. Next, the study examined how dogs draw the attention of their owners when they are trying to get at a toy made inaccessible behind a heavy wooden box. Here, too, the same pantomime of looking back and forth between the owner and the toy went on, irrespective of whether the owner could see it or not. Other scenarios produced similar results, such as the owner offering the dog a different toy instead of the one it wanted: again, no difference. There was no indication that the guide dogs knew that their owners were blind, and that they thus had to rely on other cues, such as sounds, to tell them which way to point their heads.

These experiments tell us that dogs have a passion for following the human gaze, but they do not tell us whether the dogs are born with this obsession, or whether they learn it. The guide dogs that were studied had not always lived with blind people; they had been raised by sighted families for the first twelve to eighteen months of their lives, before starting guide-dog training. Perhaps these are the critical months in which the habit of following a person's gaze is learned, after which it is very difficult to break. However, it is remarkable that the guide dogs seemed hardly to have altered their behaviour at all in the four years, on average, that they had been living with a blind person.

This apparent over-reliance on human eyes and arms raises the question of whether dogs actually have the ability to understand what we are thinking. They are clearly responsive to what they see us doing, but that is not at all the same as understanding that each person has a mind, one that, furthermore, is different from their own. Such an idea must seem like heresy to the majority of dog owners, but science has thus far failed to demonstrate such abilities in any species apart from our own. Even the many experiments that have been done on chimpanzees have failed to provide conclusive evidence that the great apes know that other minds exist.

Part of the problem is that it is very difficult to design experiments that test whether dogs are able to tell what we are thinking, in other words, experiments that exclude simpler explanations for their behaviour. For example, in a study examining whether dogs understand what people can and cannot see, eleven dogs that had been trained not to steal food were taken into a room where there was a piece of food on the floor.[14] When the experimenter told the dogs not to eat the food when she was facing them, they usually left it, but when she was facing away from them while issuing the command, they often did take the food. The dogs might have 'known' that they could not be seen, but the simpler explanation is that they associated seeing a human face with obeying a command – 'If there is no face, then the verbal command doesn't mean anything'. Given that dogs are so sensitive to human faces and the expressions on them, it is very difficult to think of experiments that would rule out such an explanation.

However, a subsequent experiment showed that not all dogs are equally sensitive to being watched.[15] In this instance, the dogs were invited to take food from behind barriers of various shapes and sizes. One barrier, for example, hid the food but allowed the dog to see the experimenter when she was approaching the food; another was larger but with a small window, blocking the dog's view of the experimenter until the dogs were very close to the food. A few of the dogs behaved as if they understood which barriers blocked the experimenter's view of the food and which did not. Others seemed much more inhibited if she could see them start moving towards the food, but were oblivious to the fact that they could actually be seen eating it (for example, through the window in the barrier). So it is still not clear whether dogs can work out what people can and cannot see, or whether they are responding to simple learned 'rules' such as 'If I can see a person's face, then I shouldn't move towards food', or 'If I can see a person's face, then it is OK to move, but I mustn't actually eat'.

Such experiments show that dogs are very sensitive to whether people are watching them or not. They do not, however, provide any conclusive evidence that dogs can know what people are thinking – that they possess what cognitive biologists refer to as a *theory of mind*. Most dogs will have been fed all their lives from a bowl placed on the floor by a person's hand, so it is hardly surprising that they like to follow the direction a human hand is pointing to or moving in. Moreover, most dogs will have learned that the way a person reacts to them will be quite well predicted by the direction in which way the person is facing or moving. Consciously or not, humans expect dogs to be very sensitive to our body-language. This capacity must have been so useful to cementing the bond between man and dog that any dogs who lacked it were probably selected out of the population many generations ago.

Further evidence that dogs do not possess a 'theory of mind' lies in their susceptibility to deception. In one recent experiment, dogs were trained to expect that one person (the 'truth-teller') would always point at a container with food in it, and that another (the 'liar') would always point at an otherwise identical but empty container.[16] More often than not, the dogs preferred to go where the truth-teller pointed, but by no means every time. When the people were replaced by a simple association that a white box always contains food (truth) while a black box never does (lie), the dogs marginally preferred the white, 'truthful' box. Thus there was no evidence that the dogs had understood the difference between truthful and untruthful people; it is more likely that they had simply learned to associate one of the people with getting food.

In sum, domestication does not seem to have given dogs the ability to read our minds, or even to understand that humans are capable of independent thought. They must therefore live in a subjective world that is very different from ours, one in which we exist not as independent entities, but merely as components of that world (albeit usually the most important components). This is actually unsurprising, given what we now know evolution is capable of. The dog is stuck with a canid brain – and although this has undoubtedly been modified by domestication, it is asking too much to assume that a whole new layer of complexity could have been added during the domestication process.

So if dogs do not know what we are thinking, why do they give the impression that they do? From almost as soon as they can see, dogs seem to be especially sensitive to actions performed by humans. This difference from the wolf is almost certainly due to a genetically programmed change of focus in the dog's priorities, driven by domestication. Those proto-dogs that happened to possess a predisposition to attend to the humans around them would have been able to learn the significance of specific human gestures. This adaptation, in turn, would have given these more sensitive dogs a key advantage over more wolf-like dogs, which would have been more focused on their own species and the physical world.

Today this almost overwhelming focus on people and what they are doing enables dogs to learn very subtle aspects of human body-language, possibly even actions that we are unaware of ourselves. In addition, they almost certainly gather information about us, using their hyper-sensitive noses, based on subtle changes in odour that we are entirely unaware of. (This capacity to recognize subtle changes in body odour almost certainly lies behind the ability of trained dogs to detect impending seizures in diabetics and epileptics.) It is the shift in the focus of attention – from other members of their own species to members of the human race – that is domestication's primary effect on dogs' intellects. There has been no step-change in overall ability, just an adjustment of their primary focus. Dogs appear to be no more and no less limited than wolves in terms of what they can learn; it is simply that the priorities of what to learn and whom to observe have been changed by domestication. Although dogs appear to understand what we are thinking, no evidence has yet been found that suggests they are aware that we even do think. They are merely very well adapted to respond in the most productive way, nine times out of ten. Give them a situation that evolution has not prepared them for, such as an owner who is blind, and they continue to adhere to their standard ways of responding to people.

The dog's apparent lack of a 'theory of mind' then raises the question as to whether dogs even have distinct concepts for 'a person' and 'a dog'. The level of attachment between dog and owner is different from that between dog and dog, but is there also a qualitative difference? Dogs obviously behave differently towards people than towards other dogs, but could this simply be a consequence of one species walking upright and the other on all fours?

Play behaviour should be a useful window into this aspect of the dog's mind, since it incorporates a kind of 'lingua franca' that dogs and people can use to communicate their intentions equally well. Dogs can of course be readily persuaded to play with other dogs as well as with people, and human volunteers can be persuaded to play as if they were dogs – for example, by staying on all fours throughout the game. Nicola Rooney, a colleague at Bristol University, and I have been making comparisons between dog–dog play and dog–human play in order to gain insight into whether dogs play differently depending on which species they are playing with and, by inference, whether they therefore have different mental concepts of 'person' and 'dog'.[17] We recruited a dozen Labrador retrievers, chosen because they have a reputation for being particularly playful, as well as being a popular breed. The dogs were released, one at a time, into a large grass paddock, accompanied either by another dog (one it knew well) or by one of its regular carers. We gave the dogs two minutes for an initial exploration of the area, and then threw into the paddock a tug-toy consisting of a short length of knotted rope. All the dogs were accustomed to and enjoyed playing tug-of-war games, and thus immediately began playing with the rope, regardless of whether their play-partner was another dog or a person.

Dogs playing with a tug-toy are actually competing

The dogs spent most of their time engaged in the game, regardless of whether they were playing with a person or another dog. However, they clearly played very differently when their partner was one of their own kind, and when it was a person. When playing with the person, the dogs were much more likely to surrender the toy, seemingly in order to keep the game going. But when two dogs were playing, each tried to keep possession of the rope, attempting to guard it from the other whenever the other let go.

The behavioural distinction was even more pronounced when we added another component to the game. Three minutes after the first tug-toy was thrown into the paddock, we threw in a second one. Now each dog had the choice of continuing to play with the original toy or grabbing the second toy and going off to play with it on its own. Here, the difference between how dogs play with humans and with other dogs was dramatic. When two dogs were play-partners, they would often each take a toy and play with it for a while on their own before coming back to play together again. But when the play-partner was a person, the fact that there was a second toy available seemed almost irrelevant: the dog kept on bringing one toy back to the person and inviting her to keep on tugging.

In short, dogs appear to be in a completely different frame of mind depending on whether they are playing with a person or another dog. When the play-partner is a dog, possession of the toy seems to be most important – and indeed, it is possible that competitive play is one way that dogs assess each other's strength and character (in other words, for dogs these games are primarily a way of assessing Resource Holding Potential). When the play-partner is a person, however, possession of the toy seems almost irrelevant; the important thing is the social contact that the game produces. This finding is entirely compatible with the observation that dogs are unable to calm one another down, but can be calmed by their owners. It also indicates that dogs put humans in a completely different mental category from other dogs.

This distinction between play with people and play with dogs does not appear to be confined to Labradors, but rather appears to be a universal attribute of domestic dogs. As part of the same overall study, we also surveyed dog owners – and observed them with their dogs – to determine whether play with people interferes with play with other dogs. We hypothesized that if the two potential playmates were interchangeable as far as the dogs were concerned, playing with a person should diminish their appetite for playing with other dogs, and vice versa. But we saw no evidence for this at all: when watching owners playing with their dogs off-leash in parks, we found the quality of play to be the same whether the owner had one dog or more than one. In a related survey, we asked 2,007 owners with only one dog, and 578 owners with more than one dog, how often they played with their dogs: we discovered that the owners with several dogs actually played slightly more with each of their dogs than did those with only one. Although it was impossible to record the quality of the play, we concluded that most dogs are very happy to play with their owners, whether or not they have a canine alternative. Again, this suggests that dogs' minds have separate categories for 'people' and 'dogs'.

Play between dog and owner is such an everyday occurrence that it is easy to lose sight of the fact that inter-species play is actually very rare (indeed, virtually unknown outside the realm of domestic pets). To be successful, play requires very well synchronized communication; both partners must be able to convey their intentions precisely, while at the same time convincing each other that they are not using the game as a prelude to something more serious, such as an actual attack. The rarity of such inter-species play is probably accounted for by the limitations of communication between members of different species.

The capacity of dogs to engage in play with humans is particularly surprising given the sophistication of dogs' communication with other dogs during play. For instance, when two dogs are playing together,

Play-bow

the play-bow signal (see picture) is much more likely to occur when they are facing one other than when one is facing away, indicating that dogs are sensitive to whether or not their play-partner is paying attention to what they're trying to convey.[18] Dogs that want to perform play-bows but are being ignored have a variety of ways of getting another dog's attention, including nipping, pawing, barking, nosing and bumping. Humans are much less clever at this than they are, so the boundless appetite that most dogs seem to have for games with their owners, and even with people they do not know so well, must be due to the strength of their attachment to mankind in general.

However, our knowledge of the dog's cognitive abilities gives us no basis for thinking that dogs are aware of what they are doing when they are playing, in the same way that we are aware of (and so can talk or write about) how we play with a dog. Dogs may appear to 'deceive' their human play-partners, for example by dropping a ball and then grabbing it again before the person has time to pick it up. But there is a much more straightforward explanation for this behaviour: we know that dogs find play rewarding – 'fun' – and since it takes two to make a game, any sequence of actions that happens to stimulate play in others should quickly become part of the ritual that that dog and person engage in whenever they play, by simple association. In this instance the dog must, at some time in the past, have accidentally dropped a ball when near to a person, and then quickly grabbed it again (as a wolf would do if it accidentally dropped a piece of food). With its priorities focused on human reaction, it must have noted the person's excited reaction to this apparent 'deception'. Therefore it will repeat the sequence of actions in the hope of getting the same reaction again – which of course is likely to happen.

Indeed, although we humans are undoubtedly less good at interpreting dog behaviour than another dog would be, dogs are uniquely so focused on the reactions they get from people that they are able to adapt their behaviour to fit our own. I do not mean that they do this consciously; rather, my point is that our behaviour comprises the most salient cues available to them, such that, without having to think about it, they can adjust their reactions to us using quite simple associative learning.

Many dogs are friendly towards people in general, but it is obvious from the way they behave that they know the difference between strangers and familiar people, and between individual people that they know well. So far, science has only just begun to investigate just how dogs tell people apart from one another. Evidence suggests that they do seem to build up a single, multisensory 'picture' of people they know. In one study, researchers played for dogs a recording of the voice of one person they knew, but then showed the dogs a picture of someone else they knew. The dogs gave a look of surprise, as if the voice had already conjured up the face that should go with it.[19] (In addition, there is probably also an olfactory dimension to the picture that dogs create of us – a dimension of which we ourselves are largely unaware.)

Dogs are also very sensitive to what goes on within relationships – not just those in which they are directly involved, but also those they observe between people. In one recent study, a dog was allowed to watch three people performing a scripted transaction.[20] In this exchange, one person acted as the 'beggar' and each of the others either gave him the money he was asking for (the 'generous' person) or refused to do so (the 'selfish' person). Once the beggar had left the room, the dog was released, and allowed to interact with the other two people. The dogs preferred to interact with the 'generous' person; most went to her first and chose to spend more time interacting with her than with the 'selfish' person. It seemed to be the actual act of handing over the money that was important to the dog, because when the whole scenario was repeated but with no beggar present (meaning that the transaction had to be mimed), the dogs showed no preference for the 'generous' person.

Dogs also demonstrate some understanding of relationships between people and other dogs in the household. In an experiment that Nicola Rooney and I designed to examine this, a Labrador was placed on one side of a transparent gate, and allowed to watch tug-of-war games between a person and another Labrador.[21] Unknown to either of the dogs, the games were manipulated so that during some trials the person always won possession of the tug, and during others the dog was allowed to win. Furthermore, some of the games were made 'playful' (the person performed play-signals) while others were made 'serious' (the person did not perform any such signals). After the game, the spectators were let out from behind the gate where they had been watching. After the 'playful' games, the spectators preferred to interact with the apparent 'winner', whether dog or person; after a 'serious' game, the spectators were reluctant to approach either dog or person. Dogs not only react to dogs or people as individuals, they also react to what they have seen go on between them. However, this is not to say that they necessarily understand what a 'relationship' is, as a concept. More likely, they simply modify their behaviour towards each of the participants, depending upon what they have just seen them do.

The dog behind the barrier is watching a game of tug between a person and a second dog

If I have given the impression that I am trying to portray dogs as just 'dumb animals', it is the wrong impression. I know they can be very smart, but in their way – and not necessarily in our way. One of the problems with much of the research on canine cognition is that there is always an implicit comparison with our own: with children of what age are dogs comparable? Can dogs learn human language? And so on. The question that remains unasked is this (and it would be a very difficult question to even begin to answer): do dogs have cognitive abilities that do not have any direct counterpart in our own? For example, we know that their sense of smell is much more powerful than ours. Are they perhaps capable of processing the information they gather through their noses, in ways that we do not yet understand?

8

Emotional (Un)sophistication

Dogs are smart when it comes to learning about things, people and other dogs. Nevertheless, they have their limitations. Their lack of self-awareness, their lack of awareness that we have minds different from their own, and their inability to reflect on their own actions all restrict their capacity to comprehend the world in the same way that we humans do. Furthermore, because of such limitations, dogs' emotional lives are likely to be much more straightforward than our own, meaning that they may not be capable of feeling many of the subtler emotions that we ourselves take for granted. Nevertheless, dogs share our capacity to feel joy, love, anger, fear and anxiety. They also experience pain, hunger, thirst and sexual attraction. It is thus perfectly possible for humans to both understand and empathize with what they are feeling. Yet this facility is also a trap. It can seduce us into presuming that dogs' emotional lives are identical to ours, that in any given situation (as we see it) they are feeling what we would feel. In such instances, we are drawn into acting accordingly, treating our dogs as if they had exactly the intelligence and emotional capacities that we do. Since this is not the case, our actions may be meaningless to the dog – or indeed may mean something quite different from what we intended. Hence a thorough understanding of the full emotional capacities of dogs, and which of these capacities are simpler than our own, is essential to their well-being and to the integrity of our relationships with them.

One notable difference between dogs' emotional lives and our own is that their sense of time is much less sophisticated. Their ability to think back into their past, to mull over what has happened – even quite recently – and make sense of it, seems almost non-existent. Dogs are therefore much more inclined than we are to draw cause-and-effect conclusions based on the occurrence of two events one immediately after the other – even when a moment's reflection, if they were capable of such a thing, would make it obvious that such a connection was unlikely. Dogs do not 'do' self-reflection.

But the mere fact that dogs lack the level of consciousness that we have does not mean they lack rich emotional lives. The science of canine consciousness is still in flux, but the current consensus is that dogs do possess some degree of consciousness. In other words, they are probably aware of their emotions, but to a lesser extent than humans are. Scientists generally agree that our consciousness is much more complex than that of other mammals – in part, owing to the massively larger neocortex in the human brain as compared to that of mammals like dogs.[1] Indeed, we humans are able not only to experience emotions, but also to examine them dispassionately, to ask ourselves questions such as, 'Why was I so anxious last week?' Dogs seem to be incapable of this kind of self-awareness. All the available evidence suggests that their emotional reactions are confined to events in the here-and-now, and involve little, if any, retrospection.

Consider 'guilt', something many owners are convinced, perhaps without really thinking about it, that their dogs must feel. Does the following sound familiar? Dog does something 'wrong' (as far as owner is concerned) when owner is out of the room; owner comes back, looks at dog; dog looks 'guilty', owner smacks dog. But what if dogs do not have an emotion similar to our 'guilt'? If so, they will not be able to associate their bad behaviour with the punishment. So what does the smack teach them? Consider this possibility: 'When my owner comes into the room, sometimes I get a hug, sometimes a smack. What will happen next time?' The result: a twinge of anxiety that, if repeated enough times, can turn a sensitive dog into a cringing wreck.

The belief that dogs can feel 'guilt' and similar complex emotions is widespread among dog owners. A survey of British dog owners revealed that almost all thought that their dogs experienced affection (for their owners, presumably); almost all thought their dogs could feel interest, curiosity and joy; 93 per cent believed their dogs felt fear; 75 per cent believed they felt anxiety; and 67 per cent believed their dogs felt anger. The only emotion that the majority thought dogs were unlikely to feel was embarrassment.[2]

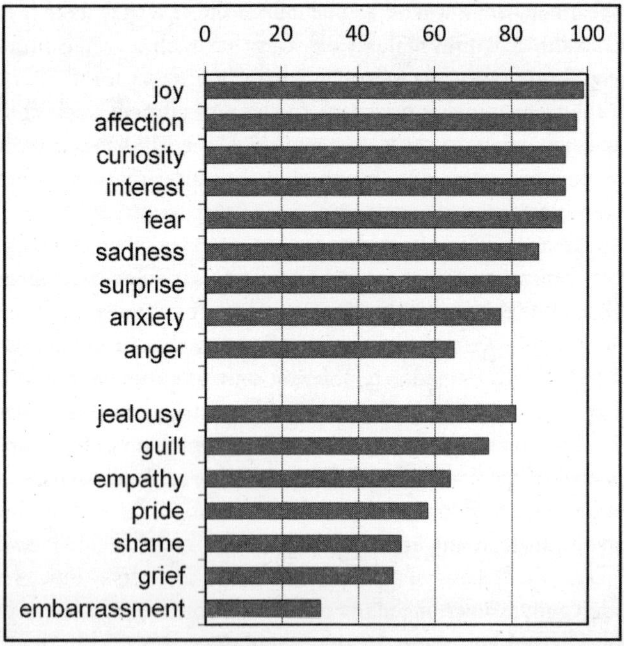

Percentages of UK dog owners who thought their dogs could feel particular emotions

Somewhat surprisingly, a high proportion of these owners believed that their dogs felt jealousy, grief and guilt. These, along with the other emotions listed in the lower half of the graph, are classified by psychologists as secondary emotions: they require some degree of self-awareness, and also an appreciation of what others are thinking – namely, a 'theory of mind' (as discussed in the previous chapter). Despite what their owners believe, it is not obvious that dogs have the mental capacity to actually experience all or, possibly, any of these six or seven emotions. Since each requires a slightly different combination of self-reflection and other aspects of intelligence, each deserves to be examined separately. I will look specifically at jealousy, grief and guilt, all of which happen to have received some degree of attention from scientists studying dogs.

Jealousy in humans springs from a suspicion that someone might displace us in a relationship with a person we love. What we feel initially may be unfocused fear or anger – the extent of which may depend upon our previous experiences with close relationships. However, this is quickly modified by our cognitive evaluation of the specific threat: what we know and feel about the person who is doing the displacing, what has been our relationship with that third party, and so on. A moment's reflection will also confirm that how jealous we feel, or how guilty, depends on how attached we are to the person to whom the emotion is directed.

To feel jealous, an animal would have to be capable of recognizing others as individuals, and to possess some concept of the quality of the relationships between those individuals. Because dogs are self-evidently very attached to their owners, it seems logical that they should feel jealous when their owner pays attention to another dog. There is also good evidence that dogs do have some comprehension of relationships between people and other dogs. Thus there is a prima facie case for taking seriously the belief that dogs can feel 'jealous'.

One strand of evidence comes from the consistency with which dog owners describe the triggers for 'jealousy' in their pets. In the study mentioned above, when asked to report what specific behaviours their dogs engaged in that suggested jealousy, and under what circumstances, all dog owners said that these behaviours occurred when they were giving attention, and especially affection, to another person or dog living in the same household. The owners consistently described in their pets what clinicians classify as attention-seeking behaviour. Half the dogs simply leaned or pushed against their owners, usually in between the owner and the object of the 'jealousy'. More than a third made some kind of vocal protest – barking, whining or growling. In connection with the growling, several owners reported aggression, to the extent of biting any other dog that the owner made a fuss over. Thus dogs' behaviour, when confronted with situations in which we might expect them to feel jealousy towards their owners, appears consistent with our expectations of this emotion. They behave as if they were trying to interfere with an interaction that (as they presumably see it) is threatening their relationship with their owner. Often, as noted earlier, they literally interpose themselves between their owner and the object of the unwanted attention – whether that is the owner's spouse or a dog visiting the household.

In short, it seems entirely plausible that dogs feel something that we would label 'jealousy'. Of course, whether or not jealousy 'feels' the same to them as it does to us humans is, essentially, unknowable. In dogs, it may be little more complex than a feeling of anxiety. But it seems to occur only at the specific moment of interaction between, for example, the owner and another dog: we have no evidence that dogs can feel jealous about their recollections of that interaction – a major feature of jealousy in human relationships. There is no sign, for instance, that they can become obsessively jealous.

The evidence that dogs can experience any emotions more complex than jealousy, however, is flimsy. Many psychologists believe that self-consciousness is required for feelings such as guilt, pride and shame to exist. Scientists point to the massive expansion of the neocortex, first in the primate brain and then again in the evolution of our own species, as the physical site where such advanced information processing takes place. By comparison, the dog's cortex is tiny, suggesting that it simply does not have the capacity to generate self-consciousness.

Nevertheless a minority of academics[3] have used largely anecdotal evidence to support the idea that some mammals, at least, do have sufficient self-consciousness to experience more than the basic set of primitive emotions (see box – 'The Changing Face of Animal Emotion'). For example, dogs have been described as capable of compassion, gratitude and disappointment – all of which require self-reflection.

Because our understanding of emotion in our own species is intimately connected with language, it is not easy for us to conceive of what the more complex emotions might feel like to animals. The basic emotions – including fear, joy and love – appear during the first year of a human baby's life. We know this intuitively because such emotions manifest as facial expressions. However, the more advanced emotions – guilt and pride, for example – are not linked to universal facial expressions. Moreover, they require learning about what is expected and disapproved of in the society the infant is being raised in, and we have no reason to suppose that dogs can form such concepts. Evidence that human children actually have such feelings does not appear until

THE CHANGING FACE OF ANIMAL EMOTION

Charles Darwin, a devoted dog-owner as well as the proponent of natural selection and the father of modern biology, appears to have been uncertain about how complex dogs' emotions might be. In his 1871 book The Descent of Man, *keen to emphasize the evolutionary continuity between man and the other mammals, he wrote: 'Most of the more complex emotions are common to the higher animals and ourselves. Every one has seen how jealous a dog is of his master's affection, if lavished on any other creature . . . a dog carrying a basket for his master exhibits in a high degree self-complacency or pride. There can, I think, be no doubt that a dog feels shame, as distinct from fear, and something very like modesty when begging too often for food.' However, in* The Expression of the Emotions in Man and Animals, *published the following year, he restricted his explanation of canine body-language to simpler emotions, such as fear and affection. So perhaps he had changed his mind.*

The nineteenth-century psychologist Lloyd Morgan, also a devoted dog owner, condemned such attributions of complex emotions as anthropomorphism. This idea was taken further by some animal psychologists, such as John B. Watson and B. E. Skinner, who restricted their concept of behaviour, even human behaviour, to observable processes and thus had no need for such hypothetical constructs as emotions. In the mid-twentieth century, zoologists studying animal behaviour were generally dismissive of the inclusion of emotions as explanations for what they observed – although Nobel Prize-winner Konrad Lorenz, in his book Man Meets Dog, *wrote: '[J]ealousy, to which dogs are very prone, can cause horrible effects' implying that he believed dogs had the capacity for such a complex emotion. Since the genesis of cognitive ethology in the 1970s, more and more biologists are invoking subjectivity as a legitimate area of study in animals, and some would now regard Darwin's original position as entirely reasonable.*

between eighteen and about forty months of age (depending upon the emotion) and few children can describe them completely until they are about eight years old; it appears that they have to go through a period of emotional education, based on the reactions of other people, before they can pinpoint precisely what they are feeling. Because we rely so much on speech to articulate our more complex feelings, it is difficult for us to imagine what form they might take in a species that is incapable of symbolic language. Indeed, I would go so far as to suggest that language and symbolic thought are sufficiently necessary to the production of such human emotions as embarrassment, guilt and pride that dogs are very unlikely to be able to feel them – or, at the least, not in a form that would be recognizable to us.

Grief, for example, requires complex cognitive abilities that we have no evidence for in dogs. Many two-dog owners report that when one dog dies, the other dog in the household stops eating, loses interest in going for walks, and generally hangs around looking sorry for itself. Other owners, if pressed, will admit that the death of one dog seemed to make little impression on the surviving dog. I do not doubt that many dogs react to the disappearance of a dog (or a person) that has lived alongside them for a long time, but I see no reason to suppose that their subjective experience of this is qualitatively different from their reaction to any other protracted separation, emotionally rooted in anxiety. Of course, if the owner of the deceased dog is visibly grieving, the survivor may be having to cope simultaneously with both the disappearance of its canine companion and an inexplicable and unprecedented change in its owner's behaviour. The finality of death is a sophisticated concept, one that even we humans do not develop until we are about six years old, and it is difficult to conceive of why or how such a capacity would have evolved in dogs.

Guilt is another emotion that requires cognitive abilities that, so far, we have no evidence for in dogs. Psychologists classify guilt, along with pride, envy and one or two others, as *self-conscious evaluative* emotions. In addition to requiring a sense of self and an understanding of relationships between third parties (as in the case of jealousy), these emotions, at least as experienced by humans, require an extra evaluative capability. For instance, to feel guilt one must be able to make comparisons between memories of one's own behaviour and mental representations of standards, rules or goals. In humans, these standards are learned and strongly influenced by culture. Moreover, it is believed that they do not begin to develop in children until their third or even fourth year, a year or more later than is the case for the simpler self-conscious (non-evaluative) emotions such as jealousy.

Guilt is widely believed to be a feature of the dog's emotional life. Owners often describe their dogs as looking 'guilty' if they return home to find that the dog has done something it is not allowed to do when they are at home. This could be something as simple as sleeping on the sofa, or more serious, such as chewing one of the owner's shoes. In order to feel guilty, a dog would have to have some mental representation of what it is and is not allowed to do – which seems reasonable. But it would then have to compare this with what it has actually done over the past few hours, while the owner was away. This seems more problematic, as the dog would need to recall not only the events in question, but also their social context (that is, owner not there). Biologists are fairly sure that dogs do not have the mental capacity to understand the impact of social context on their own actions; if they were, they should be capable of, for example, deception. Biologists are also far from sure that dogs can recall the specific contexts in which individual events occurred, after the events themselves have ended. At present, then, there has to be considerable doubt about whether dogs can actually experience an emotion similar to our 'guilt', since it is doubtful that they have all the cognitive abilities necessary.

However, let us for a moment give dogs the benefit of the (considerable) doubt, and assume that they can feel guilt. In order for dogs to communicate that guilty feeling, they would have to behave in some specific way that unequivocally signalled that feeling to their owners, before the owners became aware that the dogs had done something to feel guilty about. Although dogs could conceivably learn some specific piece of behaviour that would convey this message, it is very difficult to surmise why such an ability might have evolved. Would it be sensible for a young wolf to walk up to its father and confess that it had eaten the best piece of meat from a kill while his back was turned? Unlikely. However, let us entertain for a moment the possibility that this is one of the cognitive abilities that dogs are supposed to have gained during the course of domestication. What happens after a dog signals its 'guilt'? Most likely it will be punished by its owner. Why would a dog learn a social signal that immediately triggers punishment? The punishment should inhibit the performance of the signal, not promote it.

Thus it is probably not surprising that, when psychologist Alexandra Horowitz examined the kinds of behaviour that dog owners took as evidence of guilt in their pets, all that she found were signs of fear or affection.[4] In the first phase of her study, owners were asked to describe what their dogs did that made them believe the dogs were feeling guilty. They came up with a long list of behaviours, including avoiding eye contact, lying down and rolling over, dropping the tail, rapidly wagging the tail in this lowered position, holding the head and/or ears down, moving away, raising a paw, licking and so on. But all these behaviours are evident in other situations too, some associated with fear, some with anxiety and some with affection. None could reasonably be claimed as diagnostic of 'guilt'.

The next phase of the study was conducted in fourteen of the owners' homes, where a test was set up to make the dogs look 'guilty'. All of the dogs had previously been trained to take a food treat only when their owners gave them explicit permission. During the study, a treat was duly produced, and the owner commanded the dog not to eat it. The owner then left the room. Once the owner was out of earshot, one of two things happened, depending on the experimental protocol: either the treat was removed, or it was handed to the dog with encouragement to eat it. Once there was no longer any visible evidence of what might have happened to the treat, the owner was invited back into the room. The owners' behaviour was then manipulated to see how it affected their dog's behaviour. Just before they were allowed back into the room, the owners were told either that the dog had 'stolen' the treat, or that it had not stolen it. The owners were then encouraged to do whatever they would normally do in that circumstance, that is, they could praise the dog if they had been told that it had left the treat alone, or admonish the dog if it had disobeyed and eaten the treat. Whether this was the appropriate behaviour for the situation depended, of course, on whether or not the owners had been told the truth about what had happened when they were out of the room. The clever twist in this protocol was that all possible combinations were presented: 'right' – dog scolded after actually eating the treat or dog praised for not eating, and 'wrong' – dog praised after actually eating the treat or dog scolded having not been allowed to eat. To avoid affecting the sincerity of their reactions, the owners were not told until after the experiment was complete that they had at times been deceived about what their dogs had really done.

The results were very clear-cut. The way that the dogs behaved depended not on what they had or had not actually done, but, rather, upon the owners' behaviour, which in turn was based upon what they believed their dogs had done. If the dogs had really experienced 'guilt', they should always have looked guilty after they had eaten the treat. In fact, they performed their 'guilty' behaviour (each dog was slightly different in this regard) only when the owner had been told they had eaten it and therefore scolded them – even when they had not actually been given any opportunity to eat the treat. Moreover, the three dogs that were regularly physically punished (forced down, grabbed or hit) by their owners when they were disobedient were those that performed the so-called 'guilty' behaviour most intensely. The inescapable conclusion is that 'guilty' behaviour is in fact a mixture of fearful anticipation of punishment (hence the exaggerated behaviour of the dogs that were physically punished) and attempts by the dog to re-establish a friendly relationship with the owner (hence the dogs' so-called 'submissive' behaviour such as rolling over, licking and paw-raising).

So what is actually going on in these dogs' minds, if they are not feeling 'guilty'? Let us assume that they are using their default learning 'rule' of associating events that occur very close together in time. So the dog understands this pattern: owner comes home, owner punishes me, I can reduce the intensity of the punishment by performing affiliative (submissive) behaviour. The next time the owner comes home, the memory of previous punishment triggers this affiliative behaviour regardless of whether the owner has any intention of punishing the dog. All the dog understands is that on some occasions the arrival of the owner is followed by punishment, and on other occasions not – in an apparently unpredictable way. As a consequence, the level of anxiety rises and the affiliative behaviour becomes more frantic, the goal being to achieve reconciliation with the owner so that the anxiety goes away. We have no evidence to support the idea that dogs can, at such an intensely emotional moment, 'think back' to what event in the past might be determining whether the normal friendly greeting is replaced by chastisement.

Misconceptions about canine emotion are an important issue in pet-keeping. In general, owners want their dogs to live up to the expectations they have of them; when the dogs repeatedly fall short, they may resort to punishing them, or even disposing of them. If such expectations are based on a misapprehension of what dogs are actually capable of, then they have little hope of rectifying the situation, since they will have no comprehension of why their owners are behaving in a particular way. Hence their relationship is likely to deteriorate.

There are probably few problems in store for a dog whose owner mistakenly believes it is grieving, since the owner's reaction will presumably be an affectionate one, but the misattribution of guilt can have serious consequences for the dog. Many dogs get upset at being left alone by their owners. As a consequence of the insecurity they feel when alone, they may do things that their owner will disapprove of, chewing the frame of the door that the owner left through, for example, or trying to bury themselves under the sofa cushions and damaging them in the process. The returning owner sees the damage and immediately punishes the dog, thinking, almost certainly wrongly, that the dog will associate the punishment with the 'crime', and thus not do it again. In fact, quite the opposite will occur: because the punishment is associated with the owner returning, the anxiety felt during separation intensifies, making it more likely that the dog will be driven by its insecurity to do something the owner disapproves of while the owner is away. More punishment follows, and so a vicious cycle ensues, one that can last for years unless the owners seek expert help. At worst, a dog's life can be ruined by a simple and easily corrected misunderstanding of its emotional intelligence.

However, it is not just owners who have difficulty in interpreting and understanding their dogs' emotions. Dogs themselves, given their inability to think dispassionately about how they are feeling, are not good at dealing with their own emotions. Their lack of emotional sophistication manifests itself not only in their relatively limited emotional palette, but also in their inability to rationalize such simpler emotions as fear. Unlike us, they cannot 'tell themselves' that there's nothing to be frightened of: they cannot calm themselves down. Nowhere is this more evident than in their irrational fear of loud noises.

Given that dogs have long been used as aids for game shooting, it is odd that so many of them are frightened of noises. (If there were any genetic basis to this fear, the expectation is that it would have been largely selected out by now.) Up to half the dogs in Britain react fearfully to fireworks, gunfire and so on. Although some dogs probably habituate quickly to loud noises, so that their owners never notice a problem, many instead become sensitized. It is perfectly natural for a dog to be fearful of a loud noise that happens without warning and with no identifiable source or cause. Yet this very unpredictability is what makes it difficult for the dog to know how to react, and usually whatever it does will be only partly effective; hiding behind the sofa may provide a feeling of protection, but does not serve to reduce the volume of the next bang very much. This inability to deal with the noise triggers an inability to cope, then an escalation of the emotional reaction and, in some dogs, the emergence of a full-blown phobia, such that the triggering sound, even at a low level, will set off an extremely fearful reaction. Such phobias also occur in humans, of course, but their much greater prevalence in dogs is a sign of just how much they are at the mercy of their emotions when faced with situations that evolution has not prepared them for.

Dogs' limited capacity for emotional self-control can therefore have real consequences for their welfare. Dogs cannot 'pull themselves together'. Their instincts tell them to be frightened of sudden, novel events, and when they find such events incomprehensible (such as when they hear the loud bang of a firework from behind a closed curtain), they are not capable of dismissing the event as irrelevant. On the contrary, some dogs become more and more frightened every time. Similarly, since dogs lack the mental abilities to feel 'guilt', let alone its more abstract cousin 'shame', owners who punish them on the basis that they 'obviously know they have done wrong' are doing them a great disservice. The scientific exploration of canine emotions and moods is still in its infancy, but there will surely be new developments in the near future. In particular, a new technique allowing dogs to tell us how they are feeling may have great potential (see box – 'In the Mood?'). But there can be little doubt that emotions are part of their minute-by-minute experience of their existence.

IN THE MOOD?

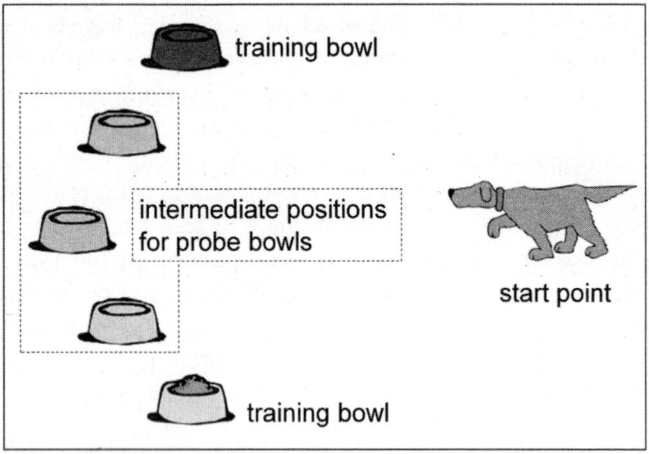

In humans, anxiety and depression are associated with negative judgements of ambiguous situations – 'the glass is half empty' syndrome. If such biases could be detected in non-human animals, they might provide a way of probing 'moods' in other animals. Following up studies done on rodents, colleagues of mine at Bristol University have examined whether dogs might also show such biases.[5] *Twenty-four dogs awaiting rehoming at a rescue shelter were first given a separation test, which is designed to predict whether or not a dog will display separation behaviour when left alone once it has been rehomed. The dogs were then trained to perform a spatial discrimination task in which one location always contained food (in the diagram, the white bowl to the dog's left – although in actuality all the bowls were the same colour) whereas another an equal distance away never did (in the diagram, the darkest grey bowl). Once they had learned which of the two locations contained food, the two bowls were replaced with one (empty) bowl, which could be in any one of five locations – two in the same locations as in the original training, and three in intermediate 'ambiguous' locations (shown as intermediate shades of grey): note that, although the diagram shows all five locations, only one was occupied by a bowl at any one time. The dogs were then tested to determine how quickly they ran to each of the locations. Faced with a bowl placed in one of the three possible intermediate locations, a 'pessimistic' dog might think 'There's nothing in that bowl, it's not where the food was last time', while an 'optimistic' dog might think 'That bowl's near the place where the food was last time, it's worth giving*

it a look'. The dogs that had exhibited separation distress when left alone ran slower than the rest, so they may be more 'pessimistic' than average. It is tempting to speculate that such 'pessimism' is the crucial underlying factor that distinguishes dogs that cannot cope when left alone from those that can.

Finally, I must allow that even the detached, scientific approach to emotion that I have tried to adopt contains at least one residual trace of anthropomorphism: I have discussed emotions using the names that we humans give them. The most basic emotions are so rooted in mammalian physiology and the more primitive parts of the mammalian brain that it is reasonable to assume that they are fundamentally the same whether experienced by a dog or by a human, even though the details of that experience may differ. However, when it comes to the simpler self-conscious emotions, such as jealousy, can we be sure that dogs possess only those that we humans have, and can put a name to? While I am reasonably confident that dogs do not feel guilt (as one example), it does not necessarily follow that their emotional lives are any less rich than ours, just different. For instance, since they are such social animals, perhaps they compensate for their less sophisticated cognitive abilities by having more fine-grained emotions? If the Inuit can have fifteen words for snow,[6] maybe dogs can experience fifteen kinds of love.

9

A World of Smells

Show any dog-lover a picture of a cute dog, and you will get an instant reaction. Show the same picture to a dog, and you will probably not get a reaction at all. (Unless it is your own dog, in which case you might get a puzzled expression that clearly signifies 'Whatever are you up to?')

Dogs may inhabit the same physical space as us, but they do not experience the world the way we do. We like to think that our version is 'the' version, but it is not. Like every other species, we pick up the information about the world that we need in order to survive, and we discard the rest. Or, more accurately, we pick up information that helped our primate and hominid ancestors survive (we have not lived our current lifestyles nearly long enough for our senses to have been modified by evolution). Dogs live in a world that is dominated by their sense of smell – a world that is quite unlike ours, which is constructed around what we see.

It is easy to ignore the fact that we, too, get an edited version of what is going on around us. We cannot 'see' the light beam that comes out of our television remote controls, but it does consist of light – it is just that its wavelength is too long for our eyes to pick it up. The mere fact that it is invisible to us does not mean it is not there. Hence it is worth reminding ourselves of what we do and do not pick up from our surroundings before going on to consider what dogs could tell us about what we are missing out on, if only they could talk.

First of all, we are colour junkies, at least by comparison with most other mammals. Although we have only three types of cone – yellow-, green- and violet-sensitive receptor cells (many animals have four, some even more) – it has been estimated that our eyes can distinguish about

10 million different colours. (When I say 'our', strictly speaking I am referring only to men; some women, possibly as many as half of them, have a fourth type of receptor in the yellow-green area and thus are able to distinguish between millions more shades of red, orange and yellow than the rest of us.)

Our ability to see all these colours has evolved only recently. Although reptiles (and birds) can see the full range of colours and ultraviolet as well, sometime during the course of the early evolution of mammals the ability to see both ultraviolet and red disappeared. It is possible that, because those early mammals were nocturnal, they needed the space on their retinas for rods, the receptor cells that are used in low-light vision, which are responsive only to black and white. The Old World monkeys and apes, most of which forage in daylight, 're-evolved' trichromatic vision about 23 million years ago, probably as a way of fulfilling a need to distinguish tender leaves and ripe fruits by their colour alone.

What the eye can detect is only half the story; the brain still has to turn raw data into pictures. All the information gathered by our eyes is integrated together in the brain to form the three-dimensional colour image that we consciously perceive as 'seeing'. Although our brains can put together a 3-D image using the information from just one eye (try closing one eye and moving your head around very slightly), the most accurate and instantaneous information comes from our binocular vision. Our brains constantly compare the pictures coming in from each eye, using the small discrepancies between them to generate a full-colour 3-D image. To make this process as efficient as possible, our eyes point in exactly the same direction. (This is unusual among mammals; even cats, with round flat faces like ours, have eyes that point slightly out to the sides, at about an eight-degree angle. By contrast, animals like rabbits that primarily use their vision to detect approaching danger have their eyes on the sides of their heads, sacrificing binocular vision completely in order to have the widest possible field of view.) And so humans are extremely visual creatures. Scientists estimate that our brains receive about 9 million bits of information from our eyes every second, ten times more than a guinea pig does, for example. There are various theories as to why we evolved this ability; among them is the supposition that as primate society became more complex, so the need to monitor the facial expressions of everyone else in the group increased, resulting in especially detail-orientated visual acuity.

Although humans see more than most mammals do, we do not hear nearly as much; hearing is evidently not as important for primates as it is for many other mammals. Mice and bats can hear much quieter and much higher-pitched sounds than we can, and dogs and cats can hear pretty much everything we can, and much more besides. We are also not as good as most other mammals at judging where sounds are coming from. Looking back to our evolutionary roots as hunter-gatherers, we can surmise that vision would have been much more useful than hearing for gathering edible plants and fruits, and for tracking game as well. However, our brains are probably much better than dogs' brains when it comes to distinguishing between very similar sounds, a skill we have evolved in order to decode speech.

It is our sense of smell that is really feeble compared to that of the rest of the animal kingdom (except birds). We can train ourselves to discriminate between different smells, provided they are strong enough for us to detect in the first place, but most of the odour information in the world around us simply passes us by. As a consequence, apart from a few professionals such as wine tasters and perfumiers, we do not even have much of a language to describe the quality of odours.

Why is the human nose so insensitive? First of all, we have a tiny olfactory epithelium, which is the skin inside our nostrils that removes odour molecules from the air we breathe and sends messages to the brain about what they are. Second, the parts of the brain that deal with incoming odour information are greatly reduced in all the Old World primates and apes, and there has been, if anything, a further reduction during our own evolution. Third, by comparison with almost all other mammals, we have a very limited repertoire of odour receptors, which cuts down on the amount of subtlety we can extract from any particular odour. We still have the relics of the genes that mice (for example) use to make the much greater range of receptors that they possess, but our versions of these genes do not work, indeed they stopped working millions of years ago, during the evolution of the higher primates. As a result, although we can probably detect the same range of odours as mice, we extract less detail from them. And of course we also need much more of the odour to be present to smell anything at all.

The phasing-out of odour perception in humans roughly coincided with the evolution of three-colour vision, and scientists believe that these changes are connected. The original primates were mainly nocturnal, like many mammals then and now, and had the standard mammalian two-colour vision. When our ancestors evolved three-colour vision, this new ability was accompanied by a substantial enlargement of the visual cortex in the brain, and a simultaneous shrinking of the areas that process olfactory information. (There appear to be limits on how much information any brain can process, and so enlargement of one area is often accompanied by shrinkage of another.) Then, as the apes and man evolved, the brain enlarged further, becoming a processor of social information, especially information gathered visually. In the process, the 'ancient' olfactory part of the brain became buried underneath the cerebral cortices.

Thus the version of the world as perceived by mankind is rather atypical, even among mammals in general. Humans have highly refined colour vision, reasonable night vision (which most of us rarely use), average hearing, and an utterly puny sense of smell. Dogs, by contrast, have poor colour vision, good night vision, excellent hearing and a very sensitive and sophisticated sense of smell. Mankind has exploited these differences throughout the domestic dog's history, valuing the dog's sensitive nose especially as an aid to hunting. However, pet dogs are often so anthropomorphized that it is easy for their owners to ignore these differences, and to treat their dogs as if they perceived the same world that we do.

The visual world that dogs inhabit is similar to ours in many ways – indeed, close enough that the differences are rarely apparent, and present no problems for the dogs themselves. Dogs can see slightly more than we can during the night, slightly less in daylight. With one notable exception – namely, their perception of colour – their visual abilities are not so different from ours that their subjective world and ours would look substantially different. Whatever we can see, they are likely to see also, if in slightly less detail.

For dogs, like most mammals, it is more important to see all the time rather than to see particularly well, in order to remain vigilant to danger. We humans have sacrificed some of our ability to see in the dark in order to be able to see in colour and in great detail during the day; presumably our tree-dwelling ancestors had few nocturnal predators. For this reason, dogs' eyes are adapted to see much better in the half-dark than we do, but less well (though perfectly adequately) in bright light.

In order to be more efficient at night, dogs' eyes contain a structure that ours do not. Most dog owners who walk their dogs at night will have noticed that their eyes shine when a light is pointed at them. This is due to a reflective layer of cells behind the retina called the tapetum, which almost doubles the sensitivity of the eyes in low light. Furthermore, dogs' eyes are connected to their brains differently from ours. We have a staggering 1.2 million nerve fibres in our optic nerves, which allows us to resolve a lot of detail, provided there is enough light. Dogs have a mere 160,000 connections, and, unlike our optic nerves, theirs are connected to multiple rods or cones, and can be triggered if any one of these receives a scrap of light. This enables dogs to see at lower light levels than us, but their perception of detail is inevitably reduced, by a factor of about four, since their brains have no way of knowing which particular one of a bundle of light-sensitive cells has been triggered. Put another way, perfect vision in humans is described as 20:20 whereas dogs can manage only 20:80 at best. Some may have even worse eyesight than this – it has proved difficult to design an eye test for dogs that is as sensitive as those opticians use on us. (Wolves, incidentally, have rather clearer vision than dogs; it is possible that dogs are descended from a more nocturnal wolf than those that survive today.)

Dogs' eyes also produce a wider picture than ours, a picture that is less centred on straight-ahead vision. They can see more of their surroundings without moving their heads. The average dog's field of view is about 240 degrees, compared to our 180 degrees – so that, unlike humans, they can see a limited amount of what is going on behind them. Each eye points about ten degrees off the centre-line of the muzzle, so there is a considerable area of overlap to the front, and dogs do use this to produce true binocular vision. Some breeds probably have better binocular vision than others; indeed, the degree of overlap is less in breeds with long muzzles.

But while dogs' field of vision is larger than ours, their close vision is not nearly as good. Most dogs cannot focus much closer than 12–20 inches from their noses, even when they are young (though, as with humans, that minimum tends to increase as they get older). Once they get their snouts within a foot or so of anything they are interested in, other senses take over, especially their keen sense of smell.

The most notable difference between canine vision and our own, however, lies in the limited range of colours that dogs can see. Like most mammals, they have only two types of colour-sensitive cells (cones) and so can see only two primary colours – blue-violet and yellowish-green.[1] Of course, like all mammals they can distinguish many different colours based on the relative strength of the signals coming from these two, but the absence of the yellow cone (which humans have) means that they cannot distinguish red from orange, or orange from yellow. There is also a gap between the colours that their two types of cones are sensitive to, such that dogs see turquoise as grey. Nevertheless, scientists who have measured dogs' colour vision found that they were more attentive to colour than most other mammalian species (apart from ourselves and our trichromatic relations, of course), so it is likely that dogs do sometimes use colour in their everyday lives.

Thus, for instance, dogs running around in a park in the daylight will see much of what we see, with some small differences. They see more, because they can see to the sides of their heads as well as straight ahead; but also less, in the sense that the leaves on the trees and the grass will be rather similar muted shades of greyish-green, and red and yellow flowers will be similar to each other in colour. As the dog's carnivorous ancestors did not need to pick out the ripest fruits or the most tender leaves, the latter deficiencies were most probably of no particular consequence to them, and probably matter little to dogs today. As darkness falls, however, the dog's superior night vision comes into play, enabling dogs to continue running about happily in the undergrowth long after their owners need a torch to find their path.

Despite these minor differences, the degree of overlap between the dog's visual world and ours means that misunderstandings of what they can and cannot see rarely cause problems. Anyone trying to train dogs to respond to visual cues based on their colour would do well to avoid using both red and orange, but this suggestion is unlikely to apply to more than a handful of specialist trainers; most everyday training uses sound and movement cues. Their general lack of interest in colour probably explains why few dogs display much interest in watching television – though the poor quality of television sound (as far as they are concerned) may also play a part.

Our restricted hearing, compared to that of dogs, can lead to situations where they are inconvenienced or, at worst, even suffer. Dogs' hearing is significantly more sensitive, and more versatile, than ours. Their low-frequency hearing has a range similar to ours, but they can hear high-pitched sounds that we cannot hear at all. We refer to such frequencies as 'ultrasound' – although, if they could, dogs would describe us as having high-frequency deafness. Cats, which can hear even higher-pitched sounds than dogs can, would presumably describe dogs as having high-frequency deafness.[2]

It is easy to forget that dogs can hear sounds that we cannot. Some researchers into canine responses to sounds have used ordinary audio playback equipment, apparently unaware that this is designed to mimic just what we humans hear and does not reproduce the high frequencies that are presumably an important part of all sounds as far as dogs are concerned. Unsurprisingly, therefore, dogs sometimes react to 'live' sounds but do not necessarily react to recordings or broadcasts (television, for example) that are, to our ears, virtually identical. The equivalent experience for us would presumably be something like the difference between FM radio and long-wave AM (which does not reproduce high frequencies).

It is not clear why dogs (or wolves) would ever have needed to hear such high-pitched sounds; this ability is probably a legacy from their smaller canid ancestors. Foxes, which can hear the ultrasonic squeaks made by mice and other small rodents, use their high-frequency hearing to locate these animals when hunting. But wolves do not routinely seek out such small prey. 'Silent' dog whistles make use of the high frequency sounds that dogs can hear and we cannot, but they are something of a gimmick: whistles that produce at least some sound audible to human ears are much easier for us to control (how can you tell when a silent whistle is not working?). Dogs are, however, very skilled at distinguishing between quite similar sounds, probably using mainly high-frequency information. For instance, although research into how dogs discriminate between different types of barks is still in its infancy, there is little doubt that they can extract a great deal of detail from what they hear, as well as being able to detect very quiet sounds.

Dogs also have much more sensitive ears than ours, and as owners we should be attuned to this difference. Within their optimum frequency range, their hearing is approximately four times more sensitive than ours. This means that dogs' hearing is probably damaged when they are subjected to the din encountered in some noisy kennels (which can be unpleasant enough even for us cloth-eared humans). Because of our own insensitivity to ultrasound, we are likely to be unaware of the discomfort that dogs must experience when subjected to noises that contain a lot of high-frequency sound, such as the banging of metal gates or the scrape of metal buckets on concrete floors.

In their sense of smell, dogs are miles ahead of us humans. And it is we humans who are unusually insensitive, not the other way around. Compared to other carnivores, dogs are about average. For example, grizzly bears have even more sensitive noses than dogs do, allowing them to find food underground even in the dead of winter. Nevertheless, dogs possess a unique combination of trainability and olfactory ability, one that we humans have made extensive use of throughout history – and indeed are finding new uses for almost every day.

It is hard to convey how sensitive dogs' noses are without getting into some almost incomprehensibly large numbers. They can detect some odours, probably most, at concentrations in the parts per trillion. By comparison, humans generally detect odours in the range of parts per million to parts per billion, a sensitivity between 10 thousand and 100 thousand times lower than that of dogs. Dogs' noses are as responsive as they are because they possess a very extensive olfactory epithelium. Although the area of this surface varies from breed to breed, the German shepherd's, at 20–25 square inches (roughly the area of a CD cover, spread over a labyrinth of bony structures called turbinates) is typical – and over thirty times larger than ours. And between 220 million and 2 billion nerves, a hundred times more than in our own noses, link the epithelium to the brain. Why so many? Not only is the area of epithelium larger in the dog, but also the receptors are packed in much more densely on the dog's epithelium than they are on ours. So that dogs can process all this information, their olfactory cortex – the part of the dog's brain that analyses smells – is roughly forty times bigger than ours.[3]

Dogs can also pick up much more detailed information from odours, because they have a greater diversity of olfactory receptors than we do. So far, more than 800 functional olfactory receptor genes have been identified in the dog genome (along with a further 200 'pseudogenes' that do not appear to make receptors, although they probably did at some time in the dog's evolutionary past). Each gene codes for a slightly different receptor, each of which is sensitive to a slightly different shape in the odour molecules. Most odours trigger many of these receptors, and the brain then compares the relative strength of all the signals it receives in order to characterize each odour. Humans have a range of receptors similar to that of dogs, but fewer of each type. The implication is that everything that dogs can smell, we can too, but with less detail extracted. We also need a much higher concentration of most odours before we can detect anything at all. Humans can discriminate between thousands of different odours. Dogs' much greater diversity of receptors suggests that they can detect a great many more.

In practice, the range of smells that dogs can detect seems almost limitless, judging by the proliferation of odour detection tasks they are asked to perform. Traditionally, mankind has exploited the dog's nose in locating food, from the tracking of game to the detection of delicacies such as truffles. More recently, dogs' keen sense of smell has been used to detect various types of cancer (melanomas as well as ovarian and bladder tumours) and impending epileptic seizures in humans. Dogs are able to smell pests such as the nematodes that can infest sheep as well as the bedbugs that can infest humans. They have even been put to use in conservation efforts: for instance, they are employed to sniff out illegal exports of sharks' fins and sea cucumbers in the Galapagos. Scientists have likewise drawn on them to map populations of rare South American maned wolves and bush dogs (based on locating their faeces by their odour).

Dogs are much more capable than humans of discriminating between very similar scents. For example, they can distinguish between the odours of non-identical twins living together, and those of identical twins living apart. (However, they seem unable to reliably distinguish between the odours of identical twins living together.)[4] In short, dogs can identify us using not only odour cues derived from the environment that we live in (for example, the food we eat and the fabric conditioner on our clothes) but also genetically based factors that contribute to our characteristic individual odours. Only when the genes are the same, and the environments also, do dogs begin to get confused. Dogs' acuity at distinguishing particular human odours is now being used in several countries, including the Netherlands and Hungary, as a way of linking criminals to crime scenes.

Because we make so little use of our sense of smell, we have to exercise considerable imagination in order to understand how dogs experience this unfamiliar world. Odours do not behave in the same way as beams of light or sound waves; they are much less predictable than either. The rate at which they get into the air varies with temperature, humidity and the kind of surface that they are coming from. Moreover, the speed with which – and direction in which – odours travel is much more haphazard than is true of either light or sound. These factors do not matter much to us, and indeed rarely impinge upon our consciousness at all, because we use our visual sense to find our way around. Dogs, by contrast, have of necessity developed strategies to glean useful information from the odours that they rely on to locate objects of interest – whether those are scent-marks left by other dogs, potential food items, or odours that we have specifically trained them to find.

Finding interesting odours is not as simple or as instantaneous as gathering visual information. When we go somewhere new – for example, we enter a room we have not been in before – we look around and check our surroundings. Because light travels in predictable straight lines, it is immediately obvious if there are any parts of the room that we cannot see; we know without having to think about it that we cannot see into cupboards if the doors are closed, or behind screens or large pieces of furniture. Unfortunately for dogs, smells do not travel nearly so predictably as light. They spread very slowly of their own accord, by molecular diffusion, but the distances involved in this process are so minute (no more than a few inches) that they are relevant only to small insects like ants that live in the thin 'boundary' layer of still air close to flat surfaces.[5] For an odour to travel any distance greater than this, it has to be transported by air movements, and these are very unpredictable and erratic.

To understand what a dog experiences, imagine opening a food cupboard and not being able to tell instantly whether something you are looking for is on a shelf inside, in a rack on the back of the door, or on the work-surface beneath. Try turning the lights out and locating a spice jar by its odour alone. We humans do retain some vestigial ability to navigate by smell, but it is a slow and cumbersome process. Even when we can smell something, tracing the source of the odour is rarely straightforward. Air movements are too unpredictable, especially indoors. That is why, if you watch dogs for a while, you will realize that they spend a lot of time and energy looking for visible indicators of likely places to find an interesting odour. How do they know where to sniff first? Presumably this is largely a matter of experience, though if they are leaving their own scents for others to find, they will either leave them somewhere obvious (on the proverbial lamp-post, say) or leave a visible indicator (such as the 'tramlines' that some dogs scratch in the soil, pointing to where they have just urinated).

If there are no visible cues, then dogs have to use their legs to work out where the smell is coming from. If there is not much air movement, they will run around sniffing, working out by trial and error where the smell is strongest. In situations where the odour is coming from a point source, this strategy is usually successful, sooner or later, but, if it is not, the dog can become very confused and frustrated. There is an apocryphal tale of a trained narcotics-detection dog that went crazy inside a container full of oriental furniture. There was a strong odour but he was completely unable to identify where the smell was coming from. As the story goes, it turned out that the whole consignment had been lacquered with cannabis resin – so the container itself was the source!

Dogs are particularly adept at following scent-trails, such as those left by other animals, or made deliberately by people, as in drag-hunting. Dogs will follow a trail by zigzagging to and fro. They find the edges of the 'corridor' of odour coming off the trail, and, if they lose it, will head back in the opposite direction, back across the invisible trail. As well as keeping to the trail, dogs have to make up their minds about which direction it is going in. It is likely that wherever possible they use visual cues, such as the flattening of grass or undergrowth in the direction of travel. However, some dogs, though probably not all, seem able to follow a trail in the correct direction even if the visual cues are misleading. In one set of experiments, human subjects were persuaded to walk backwards across a grassy field, so that if the police dogs that then followed the tracks used heel-to-toe cues to determine direction, they would go the wrong way.[6] Instead, they headed in the direction the persons had travelled. (It is possible, however, that they were picking up on the detail of which way the grass had been flattened, rather than simply the heel and toe impressions, even though the trails were by then an hour old.)

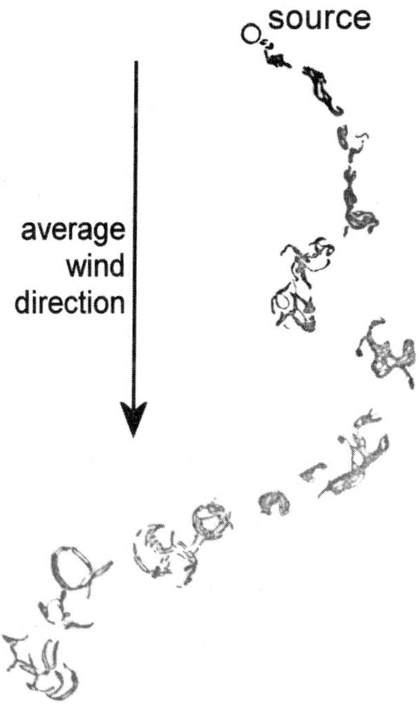

Bird's-eye view of an odour plume. The average wind direction is shown from top to bottom, but changes in direction lasting a few seconds cause the plume to 'snake'. Eddies (caused by irregularities on the ground) cause the plume to swirl and break up into pockets.

Dogs often face the problem of finding the source of an odour when there is no track along the ground. Outdoors, there is usually some kind of breeze to carry the odour to the dog, but breezes are not very predictable when it comes to carrying odour. You might think that odour travels in a straight line downwind from the source, but in fact it spreads out sideways as it travels downwind, resulting in a conical distribution with the source at the apex. Nevertheless, at any one instant, the distribution of odour would look, from above, more like a snake – one that is solid in some places and thin and wispy in others. The reason is that, as the wind blows over any surface, friction between the two causes eddies to develop. Some are several yards across, causing the snaking effect; others are smaller, causing the snake to spread out or bunch up. As a result, a dog that is standing still, even directly downwind of the smell's source, will be outside the odour plume for a longer time than within it; conversely, a dog that is downwind but well away to one side will occasionally receive a burst of odour as the snake wiggles particularly violently.

In short, when dogs first pick up a trace of an odour they are trying to locate, they can only guess roughly where it is coming from. This is where their wet noses are helpful. Technically known as the rhinarium, the 'pebbled' area of specialized skin around the nostrils is crammed with pressure and temperature sensors. (The rest of the skin on their heads is generally rather insensitive.) Those wet noses are not only directly sensitive to the wind going by, but are also simultaneously cooled on the upwind side, giving them an instant readout of which direction to head in.

Yet because of the wind's intrinsic vagaries, this tactic will almost certainly immediately take the dog out of the scent pocket. Inexperienced dogs will immediately switch to quartering, running mainly across the wind in an attempt to relocate the odour. As soon as they pick up the smell again, they will check their pace and revert to running upwind, until the scent is almost inevitably lost again, whereupon the whole process starts again. More experienced dogs, for instance those that have regularly competed in gundog trials, will tend to go on running upwind for a few seconds after they have lost the odour, confidently expecting that they will soon run into another pocket of odour. If they do not, they will then switch to the quartering tactic. A prolonged period of running without encountering any odour will usually cause most dogs either to give up, or, if their motivation remains strong, to start a purposeful loop back downwind to the general area where they first detected the odour.

Once dogs get close to the source of the odour they change their tactics. The average strength of the odour will be increasing at this point, but the dogs will probably be alerted more reliably by the sudden disappearance of the gaps of clean air between the pockets of odour. Now they will slow down abruptly, tails wagging furiously, and start to use their eyes to locate the target, because the olfactory information is no longer sufficiently detailed to be of much help. Only if they accidentally blunder on past the source and hence lose the scent will the dogs loop back around into the odour corridor and go back to using their noses.

Whether tracking or following an air trail, dogs can ramp up the sensitivity of their noses. Rapid sniffing makes the air entering the nose more turbulent, so that more of it comes into contact with the olfactory membranes. They can also change the airflow in their nostrils: by widening the nasal valve, dogs can send more information into the olfactory area. Dogs that are tracking along the ground need to travel quite slowly in order to maintain contact with the trail, and so can sniff all the time, at about six sniffs each second. They can also temporarily increase their rate of sniffing if they need to, up to twenty sniffs for each inhalation. Indeed, they may even be able to perform the saxophonist's trick of breathing in through their noses, sniffing continuously, while simultaneously breathing out through their mouths. But dogs cannot be sniffing all the time, particularly while running – they would simply run out of air. When attempting to follow an air trail, as opposed to a track on the ground, dogs often move at a canter. At such a pace, they of course use up a great deal of oxygen, which requires them to breathe more heavily. Because of that, they have to make a trade-off between maximizing the amount of odour they can analyse and locating their target quickly. When gundogs follow a track laid on the ground, they sniff five or six times a second. However, they sniff only about twice per second when following a scent upwind, and even less frequently – once per second or so – when running crosswind trying to locate the scent plume.

*

Once inhaled, the contents of each sniff are analysed by the dog's olfactory system. The air in each sniff passes up the nasal passages and swirls around the turbinates, scroll-shaped bones that carry the olfactory receptors. The receptors encode the nature and strength of the odour, and then pass on this information to the olfactory nerves and thence to the brain, where the sensation is generated and comparisons can be made with odours that have been sampled in the past.

Until recently, not much was known about how mammals detect and analyse odour, but now that the canine and other genomes have been sequenced, an increasingly detailed picture is emerging. The molecules that make up the odour – and there will be many different types in any natural odour – first have to be extracted from the air and passed on to the receptors. Because odour molecules move very slowly, the receptors need to be very close to the air; otherwise, it would take so long for the odour molecules to reach them that they would not be able to give the instantaneous response a dog needs in order to keep up with its six sniffs a second. Thus in the dog's nose, the receptors are just a few thousandths of a millimetre from the open air. Exposed like this, the receptors are very susceptible to damage. The olfactory equipment protects itself in two ways. First, it cleans, warms and humidifies the incoming air by passing it over mucus-covered membranes before it can reach the olfactory epithelium itself. Second, the olfactory neurons, on which the receptors sit, are constantly renewed, undergoing replacement roughly every month.

Once absorbed by the olfactory epithelium, a specific odour triggers the corresponding receptors. The odour molecules diffuse through the mucus that covers the receptors' exposed ends. In the dog, there are hundreds of types of olfactory receptors. All those of a particular type are connected to a single ball of nervous tissue about a tenth of a millimetre across, which in turn relays its information to the brain through a small number of nerves, the mitral cells. This combining of information maximizes the capacity of the nose to detect tiny amounts of odour. In contrast to the eye, what matters is not where in the nose each molecule is being picked up, but how many receptors are being activated at any one time, so it makes sense for all the signals to be gathered together before relaying the information to the brain.

The olfactory bulb in the brain then compares all the signals produced by specific receptors to generate much more nuanced information – much as our brains enable us to 'see' millions of colours even though our eyes can detect only three. Clearly, since dogs can distinguish tens of thousands of different odour molecules, even though they have only 800 or so types of receptor, there cannot be one receptor for each odour. Rather, a particular odour molecule binds to a greater or lesser extent to several different kinds of receptor and the 'odour brain', the olfactory bulb, combines the information to decode what has been detected. Finally, once the odour molecules have interacted with a receptor, special enzymes degrade them quickly, otherwise the sensation of the odour would persist for too long. The receptor is then clean and ready to receive the next incoming molecule.

Dogs have yet another way of perceiving odours, and it is one that we humans do not share at all. Running between their nostrils and the roof of their mouths, just behind the front teeth, are a pair of fluid-filled tubes, the incisive ducts. From each of these runs a cigar-shaped, blind-ended tube called the vomeronasal or Jacobson's organ. If you look behind your own incisors in the mirror, you will see nothing – we do not have incisive ducts or functioning vomeronasal organs, although most other mammals (and reptiles) do. Like much of our olfactory sense in general, these organs disappeared in our distant ancestors, way back during the evolution of the higher primates.[7]

The purpose of the vomeronasal organ (VNO) is not easy to determine. Both the VNO and its ducts are fluid-filled, so at first glance they would seem to be rather awkwardly placed to perceive odours. However, there is a muscular pump that can move the fluid in and out of the nose and down into the VNO, providing a possible mechanism for odour molecules to get from the outside world into the VNO. Potentially, scent molecules can first be absorbed into the saliva, or into fluid in the nostrils, and then be pumped to the VNO. The resultant delay means that the VNO cannot be much use for detecting information that changes by the second, such as an airborne scent-trail, but should be adequate for an animal to analyse the scent of another member of its own species, which should remain constant. Thus the VNO is thought to be the sense organ that specializes in social odours, although not exclusively so: the roles of the VNO and the nose overlap considerably in this respect.

It is still not clear precisely what dogs use their VNO for. Part of the problem is that there is no obvious external sign that indicates when a dog's VNO is being brought into play. Cats and some other mammals – including the dog's close relative the coyote – make a characteristic facial expression when employing the VNO: the mouth is held slightly open and the upper lip is curled back, and the cat/coyote seems momentarily lost in thought. This expression is exhibited not when the animal is sniffing food – food odours are analysed by the nose in cats and coyotes – but when it is sniffing a scent-mark left by another member of the same species. Although dogs do not display the same expression, some dogs do chatter their teeth when they are sniffing scent-marks, and others make a kind of chortling noise. These sounds may be indicators that the pump that transfers odours into the VNO is in use.

The canine VNO thus certainly does *something*. Most likely it is used to analyse social odours, which the dog either licks up or inhales, simultaneously activating the pump that carries them to the VNO itself. Odours can thus be analysed twice – first, more or less instantaneously, by the nose and then for a second time, in a more leisurely fashion, by the VNO. The highly detailed information that emerges can then be stored away in the brain for use in future social encounters. This is yet another example of the dog's superiority over humankind in its ability to decode smelly information – but one that has thus far proved difficult for scientists to decipher, probably because we have difficulty appreciating a sense that we do not possess ourselves.

Whether they are perceived through the nose or the VNO, smells are very important to dogs, much more so than they are to us. Dogs use odour not just to decide what to eat and what not to: odour is their primary means of identifying people, places and other dogs. Smell is their dominant sense, the one they use in preference to all their other senses, whenever they can.

Because odours are so complex, and because they differ depending upon the environment in which the individual dog lives, it would be impossible for dogs to be born with the ability to recognize more than a handful of odours. Dogs therefore have to learn what each odour means. They start learning how to use their sense of smell even before birth, in much the same way that human babies learn the sound of their mother's voice while still in the womb.

Using ultrasound, scientists have observed puppies exercising their breathing muscles in the womb during the two weeks before they are born. This 'breathing' almost certainly allows the puppy to learn something about its mother's characteristic odour, including the type of food that she is eating most. In one experiment, pregnant bitches were given food flavoured with aniseed throughout the last three weeks before they whelped.[8] As early as a quarter of an hour after they were born, and before they had even begun to suckle, their puppies moved towards the smell of aniseed. The smell of vanilla, an odour that the puppies had never been exposed to, did not have the same effect, so clearly they were not simply investigating the aniseed because it was an unfamiliar smell. What had caused this preference for aniseed? Presumably it had flavoured the mother's amniotic fluid, where the pups had 'smelled' it before birth.

It is not clear precisely why puppies need to learn their mother's smell before they are born; it would probably be equally helpful if they learned it immediately after birth, since at that stage they are in any case too helpless to move far from their mother. (Prenatal learning is especially useful in animals such as sheep, where the young are much more mobile at birth, and thus run the risk of getting separated from their mothers.) Perhaps dogs have simply retained this ability from their mammalian ancestors, even though it is not of much use to them now.

From the moment they are born, puppies use odours to help them make sense of the world around them. Initially, this attention is focused primarily on the mother. Three days after she gives birth, the bitch produces a substance around her mammary glands that, in turn, is modified by bacteria on her skin to create an odour which helps her puppies locate her. It also seems to have a calming effect on them. Although the mechanism is somewhat obscure, the same substance appears to have a calming effect on adult dogs. Scientists are not agreed as to whether this change in behaviour is also caused by an instinctive, 'pheromonal' effect, or is due to a memory of being protected by the mother, but the extracted odour has proved useful in the treatment of acute fears in dogs.

As soon as they are able to move around, dogs start sniffing anything and everything they come across, a behaviour that continues for the rest of their lives. Many owners are embarrassed by their dogs' proclivity for sniffing the crotch of every person they meet; many more train their dogs not to do this. Yet this is the dog's first-choice method for identifying other animals, both human and canine. When two dogs meet in the park, their first and often only goal is to sniff each other. Sometimes they circle one another before diving in for a sniff. Sometimes one dog is so intent on sniffing the other that a chase ensues. However, in eight times out of ten the objective of the encounter is to get olfactory information about the other dog.[9]

Because both dogs attempt to be first to sniff the other, they often end up circling one another

The odours in question evidently originate at both ends of the body. Sniffing is often focused around the ears, indicating that these may be the source of an individual-specific odour. But although the ears definitely contain odour-producing glands, little is known about what kind of information is contained in the odours they produce. Sniffing under the tail must pick up odours from the preputial (male) and vaginal (female) glands that add their contributions to the dog's ubiquitous urine-marks.

However, the main target of canine sniffing seems to be the anal sacs. Located on both sides of the anus, as their name implies, these contain a pungent mixture of odours (mainly produced by micro-organisms) that varies considerably from one individual dog to another. Perhaps because the anal sacs are usually closed, their odours do not vary much from one week to the next, though they do change gradually over timescales of a few months or so.[10] They are therefore good candidates for a 'signature' odour, albeit one that will, like all chemical signals produced by mammals, require relearning by recipients as it changes gradually over time. This is presumably part of the explanation for dogs' insistent attempts to sniff the back ends of every other dog they meet; if the odour stayed consistent from one month to the next, they would need to do it only very occasionally. Such sniffing, like urine-marking, has origins that go back to well before domestication. Young male wolves have a similar fascination with sniffing this part of the body, and adult wolves sometimes actively invite other members of the pack to sniff them in this area, by standing stock-still with their tails held upright.

Scent inspections tend to follow predictable patterns. Some dogs, mostly males, go straight for the area under the tail, which produces an information-rich odour. Most females, and a few males, prefer to sniff the head of the other dog first, and then to move back, provided the other dog will let them. This difference between the sexes is so far unexplained, but it is also true of wolves, so it may simply be an inherited tendency with little functional significance as far as modern dogs are concerned.

Interestingly, while dogs love to sniff other dogs, it seems that most dogs do not much like being sniffed themselves. It is almost always the dog being sniffed that attempts to break off the interaction. While dogs want to find out as much as they can about other dogs' 'odour signatures', they seem reluctant to give away their own. (Young wolves share this reluctance, so this may be where this behaviour originated.) It is as if they see information about the dogs around them as the key to – well, something – since once the sniffing is finished the interaction usually ends. What that 'something' is, has yet to be resolved. If they are successful in their encounters, dogs go home from walks with lots of information in their heads about what the other dogs in their neighbourhood smell like. What they do with this information is currently unclear.

In fact, there is a great deal we do not know about the kinds of information dogs can get by sniffing each other. The anal sac may signify more than individual identity; for example, for a wolf it might also indicate which pack it belongs to, if members of a pack share an odour. Some components of the wolf's anal sacs may also vary according to gender and reproductive state. The same might be true for dogs, but at present we do not know. It is remarkable that we know so little about the one activity, sniffing, that dogs like to do the most. Nothing better exemplifies how human-centred we can be when thinking about our domestic animals. Somehow we fail to grasp the 'otherness' of much of what they experience. Of course, to dogs what something smells like is not 'other'; it is, if anything, more important than what it looks like.

The dog's fascination with odour must have originated way back in its evolutionary past. In particular, scent is a major mode of communication for a wide variety of animals (it is humans who are the exception, not dogs). Scent is a good way of transmitting information between animals that live far apart from one another. The early carnivores, the dog's remote ancestors, are very unlikely to have lived in groups. They were almost certainly solitary, defending territories against other members of their own kind. The only groups would have been mothers and their dependent young, who would have stayed together for a few months at most before the young were old enough to disperse. Communication between adults would therefore have revolved around establishing and maintaining territorial boundaries. Apart from courtship and mating, face-to-face meetings would have been a rarity. Not only that, they would also have been risky: being well-armed with teeth and claws, carnivores try to avoid disputes that damage both parties, not just the loser. Finally, these animals were probably nocturnal, inhibiting visual communication. In the natural world, all these issues can be circumvented by using scent-marking as the primary mode of long-distance communication. A scent-mark designed for the purpose can last for days. Messages can be left for recipients to pick up at some undetermined moment in the future, obviating any necessity for actual meetings to take place. Contemporary dogs, which have evolved from sociable animals and have become yet more sociable with domestication, may no longer need to scent-mark as frequently as they obviously think they do; but their wild ancestors must have found it very advantageous, and their legacy remains in our dogs' everyday behaviour.

Nowhere is this more obvious than in the dog's apparent obsession with depositing small quantities of urine as scent-marks. Male dogs are renowned for their routine raised-leg urinations, but females also urine-mark routinely: although they usually squat to urinate, many also use a 'squat-raise' marking posture. It is not entirely clear why females leave scent-marks; one clue may be found in the observation that bitches in Indian villages squat-raise around their lairs. The male dogs in the same villages perform their characteristic 'raised-leg urination' everywhere, but especially at the boundaries of their family-group territories.[11] Male wolves, particularly breeding males, also mark at territorial boundaries and along frequently used paths, presumably as a way of communicating with other packs nearby.

The domestic dog's passion for 'pee-mail' can therefore be traced back through its immediate ancestor, but this does not explain why pet dogs do it so enthusiastically today. Perhaps they would like to 'own' the area where their owners take them for exercise; however, because they have to share this with other dogs and their access is time-limited by their owner, they get caught up in a vicious cycle. Every time they go out, they find that the scent-marks they left yesterday have

'Squat-raise' urine-marking

been overmarked by other dogs. So they have to mark again to re-establish their claim to ownership, and so on and so on.

Scientists still do not know precisely what message is contained in each urine-mark, but it seems highly likely that dogs' urine carries an odour that is unique to each individual, one that can be memorized by others. It is also likely that in male dogs this unique odour contains contributions from the preputial gland as well as from the urine itself. What is less clear is how much other information is conveyed. For example, can a dog tell how large, how old, how hungry, how anxious, how confident another dog is, simply by sniffing its scent-mark? We cannot yet answer this question, but we do know that the main message carried by a bitch's urine, apart from her identity, comes from the vaginally produced scents that indicate the status of her reproductive cycle. Bitches that are willing to mate produce a powerful pheromone that can attract males from long distances. (Pheromones are chemical signals which are similar in all individuals of a species.)

However, scent does have one serious flaw as a communication medium, namely, that the message itself is very hard to control. Mammalian scent-signals are mainly produced by specialized skin glands (though they may be deposited mixed with normal body fluids or wastes – faeces or urine or saliva). These glands inevitably get invaded by micro-organisms; these alter the scent by adding metabolic products of their own, which can be pungent. If you had a nose as sensitive as a dog's, it would be like putting up a notice in front of your house where graffiti artists come along at unpredictable times and progressively alter whatever is on the sign, including obliterating your own name.

Some animals, dogs included, have handed over responsibility for producing the smell to the micro-organisms themselves. For example, bacteria on the mother's skin make the odour that newborn puppies use to orientate towards their mothers. Likewise, the anal glands of both male and female dogs (and many other carnivores) secrete a mixture of fats and proteins into the anal sacs to which they are attached, allowing the bugs to turn these into the more volatile chemicals that make up the odour itself. (Scientists have shown that if antibiotics are injected into the sacs, killing the micro-organisms, the secretion becomes almost odourless.) The 'graffiti artists' can now write what they like, but they can use only the 'colours' (fats and proteins) they are given, and thus the dog retains an element of control.

Such an odour is, however, both arbitrary and ever-fluctuating, placing limits on its usefulness. It is impossible to predict what it will smell like in advance, and if it is to be of any use in transmitting information, recipients will first have to learn what it means, and then relearn whenever it changes. Scent-marks that are intended to claim ownership of territory present an additional problem, since their whole point is that they should permanently identify individuals who are absent. If the odour of an owner's scent-mark changes from one week to the next, an intruder may mistakenly deduce that ownership of the territory has recently changed when in fact it has not.

A territory-holder can overcome this drawback by occasionally actually meeting his neighbours, thereby giving them the opportunity to make the connection between his appearance and his scent. If that scent is changing subtly over time, then those meetings need to be frequent enough for the connection to be maintained. This behaviour is known as 'scent-matching'; widespread in rodents and in antelope, it is less widely studied in carnivores, and not at all in dogs, despite there being every indication that they must be doing something like it.

Making and reinforcing the link between odour and appearance seems to be uppermost in many dogs' minds whenever they meet, suggesting that they do engage in a kind of scent-matching. It is likely that they memorize the odours of all the dogs they meet (why else go to the trouble of all that sniffing?) and then compare these with all the more indirect information that they get from sniffing scent-marks while they are out on walks – a kind of 'scent-matching'. If they do not find any match, then they may assume that the other dog lives far away; if they find a lot of matches, then the dog must live nearby. Since scent-matching is usually connected with territorial behaviour, perhaps domestic dogs perceive public parks and streets as a vast 'no man's land' between territories, always worth checking for occupancy in case they ever get the chance to live there.

Left to their own devices, many dogs prefer to use their sense of smell even when vision would appear to be more efficient. Trained explosives-search dogs always prefer to use their noses rather than their eyes, even in circumstances where visual cues might lead them to their target more quickly. However, dogs are also very flexible in their behaviour, and pet dogs quickly come to realize that we humans are much more attuned to visual than to olfactory cues. As a result, dogs can be successfully fooled into choosing an empty bowl rather than a bowl full of food, simply by having their owners point to the empty one.[12] Normally, of course, the dogs could have quickly identified the full bowl from its smell. This exemplifies the high priority that dogs put on social information, and also how well adapted they are to attending to the ways we, as well as they, communicate.

Moreover, since dogs can tell each other apart by smell, they can surely learn the characteristic odours of the humans they live with or meet on a regular basis. They can probably also tell a great deal about our moods from the way these odour cues vary. Dogs can be specially trained to alert epileptic or unstable diabetic owners when they are about to have a seizure or hypoglycaemic attack. There is little doubt that they do this by reacting to changes in the owner's odour (although minute changes in 'body-language', undetectable to human observers, may also be part of the cue). Even ordinary pet dogs can be trained to perform this service; no special olfactory ability seems to be necessary.[13] The implication is that all dogs are at least potentially able to monitor our moods based on the way our body odour changes. (Of course, they must simultaneously allow for, and possibly try to interpret, other causes of our changing odour, such as our state of health and the different foods that we have eaten.) If so, they are picking up, and presumably reacting to, a vast range of information about our lives that we ourselves are only dimly aware of.

Perhaps one reason why we can be so oblivious to the importance our dogs place on smell is how little they seem to suffer as a result of our ignorance. However, just as their ears can be damaged by the high levels of ultrasound produced by the clanging of metal kennel gates and furniture, dogs' noses must surely be insulted by what must seem to them to be the overpowering odours of our detergents, fabric softeners and 'room fragrances'. Presumably they just get used to them, accepting them as an unavoidable downside of sharing a living space with the humans they are so closely bonded to. In the hygiene-conscious world we live in, many of us do not like to let dogs do what they must feel compelled to do when they first meet us, which is to sniff us. I always hold out my hand to any dog I am introduced to (I make a loose fist first, in case the dog has a habit of nipping fingers). If the dog wants to lick my hand as well as sniff it, I let him. Not doing so would be as unsociable as hiding our face from someone we are being introduced to, and I can always wash my hand later if I want to.

Perhaps it is just as well that we have only recently started to become aware of this 'secret world' that dogs inhabit; otherwise we might have been tempted to interfere with it. We have certainly taken liberties with their visual communication, by breeding them into such diverse shapes and sizes. The potential for a Chihuahua and a Great Dane to misunderstand each other's visual signals seems almost unlimited, since they do not look like one another, nor indeed does either look much like a wolf. However, their scent glands, and the behaviour that enables them to use these to communicate effectively, seem for all intents and purposes to be intact. It is quite possible that dogs' reliance on scent has been their salvation, enabling even breeds that look extraordinarily different from one another to go on conversing with one another – at some rather basic, smelly level.

10

Problems with Pedigrees

Throughout most of this book, I have discussed dogs as if they were all roughly equivalent. For our purposes, this is very often true; despite some inevitable variations between breeds, all dogs share an evolutionary past, an acute sense of smell, a capacity for forming strong bonds with people and an ability to recognize one another as members of the same species and to interact with one another accordingly. However, dogs are self-evidently not all the same, and sometimes it is the differences between them that most affect their well-being. The differences between dogs are primarily imposed by us, not by the dogs themselves. Where mankind does not interfere with breeding, dogs look much the same; village dogs in Africa, for instance, are more or less similar. They

Changes in the rates of development of the basic wolf blueprint have led to today's extremes of size and shape

evolve into a type that is adapted to the environment they find themselves in. When humans start to choose which dogs to breed from, however, they generate dogs who are, by definition, less well suited to that niche. Initially, this probably did not matter at all. The capabilities that equip dogs to live on the street, alongside mankind, have gradually been replaced by those that allow dogs to live with man. These include not only changes that enable dogs to earn their living, such as helping with herding, hunting and guarding (to name but three), but also those that enable dogs to be good companions.

However, as this process continued, there must have been many dogs whose well-being was compromised by humankind's attempts to produce more extreme forms. For example, the Romans bred their mastiffs larger and larger, striving for fiercer and fiercer dogs. Some of these dogs must have been freaks – puppies too large to pass through their mother's pelvis, or dogs whose skeletons were too heavy for their joints and thus in constant pain. In those rough-and-ready days, with precious little veterinary care, a crude kind of natural selection would have prevailed. Dogs that were not viable would have been stillborn or would not have lived long enough to breed, and dogs too infirm to perform their intended task would not have been selected for breeding.

Like all animals, dogs are capable of producing far more offspring than is necessary for the continuation of their species. Unless a population is growing rapidly, this inevitably means that many individuals die before reproducing. As a general rule, those that die first are those least well suited to their environment. Many will have suffered before they died. This of course applies as much to village dogs as it does to dogs being bred by man for specific purposes. Nevertheless, the creation of new forms of dog inevitably left casualties in its wake.

Times have changed. In the West, we now believe in the right of each individual dog not to suffer. Puppies are no longer regarded as disposable items, to be drowned if unwanted. There is an outcry in the media whenever any cull of dogs is proposed, whether these be ferals, strays or unwanted pets. These are high standards indeed. We have taken upon ourselves the obligation to ensure that every puppy is a wanted puppy and will grow to be a healthy, happy dog. In many ways, we have succeeded in fulfilling these responsibilities. We have developed sufficient veterinary care to enable the majority of dogs to lead healthy lives. High-quality nutrition specifically designed for dogs is available in every supermarket, to the point that many have a healthier diet than some humans.

In other ways, however, we have failed our canine companions. In our seemingly insatiable quest for novelty, we have bred dogs which suffer from a vast range of avoidable ailments. And in our anthropomorphic need to see dogs as extensions of our own personalities, we have generated dogs that are unacceptably aggressive or have other temperamental defects. Their role as companions – a role they must fill if they are to be assured of leading physically and psychologically healthy lives – seems rarely to be the first priority. Novice owners can be faced with choosing between pedigree puppies, primarily bred for appearance rather than temperament, and rescue dogs of uncertain parentage, some of which may have been abandoned because they are the progeny of dogs bred for aggression.

Whereas dogs once made their own decisions about reproduction, nowadays in the West most matings are planned by humans. Over the past hundred years specialists have increasingly come to control dog breeding. At present, most of our pet dogs are either pedigree dogs or can trace their ancestry just a few generations back to crosses between pedigree animals. By comparison with the whole history of the domestic dog, this is a very recent phenomenon, and one that is geographically and culturally confined: genuinely ancient types of dog persist in many parts of the world. Nevertheless, most of the dogs available as pets to Westerners have pedigree ancestors.

The current rules for breeding pedigree dogs are causing profound and accelerating harm to their genetic viability. The current registration systems for pedigree dogs in the United Kingdom and many other parts of the world confine each breed to mating only with other members of the same breed. If this system were to be imposed totally, it would result in each breed becoming completely genetically isolated from all other dogs (in actuality, due to unplanned matings and occasional deliberate cross-breeding, only the pedigree breeds have been sequestered in this way).

Although most of these breeding regulations are very new – affecting only the most recent 1 per cent of the whole evolutionary history of the dog – they are already having profound effects on the dogs we see today. The genetic isolation of each breed has brought about a dramatic change in the dog's gene pool, inexorably reducing the amount of variation in each breed. The less the variation, the more likely it is that damaging mutations will affect the welfare of individual dogs: in order for a potentially detrimental mutation to actually cause harm, it generally has to have been present in both parents – and this is likely to occur only if the parents themselves are closely related. In some dog breeds today it is difficult to find two parents that are *not* closely related.

Until very recently, the amount of variation in the domestic dog was sufficient to maintain genetic health. Multiple domestications and back-crossing with wolves have meant that dogs worldwide still have an estimated 95 per cent of the variation that was present in the wolves during the time of domestication. Most of this variation lives on today in street dogs and mongrels, but pedigree dogs have lost a further 35 per cent. That may not seem much, but let us imagine the scenario in human terms. Mongrels maintain levels of variability that are similar to those found globally in our own species. In many individual breeds, however, the amount of variation within the whole breed amounts to little more than is typical of first cousins in our own species. And we humans know that repeated marriages between cousins eventually lead to the emergence of a wide range of genetic abnormalities, which is why marriages between close relatives are taboo in most societies. It is astonishing that the same consideration has not been given to dogs.

Just a handful of prize-winning popular sires are used to father the majority of puppies. This has tremendously restricted the gene pool. For example, about 8,000 new golden retrievers are registered in the United Kingdom each year, with a total population of perhaps 100,000. Over just the last six generations inbreeding has removed more than 90 per cent of the variation that once characterized the breed.[1] In a recent sampling of the Y (male) chromosomes of dogs in California, no variation at all was found in fifteen out of fifty breeds, indicating that most of the male ancestors of each and every dog in those breeds had been close relatives of each other.[2] Some of the other breeds surveyed had only a very little variation. In the context of the imported breeds in the study, such as the Rhodesian ridgeback, the boxer, the golden retriever, the Yorkshire terrier, the chow-chow, the borzoi and the English springer spaniel, this is not surprising. Assuming that all Californian examples are likely to have descended from a small founder population, limited gene pools are to be expected: much more variability might have been apparent if the samples had been taken in other countries. Of more concern was the lack of variation in the three American breeds in the study, since these are more likely to be representative of those breeds worldwide. There was no variability at all in the fifteen Boston terriers tested, and only a small amount in the twenty-six American cocker spaniels and ten Newfoundlands. Conversely, a couple of breeds recently derived from street dogs, the Africanis (or Bantu dog), and the Canaan dog, showed levels of variation similar to those in mongrels, but this can be ascribed to a deliberate policy among their breeders, who have seen the problems that popular sires have brought to other breeds of minority interest.

The inbreeding of dogs – though utterly deleterious to them – is potentially a huge boon to mankind. The canine genome was chosen by geneticists as one of the first to be sequenced, precisely because the occurrence of so many inherited diseases in today's pedigree dogs provides scientists with abundant opportunities to study, and then devise cures for, their (much rarer) counterparts in humans. The gigantic, if unintended, global experiment that is modern pedigree dog breeding promises to bring cures for many of our own diseases – and many years sooner than if the research had had to be conducted in mice or other laboratory animals. This will undoubtedly benefit our own species, but what about the dogs? If they could grasp the implications of what we have done to them, what would our dogs have to say?

The effects of selection for extreme shapes, sizes and conformations of dogs have been causing concern for more than two decades, on both sides of the Atlantic.[3] Even earlier than that, it had become apparent that the previously working origins of most breeds had been overwhelmed by the seemingly arbitrary demands of the show ring. Since then, as a result of defects due to the slavish application of breed standards, many breeds have become caricatures by comparison with their former appearance. Other problems, too, have emerged as a consequence of such breeding for extremes. For example, puppies of many of the round-headed breeds, such as bulldogs, pugs, pekes and Boston terriers, have to be born by Caesarean section because their heads are too big to fit through their mother's pelvis. By 2009, when a high-profile documentary on BBC television – *Pedigree Dogs Exposed* – raised the issue again in the United Kingdom, the extent of the suffering caused by selective breeding had become better documented.[4] Responsibility for selective breeding and its consequences must rest squarely with the breed clubs that control it.

Together, the breed clubs control a large proportion of the canine genome in the United Kingdom, the United States and most other Western countries. The competition is mainly between a few 'top breeders' within each breed, regulated by judges who are (or were) themselves 'top breeders'. Selective breeding towards the latest interpretation of the 'breed standard', leads to a variety of welfare outcomes that affect more and more dogs of that breed – not just those that become champions, but also many dogs destined to become pets. The UK Kennel Club publishes breed standards that are available to help prospective dog owners find breeds that suit their lifestyle. For example, they describe one popular companion breed, the Cavalier King Charles spaniel, thus: 'Characteristics: Sporting, affectionate, absolutely fearless. Temperament: Gay, friendly, non-aggressive; no tendency to nervousness.' No mention here that the whole of the modern breed is probably descended from just six individuals, and that the breed is prone not only to heart problems, but – more importantly, if you are one of these dogs – to cysts on the spinal cord that cause 'phantom' pains which the dog's behaviour clearly shows are very distressing.[5]

The various reports on the effects of pedigree breeding catalogue a wide range of insults to the welfare of dogs of particular breeds. They can be divided into two broad types. First, some are side effects of deliberate breeding for exaggerated characteristics. The problems of puppies with large heads that will not fit through the bitch's birth canal have already been mentioned; likewise, 'cute' folded skin on the face increases the risk of dermatitis, and the legs of the most fine-boned toy breeds are prone to painful fractures that can occur during normal canine behaviour such as jumping, to name but two others.

Second, the extreme levels of inbreeding (what those in the business refer to as 'line-breeding') have caused many heritable diseases to emerge in numerous breeds. These diseases are becoming widely documented, and although the genetic mechanisms behind them can be complex, essentially most arise because of accidental over-breeding from dogs that are carriers of a defective version of a gene. Usually, because they are only carriers, they are not themselves affected, and so the problem goes undetected until their descendants are mated together, producing some puppies with two defective copies of the same gene. Progressive retinal atrophy (an eye disease) in Cardigan Welsh corgis, is one well-documented example, as is 'rage syndrome' (episodic dyscontrol) in English cocker spaniels. Modern DNA technology, though expensive, has the potential to at least check the spread of inherited disease – specifically, through its ability to detect carriers that have no outward signs of the disease, as well as defects that do not become obvious until later in life, when the dog has already been bred from.

Other disorders are inherited in more complex ways, through interactions between many genes, but the general principle is the same. One common defect in many medium- and large-sized breeds is hip dysplasia, caused by loose ligaments around the hip joint – a condition that leads to pain, restriction of movement and lameness. In some breeds enough individuals with 'good hip genes' exist that the defect might eventually be removed from the breed by preventing dogs with poor hips from breeding. In others, such as the golden retriever, the main factor determining whether the hips fail turns out to be how the dog is exercised when young; in other words virtually all members of this breed have the genetic potential to develop hip dysplasia, and therefore it cannot realistically be 'bred out' unless the rules of pedigree are broken.

Correcting genetic defects within breeds is bound to be difficult. Removing all individuals affected by one defect from the breeding pool inevitably reduces the genetic variation within the breed, causing other defects to appear or become more prevalent. It is generally thought that such a strategy is truly effective only when several different strains coexist within a breed, as with show and working lines – *out-crossing* – and there may be resistance to this from their respective enthusiasts. The obvious solution, of course, is to open up the closed gene pools of the existing breeds, by cross-breeding, merging several breeds into one, or creating new ones by crossing two or more distantly related breeds. Paradoxically, although both of these ideas meet with strong resistance from today's breeders, they were the very mechanisms by which the nineteenth-century dog enthusiasts generated today's breeds.

With hindsight, it was inevitable that the shift in emphasis in dog breeding from function to appearance would be damaging to dog welfare. Wild animals, including wolves, are selected by the environment within which they live: a case of 'survival of the fittest'. Once one species becomes totally dependent upon another, as happened to dogs thousands of years ago, natural selection becomes relaxed in some areas. Dogs that perform arduous tasks, such as sheepdogs, have to stay fit and healthy above all else, and so their breeders are unlikely to select for traits that seriously impair welfare, hence the reluctance of many of the working-dog breed clubs to have anything to do with the show lines. In dogs that are bred for showing, deficiencies in fitness can be compensated for by their owners and through veterinary intervention. Provided they do not affect performance in the show ring, welfare problems can spread through a breed – problems due to deliberate selection for appearance as well as those that arise by accident through inbreeding. While most breed organizations make attempts to halt this process (some are even trying to reverse it), the evidence that such efforts have been largely unsuccessful in the past is there in the dogs themselves.

Selective breeding has also damaged dogs' abilities to communicate with each other. Since communication is crucial to harmonious social interaction, dogs whose repertoire of visual signals is restricted are intrinsically penalized. Those whose intentions cannot easily be gauged are often avoided by other dogs. Others, having been on the receiving end of unexpected aggression because they could not read another dog's intentions, become anxious towards all other dogs.

Indeed, the structures that the wolf uses for visual signalling have been drastically altered by the extremes of body conformation introduced by selective breeding. Jaws have been shortened, facial expressions hidden by loose skin or obscuring hair, ears permanently pricked up or hanging heavily, coats lengthened or made wiry so that hackles cannot be raised, legs shortened so that the dog cannot easily crouch, tails curled or docked. These changes have had a devastating effect on the visual signalling repertoire of many breeds; some, such as the Cavalier King Charles spaniel, seem incapable of emitting any of the wolf's visual signals (which number over twenty, at a conservative estimate). They no longer have access, therefore, to the primary mode whereby pack members can communicate with one another.

Many other breeds fare little better. In an attempt to quantify the effects of domestication on the ability to communicate, my colleague Dr Stephen Wickens and I once performed a study comparing the visual signalling repertoires of a whole range of breeds, from the least to the most wolf-like, from Cavalier King Charles spaniel to Siberian husky.[6]

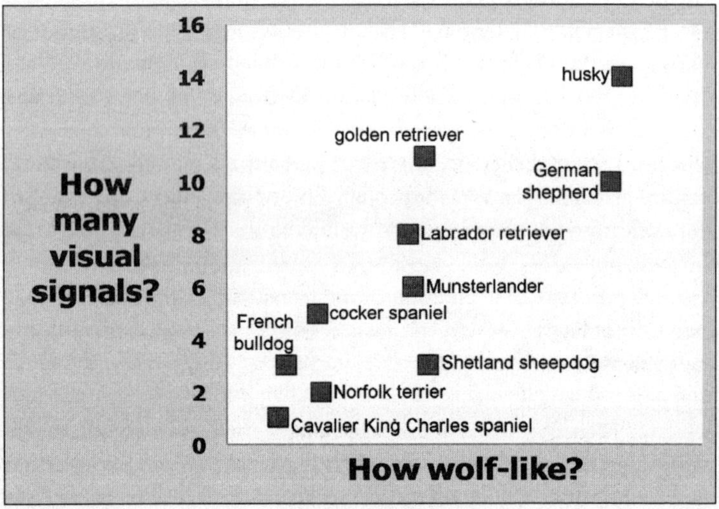

The number of wolf-like visual signals performed by a range of breeds, and how wolf-like those breeds are in general appearance (ranging from not at all on the left to very similar on the right)

Not surprisingly, the huskies were rated as the most wolf-like dogs in appearance, with a range of signals to match. In fact, their repertoire is essentially the same as the wolf's, probably retained to allow precise communication within groups kept as sled teams. Medium-sized gundog breeds such as Labradors and golden retrievers, as well as the Munsterlander, retain between half and two-thirds of the wolf's repertoire. So does the German shepherd, which was deliberately bred to look like a wolf but not to behave like one. These breeds retain a common set of signals that permit a fair range of visual communication, albeit not as sophisticated as the wolf's (see box – 'Canine Body-Language').

The smaller breeds in the study, from cocker spaniel down to Cavalier King Charles, performed very few discernible visual signals. The Cavaliers' only 'signal' was to push another dog out of the way – the universal language of shove, not really a signal as such. They could, if need be, back this up with a growl. Even more intriguing was the finding that the signals performed by the four breeds with the smallest repertoires – Cavaliers, Norfolk terriers, French bulldogs and Shetland sheepdogs – were almost without exception those that appear earliest in growing wolf cubs, such as muzzle licking and looking away. These breeds are not only arrested in terms of their growth patterns, but also in terms of the development of their ability to communicate in a wolf-like way. Although this study cannot be considered definitive, inasmuch as only a small proportion of breeds was sampled, it appears that breeds that have been derived by arresting the wolf's physical development – and are therefore, inevitably, smaller-than-average dogs – are handicapped by having the communicative abilities of a wolf cub. In addition to this general trend, more specific losses have occurred in breeds of all sizes: for example, the French bulldog's short coat, which prevents it from effectively raising its hackles, is also a feature of much larger breeds, such as Weimaraners.

Because so many dogs can no longer perform the full repertoire of canid behaviour, it is not always easy for dogs of different breeds to understand one another when they first meet. By deleting and distorting the wolf's range of signalling structures through breeding, we have messed around with the dog's visual communication system to the point where it simply does not work as well as it should.

Consider, for example, docked or immobile tails. Some breeds, such as bulldogs, have been bred to have very stiff tails that do not wag particularly easily. In many others, such as spaniels, it is traditional to amputate part or most of the tail, ostensibly to reduce the risk of injury. Docked tails are harder to see than entire tails, so dogs whose tails have been docked find it more difficult to communicate than dogs

CANINE BODY-LANGUAGE

Dog ownership can be made much richer and more rewarding by an in-depth understanding of how dogs signal to one another. This process would be much more straightforward if dogs all looked roughly the same, but fortunately there is a common underlying language that is there to enable both dogs and people to understand canine moods and intentions.

First of all, the dog's overall posture is a good indicator of its level of confidence. Dogs that are worried about the outcome of an encounter will tend to keep their body low to the ground, trying to look as unthreatening as possible, until they can be sure that the other dog means them no harm. A confident dog will stand tall.

Likewise, the lower the tail, the less confident the dog; dogs in retreat will usually tuck their tail forward between their hind legs. Precisely where 'low' is will vary from one dog to another, because selective breeding has affected where the normal, relaxed tail position is in relation to the horizontal: compare, for example, the tail position of a spitz dog (naturally curved and upright) with that of a greyhound (naturally low and straight). It is the change in position that signifies the change in intention. An upright tail with a wagging tip indicates interest; a relaxed tail that is being wagged from side to side using movement of the whole back end of the dog indicates excitement and/or a desire to play. Some dogs perform an exaggerated slow swish of their tails when they are contemplating aggression.

Moving towards the front of the dog, we find that the shape of its back can also be a give-away. If rigid, it can indicate a low level of fear or anxiety, although some breeds have naturally stiff backs. A rounded-up back may indicate indecision – the dog looks as though its back legs are trying to move forward while its front legs are trying to stand still.

Ears are easy to read in some dogs, harder in others; but even in breeds with rather rigid ears the muscles at the base of the ear may show what the dog is trying to say. Ears pricked forward suggest alertness and interest; ears pulled back indicate anxiety, and, if flattened as well, fear and an intention to withdraw. Tense eyebrows, often extending to the face in general, indicate threat, often accompanied by a fixed stare. In some dogs, this tension will also result in the whites of the eyes becoming (more) visible. A dog wishing to dissociate from an interaction will look away, often turning its head away so that it is at a right-angle to the other's. Relaxed dogs will hold their mouth loose and slightly open when interacting with other dogs; tense dogs will hold their mouths shut tight. Fear and anger alike can lead to the teeth being bared; the rest of the dog's body-language, from the ears backwards, should provide clues as to which of these two very different emotional states is applicable. The friendly 'grin' or 'smile', with teeth slightly bared, is the position of the mouth in the affiliation display, though many dogs will use it as a signal in its own right when interacting with people, presumably because it has been rewarded by extra attention due its superficial similarity to a human 'smile'. The 'cute' head-on-side posture is likewise not a species-typical canid signal but, rather, a posture that some dogs learn because it evokes a rewarding response from their owner.

whose tails have been left as they should be. In 2008, researchers studied the impact of docking on communication using a robotic model of a dog whose 'tail' could be made to wag by remote control.[7] After setting up the robot in an off-leash exercise area, they noticed that when its tail was wagging other dogs would approach it playfully, whereas when the tail was upright and motionless other dogs avoided it. These reactions are consistent with what we already know about the use of the tail in signalling. Then the scientists replaced the long tail with a docked version. When the short-tailed robot was let loose in the park, other dogs approached it warily whether the tail was wagging or not – as if they could not make up their minds how they were likely to be received. Although a real dog with a docked tail could probably overcome this shortcoming with other aspects of its body-language, the study clearly shows that tail-docking puts dogs at a disadvantage when interacting with their own kind. At the very least, they would feel anxious when encountering one another for the first time; at worst, miscommunication could lead to unintended aggression.

Unreliability of visual signals may well be a reason why dogs are so intent on sniffing one another when they meet. As far as we know, selective breeding has had little or no effect on dogs' abilities to communicate by odour. However, the very instability of odour signals as they are altered by micro-organisms means that they have to be continually relearned if a dog is to keep up to date with 'who smells like what'. Of course, to do so, dogs have to get close to one another, and in judging whether this is a safe manoeuvre, each must depend on long-distance, mainly visual signals from the other dog. Thus dogs cannot escape the problems of an unreliable body-language, even in this scenario.

As we know from observing their interactions with humans, however, dogs are very flexible when it comes to learning new signals and cues. This flexibility goes a long way to explaining why most interactions between dogs – even those with a limited repertoire of visual signals –

end without incident. Dogs are quick learners and can recall the identities of many other dogs, so they can presumably also learn to make allowances for the inevitable body-language deficiencies in dogs they have met before. In addition, they can modify, even completely alter, their responses, depending upon other information available to them. Who is sending the signal? Have I met him before? If not, have I met a similar dog before, and how did that encounter work out? What else is going on – for example, what is the context for the signal? Is the dog standing over a toy, or are other dogs watching us? It is usually to the receiver's advantage to take all of these factors into account before making its response, except on those rare occasions when the other dog appears to be about to attack, in which case immediate flight is probably a more sensible option. Moreover, each encounter provides more information about the signaller that can be stored away for use on a subsequent occasion. In this sense, dogs' native intelligence has enabled them to compensate, most of the time, for the liberties we have taken with their visual signalling structures.

Selective breeding for appearance is largely a product of the last 100 years; for far longer – probably since the earliest stages of domestication – man has been breeding dogs for behaviour. This tendency has continued right up to the present day, as dogs' roles continue to become ever more specialized and demanding. For example, the Guide Dogs for the Blind Association in the United Kingdom has developed a strain of golden retriever/Labrador retriever crosses that are particularly suited for guide-dog training. Much of this breeding has fitted dogs to particular working roles, thereby doing a great deal to strengthen the bond between man and dog. But in the contemporary West, where dogs' working roles have diminished, some of the more exaggerated behavioural traits – such as indiscriminate chasing and forceful territoriality – can be unhelpful for dogs whose primary role is to be companions.

One clear 'personality' difference between breeds lies in the extent to which they enact the predatory behaviour of their canid ancestors. Some dogs show no predatory behaviour even when you would expect them to do so: wolves, on seeing a small animal running away from them, would instinctively give chase – as would many dogs, especially the hunting breeds. Others, especially some of the guarding breeds, seem oddly uninterested. Although training plays a part, these differences between breeds are, at their heart, genetic.

The sheep-guarding breeds are extreme examples of this kind of unresponsiveness. Originating around the Mediterranean, these include the Pyrenean mountain dog, the Italian maremma, the Hungarian kuvasz, and the Turkish karabash and akbash. Many of them are entirely or largely white, bred to look more like sheep and less like wolves. Traditionally, these dogs were raised with livestock and then kept with the flock to guard it against predators. They therefore treat members of the flock as part of their own social group, confining their aggression to whatever they perceive as threatening to themselves or their flock. They do attack and kill rabbits, so some of their predator behaviour must remain intact. However, they have been reported as not knowing what to do with their kills – they simply carry their dead prey around until it falls to pieces. All dogs may be born with the ability to perform the various elements involved in predatory behaviour, but in some breeds some of these elements do not appear until adolescence, and thus never become integrated into the rest of their behaviour.[8]

On the other end of the spectrum are working collies, that display a different modification of predatory behaviour – albeit also for peaceful ends. Hounds and terriers used for hunting will complete the entire wolf hunting-sequence right through to consuming their prey, unless they have been trained not to, but this is essentially unreconstructed canid predatory behaviour; the aforementioned hunting elements are present, but subtly reorganized, in the collie. Herding sheep the collie way involves three key elements of predatory behaviour: the 'eye' (fixing the gaze, thought to be intimidating), the stalk and the chase. Collie pups start to perform these behaviours at a very early age, and integrate all three into their play. It is then possible for the shepherd to train the young dog to perform each of these separately, on command. The later and most violent parts of the predatory sequence – biting and, eventually, killing – are suppressed if necessary by training, although many collies seem to break off naturally after the chase. Herding ability in border collies is surprisingly heritable (in other words, some collies are born better herders than others), indicating some residual variation even within the breed. Thus selection for this crucial ability, while it must have been and probably still is intense, has not yet reached completion.

A working collie

Among dogs that do not work, many of the skills for which they were originally bred become redundant – or worse – in their companionship role. Sometimes this redundancy does not appear to present any problem; for example, many of the most popular companion breeds – such as spaniels and retrievers – are descended from working animals. But even in these breeds, there has been a tendency for separate 'working' and 'show' lines to emerge, with most pet animals coming from the latter. This implies that the dogs selected specifically for work may not fit the companion niche as well as they might. The conflict between working traits and the pet owners' requirements can be even more obvious in herding breeds such as border collies and hunting breeds such as beagles, both of which can require far more exercise and stimulation than the average owner is able to give.

In recent years those who regulate dog breeding have taken on more responsibility to inform prospective owners of breeds' working origins and the problems these can cause for an owner who is not prepared to adapt to them. For example, the UK Kennel Club describes the border collie thus: 'He needs a lot of exercise, thrives on company and will participate in any activity. He is dedicated to serving man, but is the type of dog who needs to work to be happy and is not content to sit at home by the hearth all day.'[9] Compare this to the official United Kingdom breed standard, which simply says: 'Temperament: keen, alert, responsive and intelligent. Neither nervous nor aggressive' – implying to the uninitiated that no collie will become nervous or aggressive, even though some that are denied the active life they crave can become both. (Some references to a breed's drawbacks are more oblique: 'There is no better sight than a Beagle pack in full pursuit, their heads down to the scent, their sterns up in rigid order as they concentrate on the chase. This instinct is mimicked in his everyday behaviour in the park: the man with the lead in his hand and no dog in sight owns a Beagle.'[10]) Nevertheless, prospective owners who take the trouble to investigate the behavioural needs of a breed that takes their fancy should nowadays be able to find fairly accurate information.

However, many of the traits that suit dogs to the companion role – strength of attachment to people, ability to cope with unexpected changes in their environment, trainability and so on – appear to vary as much within breeds as they do between breeds. While not denying that some breeds suit only active lifestyles, whereas others find it easier to adapt to the demands of modern city life, I must emphasize that it is often not so much a dog's breed as its individual personality that influences how rewarding a pet it will be – and how happy it will be in that role. Breed standards and descriptions can appear to describe a fixed personality (for example, 'Agile, alert . . . Should impress as being active, game and hardy . . . Fearless and gay disposition; assertive but not aggressive' – from the UK breed standard for the cairn terrier[11]) but scientific exploration of canine temperament has shown that this cannot be relied upon.

The most comprehensive study of dog behaviour genetics ever conducted was the Bar Harbor project, which started in 1946 and ran to the mid-1960s.[12] At the time, psychologists and biologists held diametrically opposed opinions about whether genetics influenced personality: the biologists maintained that many differences in character between individual animals (and people) were influenced by genes, while most psychologists held that personality was the product of an animal's early experiences. Dog breeds, at that point genetically isolated from one another for half a century or so, were chosen as the ideal starting point for answering such a question.

Five breeds, and crosses between them, were examined for consistent differences in behaviour. The scientists chose small-to-medium-sized breeds with reputations for having contrasting behavioural styles: the American cocker spaniel, the African basenji, the Shetland sheepdog, the wire-haired fox terrier and the beagle. They bred more than 450 puppies, many purebred, but also some that were crosses between two of the chosen breeds. They raised all of them under standard conditions, allowing the effects of any genetic differences to come through. As they grew up, the puppies were given a wide range of behavioural tests. Some of these examined spontaneous behaviour, such as play between puppies in each litter, and the response to being picked up by a person. Others tested how easy it was to train each dog to perform simple obedience tasks, such as walking to heel. Still others tested cognitive ability, such as how quickly it took each dog to learn to get through a maze or work out how to pull a bowl of food out from under a wire mesh cover.

A basenji

Surprisingly, when all the results were compiled, breed turned out to be less relevant to personality than had been expected at the outset. Although each breed was found to have some distinctive behavioural characteristics (for instance, the cocker puppies were much less playful than the others), it was only the basenjis that stood out from the rest. Although the descriptions in their breed standards said otherwise, the characters of dogs from the four American breeds overlapped a great deal. For example, although a 'typical cocker spaniel' personality could be identified (very dependent upon people, and rather unreactive and low in general intelligence), nine out of the seventeen pure-bred shelties, ten out of the twenty-five beagles and three out of the sixteen terriers (and even two of the sixteen basenjis) also had personalities of this type. Only the basenji, an ancient breed with distinctive 'village dog' DNA, were very different in their behaviour. Some of this distinctiveness could be traced to a single dominant gene, which manifested as a tendency among basenji puppies to dislike being handled until they were over five weeks old.

The basenjis aside, many of the behavioural traits that were measured varied almost as much within breeds as between them. The differences between individual dogs were found to be based upon seven different emotional traits (impulsivity, reactivity, emotionality, independence, timidity, calmness and apprehension) and only two traits of ability (general intelligence and the ability to co-operate with people). Whether the dogs performed well or badly in most of the tests had depended not upon differences in their 'intelligence' but, rather, on their emotional reactions to the situations they were put in, and their ability to glean clues from the experimenters about what they were supposed to do. Apart from the basenjis, which were much more reactive and inquisitive than the other four, the personalities of all the other breeds overlapped considerably.

Moreover, this study deliberately did not take into account a very important factor influencing a pet dog's character, its experiences during the first few months of its life. All of the puppies were raised under standard conditions, in order to minimize the effects of such experiences. In the real world in which prospective owners look for pets, such early experience can overwhelm most genetic factors. A cocker spaniel puppy born and raised in an isolated outhouse will behave much like a beagle raised under similar conditions – timid and frightened of anything out of the ordinary – and will be equally prone to developing fearful avoidance or aggression problems later in life.

Some breed organizations place insufficient emphasis on the role of environment in shaping a dog's behaviour. This is hardly surprising, as they are loath to admit that any of their breeders rears puppies under less than ideal conditions. A dog's character is the product of a complex interplay between its genetics and the dog's experiences while growing up. No breed standard for character can protect against the damage done to a puppy by keeping it in an impoverished environment for the first eight weeks of its life.

Perhaps the most important personality trait a potential dog owner will want to know about is whether or not a particular breed is inclined towards aggression. But are there meaningful distinctions between the breeds in this regard? The relative contributions of genetics and the environment in determining whether a dog is likely to bite are still hotly debated: one of the most contentious aspects of personality and breed-specific behaviour is whether aggressiveness is a genetic trait among dogs. It is universally accepted that aggressiveness can be affected by experience, but opinions differ where other contingencies are involved. Many experts now agree that much aggression in dogs overall is motivated by fear, not by anger, and that early experience and learning play a huge role in determining whether an individual dog turns its aggressive feelings into an actual attack. At the same time, however, genetic influences are hard to rule out. In the case of breeds designed for fighting and guarding, they must play a role, although rarely a deterministic one.

Since differences in experience were minimized in the Bar Harbor project, their data should be a good place to look for genetic effects on aggressiveness. All the dogs in the study were tested for aggressive tendencies according to a variety of scenarios, but these did not emerge in the analysis as one of the seven underlying emotional dimensions. Rather, aggressiveness was strongly linked to general reactivity – characterized by a generally rapid heart rate, rapid progress around obstacle courses, and so on. However, none of the five breeds selected for the Bar Harbor project, with the possible exception of the basenji, was especially noted for its aggressiveness, so this study cannot rule out the possibility that genetics may influence aggressiveness in some other breeds, especially those bred for fighting and guarding.

Aggression in such dogs is still an issue of real public concern, despite many measures taken to reduce the risks involved. Except in very carefully defined and tightly regulated circumstances, such as the training of police dogs for public order enforcement, aggressive dogs are unacceptable to most of society. In recent years, attempts to remedy the social problems caused by canine aggression have largely taken the form of breed-specific legislation, much of which has proved difficult to enforce. The laws vary considerably in detail from country to country, but most ban or place severe restrictions on ownership of pit bull terriers and similar breeds. But are pit bulls really different from other dogs, or do they simply have the right 'look' for those who wish to use dogs as weapons? The truth probably lies somewhere in between.

Pit bull

Reports of biting incidents are notoriously unreliable,[13] so care must be taken in considering whether a dog that has attacked someone was actually a pit bull. Since pit bull types generally lack authenticated pedigrees, pit bulls cannot be called a breed in the same sense that, say, cocker spaniels are. It is thus difficult to identify pit bulls as such; other breeds, most notably the Staffordshire bull terriers, are often mistakenly referred to as 'pit bulls'. Two other confounding factors may also contribute to the pit bull's reputation – (*a*) contagious over-reporting of biting incidents following one well-publicized occurrence, and (*b*) the deliberate choice of this type of dog by irresponsible owners.

Legislating against a whole breed can be justified only if there are underlying biological reasons why that breed should be aggressive. If, on the other hand, the main cause is irresponsible ownership, manifested as a desire to actually use the dog for fighting (or to merely give the impression of doing so), then outlawing one breed is unlikely to solve anything. Either the breed will be pushed underground, further into irresponsible ownership, or other breeds will take its place.

Pit bulls are certainly descended from dogs intended for fighting. The ancestry of today's pit bulls can be traced back to bulldogs. Bulldogs were used for bull-baiting in Britain until the sport was made illegal in 1835; after that, they were used for dog-fighting, on both sides of the Atlantic. Such dogs were selected over many generations for specific characteristics: a low level of fight inhibition; rapid escalation of any conflict, often omitting the usual threat communication; and absence of the bite inhibition seen in many guarding breeds, such as German shepherds, which grab and hold but usually do not shake and tear like pit bulls. (The 'locking jaw' of the pit bull is, however, a myth.) Breeders reputedly try to select against aggression towards people, for the safety of the owners and their families at least, but it is not clear that such selection is effective: since dogs in general are far more likely to choose their targets of aggression on the basis of experience than through genetically driven preference, they are apt to strike out against anyone they perceive as threatening – including their owner.

Although some pit bulls are unarguably dangerous, many are not. Granted, in 1986, pit bulls were responsible for seven out of eleven fatal dog attacks in the United States, making this breed at least thirty times more likely to have bitten than any other breed. However, none of these seven were breed-club registered animals, so it was impossible to quantify the effect of their ancestry on their aggression. Furthermore, it is likely that the way their owners had treated them, and especially the way they had trained them, had made the major contribution to their extreme aggression. Despite their fearsome reputation, the vast majority of the 1–2 million pit bulls in the United States at that time had probably never bitten anyone.

The connection between breed/personality and actual biting incidents is imprecise at best, even if one accepts that some breeds are genetically predisposed to be more likely to be aggressive than others, or that there is such a thing as an aggressive personality trait in dogs.

Even within so-called aggressive breeds, the dogs that actually attack are extreme outliers. Moreover, the reasons for their extreme behaviour are rarely investigated thoroughly – most are simply destroyed.

In short, there is no direct evidence that breed differences in aggression have much to do with genetics. A very high percentage of individual dogs in any breed, including those held to be the most 'dangerous', are not involved in attacks (see the table); in addition, the circumstances under which a dog expresses aggression are highly modifiable by each individual dog's experiences, including but not limited to training. Indeed, none of the statistics on dog attacks distinguish between the 'genetic' hypothesis on which the legislation is based, and the possibility that some breeds are much more likely to be kept by irresponsible owners.

Numbers of dogs involved in attacks on people and dogs in New South Wales, Australia, in 2004/5[14]

Breed	Number	% of breed (as registered)
German shepherd	63	0.2
Rottweiler	58	0.2
Australian cattle dog ('Kelpie')	59	0.2
Staffordshire bull terrier	41	0.1
American pit bull terrier	33	1.0
Others	619	

By contrast, genetic factors are much more evident in the inherent aggressiveness of wolf hybrids or 'wolfdogs'. Potentially more dangerous to their owners and the public than pit bulls and other fighting dogs, these crosses between wolves and dogs have achieved cult status over the past quarter-century, especially in the United States, where there may be as many as half a million of them. Wolves and dogs are adapted to such different environments that such extreme out-crossing was certain to produce animals that fit neither the wild niche nor the domestic one, and indeed wolfdogs are renowned for the unpredictability of their behaviour.

Wolfdogs have been held responsible for a disproportionate number of attacks on humans; for example, in the United States between 1989 and 1994 they were believed to be accountable for more human fatalities (twelve) than pit bulls (ten). There appear to be two distinct motivations behind such attacks. Some seem to originate in challenges over resources, as when a person tries to remove a wolfdog's food. Other attacks seem to stem from the wolfdog's perception of humans (especially children) as potential prey items, at which point they express their full range of predatory behaviour right through to the kill. Accordingly, the Royal Society for the Prevention of Cruelty to Animals, the Dogs Trust, the Humane Society of the United States, the Ottawa Humane Society and the Wolf Specialist Group of the International Union for Conservation of Nature Species Survival Commission all consider wolfdogs to be wild animals and therefore unsuitable as pets. Although the way a wolfdog is kept will undoubtedly affect whether it is dangerous or not, the wolf-type genes that it carries are undoubtedly the major influence on its behaviour.

But apart from these hybrids, the lack of any firm genetic basis for much 'dangerous dogs' legislation makes it unfair to dogs. On top of this, the slow-grinding machinery of the legal system can mean that enforcement of such legislation will make a bad situation considerably worse for dogs 'arrested' for biting. Most of these dogs are housed in kennels for months or even years while they wait for the courts to decide their fate, making retraining and rehabilitation all the more difficult or even impossible.

Aggressive dogs are clearly an issue of public importance, yet paradoxically they may not be the greatest threat to dog welfare that has been posed by selective breeding. Whenever dogs are selected for special aspects of their behaviour, there is a risk, as yet only dimly perceived, that they might suffer. This is because the choices that animals frequently have to make between one response to a situation and another are often driven by emotion. Natural selection keeps these connections functional. A wolf that is hyper-anxious or fearful or angry – or was over-attached to its mother in puppyhood – would be handicapped in its relationships with other wolves, and thus unlikely to become the breeder in a pack. Breeding dogs for specific segments of their behaviour has the potential to distort such checks and balances inherited from their wild ancestors. How do collies feel when they are unable to chase something? Wolves would not be bothered, because they feel an acute need to chase only when they are hungry. But in collies the connection between chasing, hunting and hunger must have been broken; otherwise, we could not get them to work safely with sheep. Since these connections have been broken, can we be sure that collies do not perpetually feel the need to chase something? The ease with which they become frustrated when not allowed to work, to the point of displaying stereotypical repetitive behaviour, suggests that this is entirely possible. Equally, it is plausible that protection dogs, bred and trained to have heightened sensitivity to challenges, feel anxious and/or angry much of the time, without necessarily displaying any outward signs. If such distortions are widespread, and the breed-specificity of many behavioural disorders suggests they are, then all breeders, not just show breeders, need to examine what they are doing.

Indeed, if dogs are to continue to remain popular as pets, they need some focused selection for the specific qualities that make them rewarding companions; it is no longer enough to put these in third place, after external appearance and behavioural traits that reflect the original working role. Selection for such behavioural traits may be complex, but is achievable, as evidenced by the many dogs that (perhaps more by accident than design) comfortably fit into this niche today.

Prospective owners, however, often select dogs more by appearance than by personality. Perhaps if dogs were not so variable in appearance, thereby offering owners so much choice on the 'outside', more emphasis might be placed on the 'inside'. Breed often determines how active a dog needs to be, and hence whether that type of dog will suit the owner's lifestyle. But personality and the likelihood that a lasting bond with the owner will develop are much less influenced by genetics than by environment, so owners would do well to focus instead on whether the environment in which the dog was raised has given it the best possible start for life as a pet.

11

Dogs and the Future

Dogs have been man's best friend for thousands of years, and maybe that is why we take them so much for granted. They have shown themselves to be supremely versatile, carrying out a vast range of tasks in addition to being rewarding social companions. But do they have the capacity to continue reinventing themselves as human society changes ever more rapidly? In my opinion they do, but they will need help along the way, help that canine science is ready to provide. Dogs and humans have rubbed along pretty well so far without either completely understanding the other. As I see it, we humans – as the senior partners in this arrangement – must take primary responsibility for ensuring that the relationship continues effectively into the future. Indeed, we should be working to improve the understanding between humans and dogs, using the most up-to-date science, so that dogs can continue to live harmoniously alongside us.

Dogs provide mankind with many benefits. Not only do they continue to work for us in the old, traditional ways, but we are continually finding new roles for them – tasks for which their agility, intelligence and ability to interact with the world are superior to our own. They also bring us the psychological benefits of companionship, providing relationships that complement those we have with members of our own species. Moreover, if we understand them properly, they can provide us with a fascinating glimpse into a different world, physically the same but perceived through different senses.

Canine science has brought us rich new insights into dogs' uniqueness. Until about a hundred years ago, man's understanding of dogs was no more than a branch of folk psychology, a tradition built up over thousands of years of trial and error. Science began to intrude towards the end of the nineteenth century, on two fronts: several of the early comparative psychologists, Thorndike and Pavlov among them, used dogs as convenient experimental animals, while Victorian naturalists and zookeepers provided the first comparisons with the wolf. A further burst of activity in the mid-twentieth century, an exchange of ideas between wolf biologists, canine geneticists and the first veterinarians to take an interest in behaviour, led to the first systematic understanding of the socialization process, yet also contributed a misinterpretation of wolf behaviour that has dogged canine biology ever since.

Now, at the beginning of the twenty-first century, a new opportunity has arisen to integrate concepts pertaining to wolf and dog behaviour, modern animal welfare science and new knowledge about learning and cognition, thereby allowing us to update our understanding of dogs and how they would like us to care for them. As is always the case with science, this understanding will need constant revision in the light of new information, but we know vastly more now than we did a hundred years ago about how to treat our canine companions. For one thing, dogs are recognizably canids, but they do not behave much like wolves. Superficial comparisons between any wild animal and the dog, which is perhaps the ultimate domesticated animal, are rarely helpful. Second, dogs have a unique capacity to form attachments to humans, and it is to people that their primary allegiances are directed. But it is only the capacity to form such attachments that is inborn: these have to be nurtured, primarily during the first three to four months of the dog's life. Third, dogs' sense of smell is much more sensitive than ours, and should be respected as such, not simply exploited.

These ideas are no-brainers, notions that any dog lover should find straightforward to accept, provided they have respect for the science that created them. As the scientific research becomes more widely disseminated through both the academic and mainstream media, it will be incorporated increasingly into the folk psychology of dog-keeping.

Dog training is one area in which the new canine science has met with strong resistance, to the point where some trainers and self-proclaimed 'behaviour experts' have openly and deliberately attacked the credentials of those trying to disseminate reliable, science-based information. The idea that the majority of dogs are continually trying to take over control of the households in which they live is proving very slow to die. So indeed is the use of physical punishment: shock collars, already widely available in the United States, are catching on in some quarters in the United Kingdom.

However, the situation is not simply one of punishment to prevent dominance versus rewards to encourage attachment. Some trainers decry the use of any kind of physical punishment, others see it only as a last resort, and still others as an essential and everyday part of the trainer's armoury. Disagreements over methods have sometimes spilled over into personal attacks. Those who decry physical punishment portray it as unnecessarily cruel, sometimes going so far as to suggest baser motives in those who use such techniques.[1] On the other side, some trainers accuse their opponents of actively promoting bad behaviour in dogs.[2]

All this polarization and recrimination may obscure the fact that there are several humane methods for training dogs, though their relative effectiveness has yet to be evaluated. There are probably as many ways of conceiving how to train a dog as there are dog trainers, but there appear to be four specific different facets of dogs about which trainers and behaviour experts disagree most vehemently.

The first is whether or not to portray dogs as 'pack animals'. Those supporting the 'pack' notion often appear to use it as a wake-up call for owners who over-anthropomorphize their dogs, treating them as little people. Since dogs are not little people and, indeed, can suffer if treated so, such reminders may be salutary, if applied in moderation and not to justify physical punishment.

The second is an ethical and philosophical dimension, related to welfare and well-being. Some trainers place no emphasis on the question of whether or not physical punishment will cause suffering, rationalizing it as an experience that the dog, as a barely reconstructed wolf, will expect to receive as part of its upbringing. At the opposite extreme are those trainers who abhor all forms of punishment, on the grounds that it will – by definition – cause suffering for the dog. Still others adopt a more moderate approach, maintaining that a certain amount of suffering can be balanced against the longer-term benefits that will accrue to the dog if it corrects its behaviour. They usually regard physical punishment as a last-resort technique, justified only when the dog's long-term well-being would otherwise be threatened.[3] For example, some justify the use of shock collars to punish livestock chasing, on the grounds that if the dog continued to engage in this behaviour, it would run the risk of being shot by a farmer, or euthanized. Bear in mind here that it is almost impossible in any training regime to avoid all negative feelings in dogs – even just ignoring them when they are performing unwanted attention-seeking is likely to make them anxious. Where these trainers may disagree is in where to balance the trade-off; suffering now versus benefit later.

Third, trainers make very different assumptions about dogs' cognitive abilities. Paradoxically, perhaps, trainers who work within the dominance framework have to presume an almost Machiavellian level of canine intelligence: the dog needs to be very smart indeed, smart enough to hoodwink its owner and thereby attain 'dominant' status in the household. In the other camp, reward-based pet dog trainers rely on quite straightforward associative learning, both because it works, and because it is easy for owners to understand how to implement it. Their methods tap into some of the most primitive parts of the dog's brain; they essentially sidestep the issue of how smart dogs may or may not be, relying on learning methods that evolved many millions of years ago. The point here is not that reward-based trainers think dogs are dumb, but rather that simple training methods are easier to teach to owners than complex ones. Guide-dog training, for example, while reward-based, makes much fuller use of the dog's cognitive abilities.[4] But ideally, all training could take advantage of these abilities, including, for example, the dog's capacity for social learning which canine science is still in the process of revealing. Exploring such possibilities should be more profitable in the long run than pursuing ideas for which science has found no supporting evidence.

Fourth, some trainers – especially those who train gundogs, sheepdogs and guard dogs – come from traditions that portray dogs primarily as tools. One method they advocate is to keep the dog in a kennel, away from what they view as excessive human influence. Others see the dog's natural place as an integral part of human society, and insist that training should first and foremost serve to reinforce that bond, even if the dog also fulfils a function. For example, the security services in the United Kingdom are currently divided over whether patrol dogs can be kept at the handler's home or must be confined to kennels when off duty. Given that such dogs need to be acutely attuned to people when they are working, it seems unlikely that this ability would be refined by long periods of isolation; moreover, no evidence has yet emerged that the kennel-housed dog is actually the more effective worker.

The differences between various schools of dog training are thus much more complex than the question of whether punishment is considered cruel or not, or whether or not trainers conceive of dogs as wolves. Their underlying philosophies and ethical standpoints are also different, so it is perhaps not surprising that they so often misunderstand, even misrepresent, one another. This is not helpful at a time when society expects dogs to be under the control of their owners to a greater extent than perhaps ever before.

Discipline in the sense of control, not discipline in the sense of punishment, is what is needed. Clearly a dog is not going to learn how to behave well simply and solely because it is loved, even though I suspect that is what many owners would like to happen – and may even expect to happen. Today, as I went jogging in the park near my house on the first sunny day of the year, I encountered nine dogs being walked off-leash by their owners. Only one out of the nine responded immediately when their owners wanted to recall them. The others all caused mild embarrassment for their owners, bouncing up at children, chasing cyclists, getting in the way of walkers, trying to scrounge food from picnickers, and so on. Assuming this very small sample is typical, such behaviour must contribute to giving dogs a bad name.

I do not know what methods, if any, these owners had used to try to train their dogs to come back to them on command, but I am willing to bet that many had tried punishment. Certainly I saw several owners remonstrating with their dogs once they were able to prise them away from whatever they had been doing. Although this may have been more for the benefit of the people their dogs had been annoying than for the dogs themselves, it is unlikely to have promoted the idea in dogs' minds that coming back to their owners is a pleasant thing to do. It is more logical and straightforward to train dogs to come back to their owners because they want to, rather than because they are scared not to, so there is clearly still a big gap between the ideal and the realities of dog ownership.

Proper understanding of training techniques and their diligent application are not only essential from a social perspective, but also good for the dog–owner relationship. Moreover, it has been known for nearly two decades that attending training classes results in a more fulfilling dog–owner relationship.[5] Most dogs and their owners, whether they know it or not, desperately need easier access to better standards of dog training, but at present they are faced with what must be a bewildering variety of claims and counterclaims from the various schools of trainer.

Unfortunately, there are no universally recognized standards for dog trainers.[6] The deep divisions between the various camps within the world of dog training, fuelled by the rise of the Internet, have instead resulted in an explosion of 'registers', 'associations', 'guilds' and 'institutes', each claiming to be the last word in training and the treatment of behavioural disorders. Currently, the list of associations in the United Kingdom includes the Association of Pet Dog Trainers, the Centre of Applied Pet Ethology, the Association of Pet Behaviourists and Trainers, the Canine & Feline Behaviour Association, the Association of Pet Behaviour Counsellors, the UK Registry of Canine Behaviourists, the Professional Association of Applied Canine Trainers, the British Institute of Professional Dog Trainers, the Guild of Dog Trainers, the Academy of Dog Training & Behaviour Approved Instructors, and the Kennel Club Accreditation Scheme for Instructors in Dog Training and Canine Behaviour. Faced with such a bewildering array of titles and their even more confusing acronyms, how are novice owners to choose a trainer who not only can satisfy their needs but also matches their ethical standpoint? In the United Kingdom, the Animal Behaviour and Training Council is attempting to bring some clarity to this confusion. In the United States, at least three sets of dog-training guidelines exist, one in the mission statement of the Association of Pet Dog Trainers (APDT), one published by the Delta Society and one disseminated by the American Humane Association. Effective self-regulation of the dog-training industry will be essential if we want to improve the lives of dogs (and their owners) in the twenty-first century.

*

Just as vexed as the question of proper training techniques is the question of what the next generations of dogs should look like, and where they should come from. The majority of dogs in Western countries are pedigree animals, produced by breeders who, to a greater or lesser extent, are associated with the world of dog shows and breed standards. It is now abundantly clear that this bias, and its genetic consequences, do not serve the best interests of dogs.

That said, rescue dogs can also be problematic. Many of the dogs that end up in rescue are already psychologically troubled. They are therefore ill-equipped to cope with the 'rescue' itself, which involves an indeterminate period of kennelling, and, if they are lucky, rehoming. Such dogs find unfamiliar environments and new routines highly stressful, so the rescue process, however necessary, must be managed carefully if it is not to tip an already fragile personality further towards instability. Although some dogs are rehomed because of genuine changes in the owners' circumstances, many more are given up due to behavioural problems. Of the dogs relinquished to the Dogs Trust rehoming charity in 2005, 34 per cent were due to problematic behaviour, and 28 per cent more were abandoned because they 'needed more attention than could be given'[7] – a category which sounds as though it could include many dogs with separation disorders.

Improved understanding of how to deal with behavioural disorders, and indeed how to prevent them in the first place, might therefore eventually revolutionize dog 'rescue'. For now, however, the best strategy is prevention, mitigation of the circumstances that put dogs into shelters in the first place. Each year, millions of dogs end up in kennels run by local authorities and charities, in many cases because their owners have, largely through ignorance, mismanaged their behaviour. Once sufficient numbers of people are properly trained in how to recognize and deal with the simpler behavioural problems of dogs, it may be possible for the charities to shift away from their current default of taking the dog into rescue kennels. They might then be able to focus more on working with owners to correct the behaviour in their own home, thereby eliminating the need for the stressful intermediate of kennelling. (The dogs which find kennelling least stressful are generally repeat offenders – a finding which further emphasizes this point.)

Of course, even in the West, more dogs are born each year than there are owners for, and thus many abandoned dogs never make it to new homes. Tens of thousands of unwanted dogs are destroyed in the United Kingdom each year. In the United States, more than a million abandoned dogs are euthanized annually. Although as many as a quarter of these may be essentially unhomeable because of chronic disease or extreme old age, the number needlessly destroyed indicates a serious mismatch between supply and demand for pet dogs. Euthanasia, when properly conducted, should not be a welfare issue in itself, since the dogs are presumably unaware of their fate. However, it is most definitely an ethical issue, one whose acceptability must ultimately be decided by human, not canine, society. Canine science itself cannot therefore provide any kind of answer.

Moral trade-offs regarding animal euthanasia have changed considerably with time, and today vary substantially between cultures. Dogs in many non-Western countries (and, albeit to a declining extent, in some Western countries as well) experience a spectrum of welfare issues very different from those in the United States and Western Europe. In some societies, it is still commonplace to let dogs roam the streets, and traditions of ownership may be different; for example, dogs may be fed and cared for by a whole community rather than having a single, legally identifiable 'owner'. But free-roaming dogs contribute to numerous problems: they may potentially transmit diseases such as rabies, become a nuisance through fouling and noise, cause traffic accidents and injure livestock or humans. Population control under these circumstances is often a necessity, whereby the welfare emphasis has to shift from the individual dog to that of the population as a whole: for every dog that is euthanized in a cull, another's welfare may be improved as reduced competition allows it an adequate share of the community's resources. (This is particularly true if a sterilization programme is put in place simultaneously to prevent the population from rebounding to its former level.)

Although village dogs have more control over their own lives than pet dogs and are in that sense more 'natural', their individual welfare is often compromised. They have little or no access to veterinary treatment for disease or injury; they may go hungry, they may be mistreated by people who know that they will not be penalized for doing so. Those village dogs that are alive today are a population of survivors; over the generations, vast numbers less suited to the environment they live in (for example, less resistant to local diseases or parasites) will have died without leaving offspring, and most will have suffered before they died.

The modern pedigree dog lies at the other end of this spectrum, inasmuch as we aim to protect the welfare of each individual animal throughout its lifespan. We shield our dogs from the most dangerous aspects of the man-made environment, for example leashing them near traffic. We feed them nutritionally complete and biologically safe foods. We give them veterinary care that seeks to reduce discomfort and pain. None of these advantages are routinely extended to village dogs.

In taking dogs into full ownership, removing their 'right' to breed at will, we should be able to improve their individual welfare. Unfortunately, although all concerned state that they have dogs' welfare at heart, the result has not been an unqualified success. One set of challenges to welfare – those imposed by the outside world and by competition between dogs – has been replaced by another: those that have emerged as the inexorable consequences of inbreeding.

No one is advocating a return to a free-for-all where pet dogs choose their own mates in the way that village dogs do. Controlled breeding is not inherently bad for dogs. By artificially controlling breeding, we have the power to prevent the birth of those dogs that are more prone to suffering, thus raising the overall level of canine welfare. Unfortunately, and despite many good intentions, mankind has not entirely succeeded in this endeavour. Many pedigree dogs suffer from debilitating conditions that are the direct result of our choosing which animals to breed from, and which not to.

We must radically change the way that dogs are bred – not only to eliminate genetically based defects, but also to establish temperaments that maximize dogs' capacity to become rewarding pets. Currently, most dogs born each year are the outcome either of the 'show ring' mentality, or of unplanned matings. Neither approach is primarily designed to produce pet dogs.

One possible alternative is the commercial breeding of dogs specifically intended to be pets, with no regard for the artificial demands of the show ring. After all, if owners are prepared to pay several hundred pounds for a puppy whose parents have been selected primarily for conformity to a breed standard, might they not be persuaded to pay the same amount for a dog designed specifically for life as a pet? So far, commercial pet breeding has not lived up to its potential. 'Pet factories' are beginning to appear in continental Europe, producing dogs specifically for the pet market; some are derived from existing breeds such as golden retrievers, but there are others too, such as the 'boomer', which is usually a fluffy, mainly white, toy dog that trades on the popularity of the fictional (dog) star of the television show *Boomer*, and can thus claim to be a new type of non-pedigree companion dog. However, there is little indication so far that the products of these establishments make better pets than the average dog from show-ring breeds.

While it should theoretically be possible to get the genetics right in a commercial setting, there is some doubt as to whether it will ever be commercially viable to provide puppies with all the socialization that they need during the first eight weeks of their life, before they are put on sale. In a strictly commercial setting, it would simply be prohibitively expensive to arrange for all the experiences that puppies require during their socialization period, to say nothing of the logistical difficulties that would accrue once the puppies are the right age to be displayed for sale. Commercial breeding is therefore unlikely to produce perfect pet dogs for any but the well-off few.

If dog-keeping is to retain its mass appeal without compromising the welfare of the dogs themselves, small-scale enthusiast breeders should be encouraged to continue to provide the majority of pet dogs. These hobby breeders, who breed dogs because they love them, have the opportunity to provide adequate socialization at no financial cost to themselves, simply by keeping the puppies and their mother within their own home rather than in an isolated pen or kennel. Indeed, small breeders – provided they start with the right stock, and implement the most up-to-date information on how to provide socialization – still have the potential to turn out the best pet dogs.

Genetic engineering, on the other hand, is unlikely to significantly improve the welfare of dogs. Despite the myriad shapes and sizes that dogs already come in, some constraints still linger on, imposed by the developmental trajectories of the wolf. Radically new kinds of dog could hypothetically be generated if the dog's gestation period, currently fixed at from sixty to sixty-three days, could be altered from that of the wolf. Incorporation of genes from other canids might make it possible to generate dogs that look more like foxes, or like the round-headed and undeniably cute bush dog.[8] Yet while this approach would undoubtedly generate novelties, along with a great deal of controversy, it is not what is needed to save the dog. More than enough genetic variation already exists among today's dogs to generate a wide variety of animals well suited to life as pets; what is needed, then, is to recognize this role as the dog's main function, and take the initiative away from those who conceive of dogs as a means to win prizes, whether in the show ring or the working trial.

Nor is another application of genetic engineering, cloning, the solution to producing the perfect companion dog. Texas billionaire John Sperling had his border collie/husky cross Missy cloned, and the clones certainly do look like her. But was he primarily fond of Missy's looks or her personality? Because dogs' personalities are largely the product of their early life experiences, they cannot be replicated using *in vitro* genetics.

So what are the barriers that impede the development of a better companion dog? Leaving aside the appearance of such a dog for a moment, there seem to be at least two. The first is that dog breeders rarely decide which dogs to breed from based on which ones have proven themselves the best companions. They may lack information concerning how well the animals they have produced have fulfilled their function as companions. Or they may be primarily focused on whether or not their dogs will be competitive in the show ring, even though most dogs are not purchased for competition. Moreover, it is difficult to hold breeders to account for the quality of the puppies they produce. Failures can readily be blamed on mistakes made by inexperienced owners who have purchased puppies – feeding them the wrong diet, not giving them enough exercise, giving too much exercise, and so on.

The second barrier is a classic Catch-22: the more responsible the owner of a dog, the more likely that dog is to be neutered. In short, many of the most carefully selected and nurtured dogs, those that fit the companion niche perfectly, almost never pass on their genes to the next generation. Filling their place in the population are puppies produced more or less by accident by irresponsible owners, many of whom are attracted to 'status' dogs such as Staffordshire bull terriers and German shepherds (hence the large numbers of these breeds and their accidental crosses that end up, and often end their days, in rescue). While all dog owners are rightly encouraged to neuter their pets in order to reduce the oversupply of dogs, doing so unfortunately works against the goal of creating a more companionate population of dogs.

Also unfortunate is the fact that breeding for personality is not as straightforward as breeding for looks. Part of the explanation is that genes do not code for behaviour as such, but another part is that the companionship role itself is not clearly defined. Presumably every dog owner and prospective owner has an ideal dog in mind, so there are many such ideals. Yet certain traits seem universally desired. According to research conducted in Australia by Pauleen Bennett, most people there believe that companion dogs should be friendly, obedient, robustly healthy, easy to manage, safe with children, easily housetrained, and able to show affection to their owners.[9] (It seems plausible that such traits would be valued in most Western countries.) Many owners also value physical contact with their dog – an unsurprising finding, given that we now know that stroking a dog not only reduces stress hormones but also leads to a surge of the 'love' hormone, oxytocin.

Other characteristics are rated differently by different owners. Some people prefer a dog that is friendly towards everyone, others, especially men, value a degree of territoriality that they see as helping to protect their household. Men also tend to express a preference for energetic, loyal dogs, while many women give a higher rating to calmness and sociability.

But more importantly, most owners simply do not prioritize personality when they are picking out a dog: for example, many rate looks over good behaviour, and view trainability as relatively unimportant, even though they expect dogs to be obedient. In addition, the reality of what type of dog best fits a person's lifestyle will also change as that person's circumstances change. Although dogs' lifespans are shorter than our own, they are still long by comparison with the modern pace of change in lifestyles.

That said, personality-based selection becomes even more challenging when we consider how many variations there can be, even within a breed. Many of the 'companion' traits listed above are only marginally influenced by genetics. Genetically based physical abnormalities and predispositions to disease can – and should – be targeted through more enlightened breeding, but many other desirable traits such as friendliness, obedience, lack of aggression and a predisposition to affection are strongly influenced by early environment and learning. It is difficult to see how such traits could be actively selected for without, in parallel, improving owners' understanding of how to inculcate them into their new dogs or puppies.

Companionship traits may be difficult to select for, but certain other type-specific, behavioural traits need to be reduced in companion dogs. Most of the genetic selection imposed upon dogs during their long association with man has been directed towards useful traits such as ability in herding, hunting and guarding. But now that most dogs in the West are no longer required to carry out such tasks, we need to reduce these links; otherwise, frustration will ensue. I have lost count of the times that I have been asked for advice on whether a cute sheepdog puppy will make a good pet. I always say 'No, these dogs are bred to work and will probably find living in a town intolerable.' Yet most of the people I have advised in this way have gone ahead and got sheepdogs anyway, and most have regretted doing so – though not as much as would the dogs concerned, if regret was in their emotional armoury. If such breeds are ever to fit the companion niche, we need to reconfigure them so that they no longer feel this way.

Finally, although the extent to which we can breed dogs for companionship roles is limited, we must also be careful about going too far in the opposite direction – by increasing our dogs' capacity for affection to the point where it becomes a burden to them. There is already an epidemic of separation disorders among companion dogs; a dog that was overwhelmingly motivated to be with people would presumably also suffer disproportionately if left alone. Most owners do not want their dog to be too 'clingy' (or indeed too bouncy: companion dogs are required to be inactive an average of three-quarters of their lives).

There is no reason why more dogs cannot be better fitted into the companion role that many of them clearly already fulfil well today. It is to be hoped that the pressure now placed upon breed clubs to produce happier, healthier dogs will not only succeed, but also spark a reappraisal of what the show ring is intended to produce: greater emphasis on dogs' role as companions and less on their largely outmoded roles as working animals. Furthermore, dogs not only need to be bred as companions, they need to be raised as companions, and the most efficient way for this to happen is for puppies to be born in domestic environments, not in barren outdoor kennels or sterile commercial production units. There are considerable challenges to be faced before rearing methods improve, not only because many breeders still underestimate puppies' need for socialization, but also because there is no obvious mechanism whereby best practice will become widespread, given the sheer number of people involved. The information that breeders need in order to produce well-socialized puppies is now widely available, and its universal adoption should be just a matter of time.

Even if this information is thoroughly disseminated, however, irresponsible breeding is unlikely to go away. The rehoming charities will inevitably take the brunt of coping with the unwanted dogs that result. But fortunately, they increasingly have available to them the information to adopt more science-based methods for rehabilitating such dogs, and for raising understanding among adopting owners of what makes dogs behave the way they do.

Looking into the future, I predict that dogs will need all the help they can get, from scientists and enthusiasts alike. Dogs were first domesticated to live in small villages and rural communities, and there is no doubt that tensions arise, both between dog and owner and between owner and non-owner, when dogs live in modern cities. As the globe becomes progressively more urbanized, such unease may spread.

Dogs in the West will never be able to return to the freedoms they enjoyed in the first half of the twentieth century, when many were allowed to roam city streets during the day, meeting (or avoiding) other dogs as and when they chose, before returning to their owners in the evening. Society requires much more of dogs, and dog owners, than it did then. The public's attitudes towards hygiene in particular have hardened in the past twenty years, with poop-scoop laws becoming almost universally adopted, and more people openly expressing a dislike of touching or being licked by a dog. More people also seem to be allergic to dogs than ever before (although, paradoxically, scientists now think that contact with dog allergens in infancy is actually protective against the development of this allergy). Dogs are now expected to behave well at all times, especially in public, and the number of places where owners can exercise dogs off-leash has been considerably reduced. If this trend continues, pet dogs could potentially turn into a barely tolerated minority interest, especially in cities.

There was a time in the early years of this century when it looked as though the dog populations in both the United Kingdom and United States were beginning to shrink, as though every dog had, indeed, had its day; the best estimates now suggest that the dog population may be at least levelling off. Cats are now at least as numerous as dogs in both countries, mainly because they suit modern lifestyles whereby all members of a household work, and the time and space for exercising a dog are restricted. How popular will dogs be at the end of the twenty-first century? Addressing the twin pressures of misguided breeding and poor understanding of canine psychology is crucial to ensuring that dogs remain as significant a part of human life as they have been for the past ten millennia. My hope is that this book will make some contribution towards that goal.

Further Reading

Most of the source material for this book has consisted of papers in academic journals, which are often difficult (and often expensive!) to access for those without a university affiliation. I've included references to the most important of these in the notes, but in addition I can recommend the following books, most of them written by knowledgeable academics but with a more general audience in mind.

Wolves: Behavior, Ecology and Conservation, edited by L. David Mech and Luigi Boitani (Chicago: University of Chicago Press, 2003), provides detailed up-to-date information on wolf biology from a host of experts. Older books on wolves are less useful because they contain misconceptions about the organization of wolf packs.

Dog Behaviour, Evolution, and Cognition, by Ádám Miklósi (Oxford: Oxford University Press, 2007), is currently the standard textbook on dog behaviour and contains a great deal of detailed information on domestication, on canine cognition, and on the way dogs perceive people, although Miklósi's conclusions are not identical to mine.

There are few readily accessible accounts of social behaviour in dogs that draw on up-to-date science, apart from Ray and Lorna Coppinger's *Dogs: A New Understanding of Canine Origin, Behaviour and Evolution* (London: Crosskeys Select Books, 2004).

Carrots and Sticks: Principles of Animal Training (Cambridge: Cambridge University Press, 2008) by Professors Paul McGreevy and Bob Boakes from the University of Sydney, Australia, is a fascinating book of two halves: the first half explains learning theory in accessible language, and the second contains fifty case-histories of animals (twelve of them dogs) trained for specific purposes, ranging from film work to bomb detection, each illustrated with colour photographs of the animals and how they were trained.

Karen Prior, Gwen Bailey and Pamela Reid are among the dog-training experts whose many books are worth looking out. Paul McGreevy's *A Modern Dog's Life: How to Do the Best for Your Dog* (New York: The Experiment, 2010) is full of indispensable advice for dog-owners.

For more information on the effects of early life events in humans and animals, I can recommend *Design for a Life: How Behaviour Develops* by Patrick Bateson and Paul Martin (London: Vintage, 2000). If you're looking for practical advice on choosing and raising a puppy, I suggest *Before and After Getting Your Puppy: The Positive Approach to Raising a Happy, Healthy, and Well-Behaved Dog* by Ian Dunbar (Novato, Calif.: New World Library, 2004), or *The Perfect Puppy: How to Raise a Well-Behaved Dog* by Gwen Bailey (London: Hamlyn, 2008).

Patricia McConnell's *For the Love of a Dog: Understanding Emotion in You and Your Best Friend* (New York: Ballantine Books, 2007) is an excellent and accessible account of current understanding of canine emotions. Alexandra Horowitz provides an enlightened integration of recent research into dogs' sensory and cognitive abilities in *Inside of a Dog: What Dogs See, Smell and Know* (New York: Simon & Schuster, 2009). Sophie Collins's *Tail Talk: Understanding the Secret Language of Dogs* (Chichester: Bonnier Books, 2007) is a good pictorial guide to canine body-language. David McFarland's *Guilty Robots, Happy Dogs* (Oxford : Oxford University Press, 2008) is more about robots than dogs, but covers the various and highly complex philosophies of self-awareness and consciousness.

The sensory worlds of animals is a rather neglected topic. For a general introduction into how the sensory worlds of animals affect their behaviour, the late Professor Chris Barnard's textbook *Animal Behaviour: Mechanism, Development, Function and Evolution* (Harlow: Prentice Hall, 2003) is excellent. Tristram Wyatt's *Pheromones and Animal Behaviour: Communication by Smell and Taste* (Cambridge: Cambridge University Press, 2003) provides a thorough coverage of odour communication across the whole of the animal kingdom.

The pioneering work on breed differences in behaviour, John Paul Scott and John L. Fuller's *Genetics and the Social Behavior of the Dog*, has been reprinted (Chicago: University of Chicago Press, 1998). More up-to-date information can be found in Kenth Svartberg's chapter on personality in Per Jensen's multi-author textbook *The Behavioural Biology of Dogs* (Wallingford: CAB International, 2007).

Notes

INTRODUCTION

1. Including, I have to confess, by myself – an article I wrote for a Waltham Symposium in 1990 takes this approach. At that time, there was no research contradicting it. The situation is very different today.

CHAPTER 1. WHERE DOGS CAME FROM

1. Carles Vilà *et al.*, 'Multiple and ancient origins of the domestic dog', *Science*, 276 (13 June 1997), pp. 1687–9.
2. Biologists often name whole groups of animals after their best-known member. Hence the Roman name for the domestic dog – 'canis' – is used to refer to all the domestic dog's relatives – *Canis* for the closest, canid for the extended family. (The confusion that this causes isn't deliberate, honest.)
3. Michael Fox, one of the pioneers of dog behaviour in the 1960s, thought that for each species there was a distinct limit on how large and complex a pack could become, with the wolf at the pinnacle. His theories still linger on even today in books about dogs, but since he formulated his ideas a great deal more has been discovered about the behaviour of many of these species.
4. This term appears in Hungarian expert Dr Ádám Miklósi's book *Dog Behaviour, Evolution, and Cognition* (Oxford: Oxford University Press, 2007).
5. Randall Lockwood, 'Dominance in wolves: useful construct or bad habit?', in Erich Klinghammer, *Behaviour and Ecology of Wolves* (New York: Garland STPM Press, 1979), pp. 225–43.
6. See Dr David Mech's illuminating article on the new conception of wolf biology at http://www.npwrc.usgs.gov/resource/mammals/alstat/alpst.htm. Accessed 25 August 2010.
7. There is some controversy about just how many kinds of wolf occur in the wild in North America today but only the grey wolf is sufficiently widespread

for its social behaviour to have been studied. The number of types of grey wolf on the American continent is constantly being reappraised; there may be five (Northwestern, Plains, Eastern, Mexican and Arctic), but I've referred to the first two generically as the 'timber' wolf. A sixth, the red wolf, is often considered a separate species. Although it is sometimes called the 'Texas' red wolf, certainly in the early part of the last century its range centred on North Carolina. Some people maintain that it is a unique and endangered animal, and a great deal of effort is being put into captive breeding and conservation. However, the red wolf looks suspiciously like a mixture between a grey wolf and a coyote, and the red wolf's DNA appears to back the idea that it is a hybrid. Wolves and coyotes can mate and produce offspring, certainly in zoos and probably also in the wild; the Eastern or Algonquin wolf that occurs in Ontario and Quebec is most probably such a hybrid, although it has also been posited as a third true species of wolf. To confuse the picture further, the DNA of red wolves suggests that they may have hybridized with coyotes for a second time in the nineteenth century, as changing agriculture and ranching practices began to favour coyotes over wolves in the south-eastern USA. And given that many apparently pure-bred coyotes also contain wolf (as well as domestic dog) DNA, interbreeding between wolves and coyotes appears to have been going on for thousands of years – leading to the coining of the tongue-in-cheek term *Canis soupus* to describe coyote, eastern wolf and red wolf alike.

8. As is most likely the story for the domestic cat – see *Science*, 296 (5 April 2002), p. 15, for a summary of my research group's study into this.

CHAPTER 2. HOW WOLVES BECAME DOGS

1. This international team, led by Carles Vilà at the University of California in Los Angeles, published its findings in the journal *Science*, 276 (13 June 1997), pp. 1687–9.

2. With the notable exception of the Egyptians, who mummified a wide range of animals, including vast numbers of domestic cats.

3. Indeed such long-distance translocations were rare until comparatively recently, when European dogs were introduced as part of colonialization. However, it turns out that, in most areas, pet dogs that escape, as well as hybrids between pets and local dogs, tend not to prosper; evidently they are less effective than the local street dogs at exploiting local conditions. The DNA of many local populations is thus largely preserved in its original form.

4. See Peter Savolainen *et al.*, 'Genetic evidence for an East Asian origin of domestic dogs', *Science*, 298 (22 November 2002), pp. 1610–13; also, Adam

Boyko *et al.*, 'Complex population structure in African village dogs and its implications for inferring dog domestication history', *Proceedings of the National Academy of Sciences* (19 August 2009), pp. 13903–8.

5. See, for example, Nicholas Wade's article 'New finding puts origins of dogs in Middle East', *New York Times* (18 March 2010).

6. More gruesome still is the Zoroastrian practice of allowing dogs, regarded as sacred animals, to dispose of human corpses.

7. This scenario, conveniently, would also explain why the mitochondrial DNA sequences of dogs and wolves appear to have diverged at an unfeasibly early date. The divergence would have to predate the genetic changes that split the 'normal' wolves from the 'socializable' wolves, because today there are no survivors of the latter, apart from the few that changed into dogs. Matings between 'socializable' females and 'normal' males might well have continued for many millennia after the split, but would be undetectable in the (maternally inherited) mtDNA of modern dogs.

8. Ludmilla Trut, 'Early canid domestication: the farm-fox experiment', *American Scientist*, 87 (1999), pp. 160–69.

9. A few anthropologists have toyed with the rather romantic notion of man–wolf co-evolution, suggesting that wolves taught us how to hunt in groups, even how to form complex societies. However, it seems highly unlikely that any two-legged human could ever have 'adopted' the wolf's lifestyle. The wolves would have outrun him before he had time to blink. When he finally caught up with them after they had made their kill, why would they have let him share it with them? The primitive spears and knives that he had at his disposal would have hardly been adequate to drive off a pack of hungry wolves. Moreover, depictions of men hunting with dogs do not feature in cave paintings until 5,000 to 6,000 years ago, almost halfway through the history of domestic dogs as revealed by the archaeological record. It is certainly true that wolves feature prominently in the symbolism of recent hunter-gatherer societies, but myths do not recapitulate origins; they merely invent a framework for explaining the uncontrollable.

CHAPTER 3. WHY DOGS WERE – UNFORTUNATELY – TURNED BACK INTO WOLVES

1. Here I am indebted to biologist Dr Sunil Kumar Pal and his colleagues, who have been studying the urban feral dogs of West Bengal for more than ten years.

2. This sanctuary is run by the rehoming charity Dogs Trust, to whom I am very grateful for providing this opportunity.

3. See http://www.inch.com/~dogs/taming.html. Accessed 28 September 2010.
4. See http://drsophiayin.com/philosophy/dominance. Accessed 16 December 2009.
5. These RHP-related ideas were first developed with my colleague Dr Stephen Wickens; see my chapter in James Serpell (ed.), *The Domestic Dog: Its Evolution, Behaviour and Interactions with People* (Cambridge: Cambridge University Press, 1995).
6. See, for example, John Bradshaw and Amanda Lea, 'Dyadic interactions between domestic dogs', *Anthrozoös*, 5 (1992), pp. 245–53, confirmed by additional analysis of data presented in Carri Westgarth *et al.*, 'Dog behaviour on walks and the effect of use of the leash', *Applied Animal Behaviour Science*, 125 (2010), pp. 38–46.
7. These examples are partly based on those included by Rachel Casey and Emily Blackwell in our joint paper, 'Dominance in domestic dogs – useful construct or bad habit?', *Journal of Veterinary Behavior – Clinical Applications and Research*, 4 (2009), pp. 135–44.
8. Specifically, by Ádám Miklósi, in *Dog Behaviour, Evolution and Cognition* (Oxford: Oxford University Press, 2007).
9. For an example of this approach and how it was initially adopted even by specialist veterinarians, see Amy and Laura Marder, 'Human–companion animal relationships and animal behavior problems', *Veterinary Clinics of North America – Small Animal Practice*, 15 (1985), pp. 411–21.
10. Summarized from the entry headed 'Understanding your dog' on the BBC's online encyclopedia *H2G2*, at http://www.bbc.co.uk/dna/h2g2/A4889712. Accessed 20 August 2010.
11. Taken from http://www.acorndogtraining.co.uk/dominance.htm. Accessed 18 March 2010. The author of this site, Fran Griffin, is not herself a supporter of these 'commandments'.
12. Published in two papers authored by Nicola Rooney and myself: 'An experimental study of the effects of play upon the dog–human relationships', *Applied Animal Behaviour Science*, 75 (2002), pp. 161–76; and 'Links between play and dominance and attachment dimensions of dog–human relationships', *Journal of Applied Animal Welfare Science*, 6 (2003), pp. 67–94.

CHAPTER 4. STICKS OR CARROTS? THE SCIENCE OF DOG TRAINING

1. Cesar Millan with Melissa Jo Peltier, *Be the Pack Leader* (London: Hodder & Stoughton, 2008), p. 11.
2. Colin Tennant, *Breaking Bad Habits in Dogs* (Dorking: Interpet Publishing,

2002), p. 18. The 'Expert Dog Trainer and Canine Behaviourist' tag is from the cover of the same book.

3. Quoted from Louise Rafkin, 'The Anti-Cesar Millan / Ian Dunbar's been succeeding for 25 years with lure-reward dog training; how come he's been usurped by the flashy, aggressive TV host?', *San Francisco Chronicle* (15 October 2006), http://articles.sfgate.com/keyword/puppy. Accessed 15 November 2010.

4. In fact, Konrad Most also promoted the idea of shaping dogs' 'instinctive' behaviour using rewards, and discussed the benefits of allowing dogs to make their own decisions – indeed, he went on to become a pioneering guide-dog trainer. But it is his philosophy of the dog–human relationship that is perhaps his biggest and most unfortunate legacy.

5. The Monks of New Skete, *How To Be Your Dog's Best Friend: A Training Manual for Dog Owners* (Boston: Little, Brown & Co., 1978), pp. 11–12. The phrase 'pecking order' appears on p. 13.

6. Ibid., pp. 46–7.

7. Ibid., pp. 202–3.

8. Veterinary behaviour specialist Sophia Yin explains this in detail on her website: see http://drsophiayin.com/philosophy/dominance. Accessed 16 December 2009.

9. David Appleby, one of the founders of the UK's Association of Pet Behaviour Counsellors, writes on their website: 'There seems to be little doubt that programmes introduced to cure a dominance problem can result in depression and withdrawn behaviour.' See http://www.apbc.org.uk/articles/caninedominance. Accessed 18 March 2010.

10. Fran Griffin, one of the founders of the UK Association of Pet Dog Trainers, writes: 'Over the years I have heard far too many stories from owners who have followed the "dominance reduction schedule" after taking advice from trainers/behaviourists, only to become very disappointed. Once it has become established that the dog has failed to respond to the regime, the owners became more and more aggressive in their attitude, in the belief that they were "asserting their alpha position over the dog". Eventually the dog bit them "unprovoked". For many this resulted in the dog's demise, whilst others were thrown into the local rescue kennels.' See http://www.acorndogtraining.co.uk/dominance.htm. Accessed 18 March 2010.

11. Another reason for horses' trainability in this context has to do with the sensitivity of their mouths. Dogs have plenty of teeth and are happy to carry things clenched between them; horses have a gap between their grazing and chewing teeth, which allows the bit to sit right on their sensitive gums.

12. This has been documented by a graduate student of mine, Anne Pullen.

13. According to another former graduate student of mine, Sarah Hall, this is

the most likely explanation for why cats get bored with toys so quickly – so it is reasonable that the same principle might apply to dogs.

14. 'Puppy parties' are structured socialization sessions for puppies in their juvenile period.

15. Karen Prior has written various books on this topic, including *Don't Shoot the Dog! The New Art of Teaching and Training*, revised edn. (Dorking: Ringpress Books, 2002).

16. Research done by Dr Deborah Wells at Queen's University, Belfast, and published as 'The effectiveness of a citronella spray collar in reducing certain forms of barking in dogs', *Applied Animal Behaviour Science*, 73 (2001), pp. 299–309.

17. Matthijs Schilder and Joanne van der Borg, 'Training dogs with help of the shock collar: short and long term behavioural effects', *Applied Animal Behaviour Science*, 85 (2004), pp. 319–34.

18. Richard Polsky, 'Can aggression in dogs be elicited through the use of electronic pet containment systems?', *Journal of Applied Animal Welfare Science*, 3 (2000), pp. 345–57.

19. Elly Hiby, Nicola Rooney and John Bradshaw, 'Dog training methods: their use, effectiveness and interaction with behaviour and welfare', *Animal Welfare*, 13 (2004), pp. 63–9.

20. Christine Arhant *et al.*, 'Behaviour of smaller and larger dogs: effects of training methods, inconsistency of owner behaviour and level of engagement in activities with the dog', *Applied Animal Behaviour Science*, 123 (2010), pp. 131–42.

21. Training discs should not be confused with the 'distractor', usually a tin can filled with pebbles thrown on the ground in front of the dog, which some dog trainers recommend. This method is one way of getting the dog to stop doing something undesirable; it gives the owner an opportunity to reward the dog for doing something else. However, in practice these are of limited usefulness, because most dogs quickly habituate to such noises. Among those that do not, the very lack of habituation is evidence that the 'distractor' is actually a punishment, inducing fear in those particular dogs.

22. For example, see the blog by David Ryan, Chairman of the UK's Association of Pet Behaviour Counsellors, http://www.apbc.org.uk/blog/positive_reinforcement. Accessed 16 August 2010.

23. Meghan Herron, Frances Shofer and Ilana Reisner (of the University of Pennsylvania's Ryan Hospital), 'Survey of the use and outcome of confrontational and non-confrontational training methods in client-owned dogs showing undesired behaviours', *Applied Animal Behaviour Science*, 117 (2009), pp. 47–54.

24. In the words of David Ryan, 'It makes good television to go head to head and dominate a dog. Unfortunately, television is not real life and tends to show short interactions where the dog is forced to submit. It is not impossible for a "handy" owner to repeatedly force their dog into submission either, but these unpleasant and unnecessary measures are not how most pet owners want to live with their dogs. Lamentably the high profile of these programmes means the on-screen warning "do not try this at home" is often not heeded.' See http://www.apbc.org.uk/sites/default/files/Why_Wont_Dominance_Die.pdf. Accessed 9 April 2010.

25. As wolf biologist David Mech points out in a recent article in *International Wolf*, it can take two decades for new scientific ideas to become fully accepted. He goes on to say: 'Hopefully it will take fewer than 20 years for the media and public to fully adopt the correct terminology and thus to once and for all end the outmoded view of the wolf pack as an aggressive assortment of wolves consistently competing with each other to take over the pack.' See 'Whatever happened to the term "alpha wolf"?', *International Wolf* (Autumn 2008), pp. 4–8. Available online at http://www.wolf.org/wolves/news/pdf/winter2008.pdf.

26. See http://www.youtube.com/watch?v=5z6XR3qJ_qY. Accessed 17 November 2010.

CHAPTER 5. HOW PUPPIES BECOME PETS

1. Daniel G. Freedman, John A. King and Orville Elliot, 'Critical period in the social development of dogs', *Science* 133 (1961), pp. 1016–17. The authors worked at the Jackson Laboratories in Bar Harbor (Maine), the site of many ground-breaking discoveries about dogs.

2. It later emerged that this idea had initially been proposed almost a century earlier, by the English biologist Douglas Spalding. However, there is no indication that Lorenz knew this, and the images of Lorenz swimming in his lake, attended by his retinue of faithful goslings, will always be the first that come to mind whenever imprinting is mentioned. Equally evocative are the orphaned Canada geese in the movie *Fly Away Home*, which were imprinted on to a microlight aircraft.

3. Peter Hepper, 'Long-term retention of kinship recognition established during infancy in the domestic dog', *Behavioural Processes*, 33 (1994), pp. 3–14.

4. Although the research to prove the occurrence of such learning has not, as far as I know, been done on wolves themselves, there is an extensive scientific literature on kin recognition mechanisms in other mammals, based on cross-fostering experiments. Something similar happens in our own species, hence

the *Westermarck effect*, whereby unrelated individuals who spend their childhood in the same household find each other sexually unattractive.

5. Given dogs' reliance on their sense of smell, it is surprising that no one seems to have taken into account the role of olfaction in their concept of what constitutes a human. Perhaps, unknown to us with our comparatively feeble noses, there are one or two smells that definitively signify 'human being'.

6. This capacity may have a parallel in the way young children learn languages. Many of the children in the world – though not so many in the UK or the USA as elsewhere – grow up hearing two or more languages spoken, and their brains adapt to this very well; each language seems to be stored separately, and the child quickly becomes competent at not mixing them up when forming sentences.

7. See, for example, John L. Fuller, 'Experiential deprivation and later behavior', *Science*, 158 (29 December 1967), pp. 1645–52.

8. Michael W. Fox, 'Behavioral effects of rearing dogs with cats during the "critical period of socialization"', *Behaviour*, 35 (1969), pp. 273–80.

9. Mother cats seem to rely on a straightforward rule of thumb to identify their offspring: 'If it's the size of a kitten and it's living where I keep my kittens, then it must be one of mine.' Hence the ease with which Michael Fox was able to persuade queens with litters to accept Chihuahua puppies as if they were their own. Many queens will also accept the introduction of kittens younger than their own, a phenomenon that some animal rescue organizations capitalize on to raise orphans.

10. David Appleby, John Bradshaw and Rachel Casey, 'Relationship between aggressive and avoidance behaviour by dogs and their experience in the first six months of life', *Veterinary Record*, 150 (2002), pp. 434–8.

11. This outcome was initially reported as an effect of simple handling by the people looking after the rats concerned; however, it later emerged that the return of the pups, smelling of human, stimulated the mother to take extra care of them. The extra care, rather than the handling itself, was what corrected their development.

12. See Susan Jarvis *et al.*, 'Programming the offspring of the pig by prenatal social stress: neuroendocrine activity and behaviour', *Hormones and Behavior* 49 (2006), pp. 68–80.

13. David Tuber *et al.*, 'Behavioral and glucocorticoid responses of adult domestic dogs (*Canis familiaris*) to companionship and social separation', *Journal of Comparative Psychology*, 110 (1996), pp. 103–8.

14. Subsequent research has shown that dogs' stress hormone levels are different depending not only on the gender of their owners or carers (lower if they are women) but also their personalities (lower if the owners are extroverts).

15. Sharon L. Smith, 'Interactions between pet dog and family members: an ethological study', chapter 4 in Aaron Katcher and Alan Beck (eds.), *New Perspectives on our Lives with Companion Animals* (Philadelphia: University of Pennsylvania Press, 1983), pp. 29–36.

CHAPTER 6. DOES YOUR DOG LOVE YOU?

1. This tradition is usually ascribed to C. Lloyd Morgan, one of the founders of comparative (i.e. animal) psychology. Writing in 1894, he proposed what has become known as Morgan's canon: 'In no case may we interpret an action as the outcome of the exercise of a higher psychical faculty, if it can be interpreted as the outcome of the exercise of one which stands lower in the psychological scale.' (For the word 'lower', we would now substitute 'simpler'.) Morgan came to realize, however, that this was unnecessarily restrictive, and in 1903 stated: 'To this, however, it should be added . . . that the canon by no means excludes the interpretation of a particular activity in terms of the higher processes if we already have independent evidence of the occurrence of these higher processes in the animal under observation.' In other words, if we can show that dogs experience a particular emotion, then that emotion can be invoked as a potential explanation for any dog behaviour.

2. In his book *The Emotional Lives of Animals: A Leading Scientist Explores Animal Joy, Sorrow and Empathy – and Why They Matter* (Novato, Calif.: New World Library, 2007), American ethologist Marc Bekoff, himself an ardent proponent of the reality of animal emotions, describes his perplexity at the seemingly self-contradictory behaviour of a colleague, whom he refers to simply as Bill (presumably to save his blushes). Apparently they had met up immediately before Marc was due to give a lecture on animal cognition, and for five full minutes Bill had regaled him with stories about his dog Reno, how much Reno loves to play, how anxiously he misses his master when Bill's not there, how jealous he becomes when Bill is talking to his daughter, and so on. However, in the discussion session after the lecture, Bill accused Marc of being too anthropomorphic in his explanations of animal behaviour. In response, Marc reminded Bill of the conversation they'd had about Reno only an hour or so previously. Bill, somewhat embarrassed, retorted that, while he'd described Reno's behaviour in terms of emotions, he had no idea of what Reno was actually feeling, and doubted that any of the words he'd used to describe his dog's emotions were an accurate picture of what had actually been going on inside the dog's head at the time.

3. Stephen Mithen, Professor of Archaeology at Reading University, has gone so far as to argue that anthropomorphism can be traced back some 100,000

years, to the merging between the part of our brain that dealt with our social behaviour and the part used to identify and classify animals, giving us the ability to 'think like animals do'. See his book *The Prehistory of the Mind* (London: Thames & Hudson, 1996).

4. According to James Serpell, Director of the Center for the Interaction of Animals and Society at the University of Pennsylvania, and a world-class expert on human–animal interactions: '[A]nthropomorphism is the primary force cementing these [i.e. pet–owner] relationships.' This quote comes from his chapter, 'People in Disguise: Anthropomorphism and the Human–Pet Relationship', in Lorraine Daston and Gregg Mitman (eds.), *Thinking With Animals: New Perspectives on Anthropomorphism* (New York: Columbia University Press, 2005), p. 131.

5. Zana Bahlig-Pieren and Dennis Turner, 'Anthropomorphic interpretations and ethological descriptions of dog and cat behavior by lay people', *Anthrozoös*, 12 (1999), pp. 205–10. This is one of only a few studies of owners' abilities to understand their dogs' body-language, which is surprising given how important this skill must be in ensuring that dogs' emotional needs are met.

6. This model was proposed – for humans – by, among others, Ross Buck, Professor of Communication Sciences at the University of Connecticut, and author of the classic text *Human Motivation and Emotion* (New York: Wiley, 1976).

7. While owners well attuned to their cats can probably detect anxiety from the cat's body-language, joy is harder to detect. For example, purring does not indicate joy, although it is often assumed to – cats will purr even when in extreme pain. It appears to be an all-purpose care- and comfort-soliciting signal, meaning anything from 'Is it OK that I've curled up next to you?' to 'Please help, I'm in distress here'.

8. Patricia McConnell gives a graphic account of such a response, exhibited by her Great Pyrenees bitch Tulip, in her wonderful book *For the Love of a Dog: Understanding Emotion in You and Your Best Friend* (New York: Ballantine Books, 2007), pp. 115–16.

9. On the other hand, allowing coyotes to find and feed on sheep carcasses laced with an emetic (lithium chloride), though it certainly put them off eating sheep meat, did not stop the coyotes from hunting and killing them. (Indeed, hunting and eating are separately motivated in many carnivores.) Sheep mortality was therefore unaffected, and other means had to be sought for limiting coyote damage to free-ranging livestock.

10. This study was performed by the late Professor Johannes Odendaal, a pioneer of studies of human–animal interaction in South Africa, working with

Professor Roy Meintjes of the Pretoria vet school. Their paper, 'Neurophysiological correlates of affiliative behaviour between humans and dogs', was published in *Veterinary Journal*, 165 (2003), pp. 296–301.

11. See the paper by John Bradshaw, Justine McPherson, Rachel Casey and Isabella Larter, 'Aetiology of separation-related behaviour in domestic dogs', *Veterinary Record*, 151 (2002), pp. 43–6.

12. See the paper by John Bradshaw, Emily-Jayne Blackwell, Nicola Rooney and Rachel Casey, 'Prevalence of separation related behaviour in dogs in southern England', in Joel Dehasse and E. Biosca Marce (eds.), *Proceedings of the 8th ESVCE Meeting on Veterinary Behavioural Medicine, Granada, Spain* (Paris: Publibook, 2002), pp. 189–93.

13. The latter figures are based on a limited number of similar interviews conducted by a student of mine in upstate New York in 2001.

14. Yet, paradoxically, some dogs that behave like this when their owners are at home seem not to be distressed when they're left on their own.

15. Andrew Luescher and Ilana Reisner, 'Canine aggression toward familiar people: a new look at an old problem', *Veterinary Clinics of North America: Small Animal Practice*, 38 (2008), pp. 115–16.

16. Some veterinary behaviourists tend to label the repetitive behaviour that biologists call 'stereotypic' as 'obsessive-compulsive', by analogy with human behaviour. Others, however, argue that such syndromes require conscious thought, and that this terminology should therefore not be applied to dogs.

CHAPTER 7. CANINE BRAINPOWER

1. See, for example, the book by guide-dog user and trainer Bruce Johnston, *Harnessing Thought: Guide Dog – a Thinking Animal with a Skilful Mind* (Harpenden: Lennard Publishing, 1995).

2. Notably Dr Brian Hare, at the Max Planck Institute for Evolutionary Anthropology in Leipzig. See his article, written with Michael Tomasello, 'Human-like social skills in dogs?', *Trends in Cognitive Sciences*, 9 (2005), pp. 439–44.

3. Sylvain Fiset, Claude Beaulieu and France Landry, 'Duration of dogs' (*Canis familiaris*) working memory in search for disappearing objects', *Animal Cognition*, 6 (2003), pp. 1–10.

4. Nicole Chapuis and Christian Varlet (from the Institute of Neurophysiology and Psychophysiology in Marseille, France), 'Short cuts by dogs in natural surroundings', *Quarterly Journal of Experimental Psychology*, sect. B, vol. 39 (1987), pp. 49–64.

5. In other experiments, we have shown that short-term stress actually makes dogs keener to learn, probably because it heightens their perception of the world around them, though they also make more mistakes than relaxed dogs do: Emily-Jayne Blackwell *et al.*, 'Rapid shaping of behaviour associated with high urinary cortisol in domestic dogs', *Applied Animal Behaviour Science*, 124 (2010), pp. 113–20.

6. Specifically, they claimed that Rico actually knew the words for each object, and could learn new words for new objects, recognizing them simply because they were new: see Juliane Kaminski, Josep Call and Julia Fischer, 'Word learning in a domestic dog: evidence for "Fast Mapping"', *Science*, 304 (2004), pp. 1682–3. Subsequent studies have cast doubt on this claim (Rico's data are also explainable by a combination of simple habituation and an ability to identify objects as unfamiliar by their smell), but this dog's memory was remarkable nevertheless.

7. See also the paper by Patricia Kaulfuss and Daniel Mills, 'Neophilia in domestic dogs (*Canis familiaris*) and its implication for studies of dog cognition', *Animal Cognition*, 11 (2008), pp. 553–6.

8. Britta Osthaus, Stephen Lea and Alan Slater, 'Dogs (*Canis lupus familiaris*) fail to show understanding of means–end connections in a string-pulling task', *Animal Cognition*, 8 (2005), pp. 37–47.

9. Rebecca West and Robert Young, 'Do domestic dogs show any evidence of being able to count?', *Animal Cognition*, 5 (2002), pp. 183–6.

10. Claudi Tennie, Josep Call and co-workers, (from the Max Planck Institute for Evolutionary Anthropology in Leipzig), 'Dogs, *Canis familiaris*, fail to copy intransitive actions in third-party contextual imitation tasks', *Animal Behaviour*, 77 (2009), pp. 1491–9.

11. Friederike Range, Zsófia Viranyi and Ludwig Huber, 'Selective imitation in domestic dogs', *Current Biology*, 17 (2007), pp. 868–72.

12. József Topál *et al.*, 'Differential sensitivity to human communication in dogs, wolves, and human infants', *Science* (Washington), 325 (2009), pp. 1269–72.

13. Both of these experiments were performed by Dr Florence Gaunet, a cognitive ethologist working in the Museum of Natural History in Paris: 'How do guide dogs of blind owners and pet dogs of sighted owners (*Canis familiaris*) ask their owners for food?', *Animal Cognition*, 11 (2008), pp. 475–83; 'How do guide dogs and pet dogs (*Canis familiaris*) ask their owners for their toy and for playing?', *Animal Cognition*, 13 (2010), pp. 311–23.

14. Josep Call *et al.*, 'Domestic dogs (*Canis familiaris*) are sensitive to the attentional state of humans', *Journal of Comparative Psychology*, 117 (2003), pp. 257–63.

15. Juliane Bräuer, Josep Call and Michael Tomasello, 'Visual perspective taking in dogs (*Canis familiaris*) in the presence of barriers', *Applied Animal Behaviour Science*, 88 (2004), pp. 299–317.
16. Mark Petter *et al.*, 'Can dogs (*Canis familiaris*) detect human deception?', *Behavioural Processes*, 82 (2009), pp. 109–118.
17. Nicola Rooney, John Bradshaw and Ian Robinson, 'A comparison of dog–dog and dog–human play behaviour', *Applied Animal Behaviour Science*, 66 (2000), pp. 235–48; Nicola Rooney and John Bradshaw, 'An experimental study of the effects of play upon the dog–human relationships', *Applied Animal Behaviour Science*, 75 (2002), pp. 161–76.
18. Alexandra Horowitz, 'Attention to attention in domestic dog (*Canis familiaris*) dyadic play', *Animal Cognition*, 12 (2009), pp. 107–18.
19. Ikuma Adachi, Hiroko Kuwahata and Kazuo Fujita, 'Dogs recall their owner's face upon hearing the owner's voice', *Animal Cognition*, 10 (2007), pp. 17–21.
20. The results of this study were reported by Sarah Marshall and her co-workers from universities in Italy, at the 2nd Canine Science Forum held in Vienna in July 2010.
21. Nicola Rooney and John Bradshaw, 'Social cognition in the domestic dog: behaviour of spectators towards participants in interspecific games', *Animal Behaviour*, 72 (2006), pp. 343–52.

CHAPTER 8. EMOTIONAL (UN)SOPHISTICATION

1. For more detail of this approach, see the seminal article by eminent animal psychologist and neuroscientist Jaak Panksepp, 'Affective consciousness: core emotional feelings in animals and humans', *Consciousness and Cognition*, 14 (2005), pp. 30–80.
2. Paul Morris, Christine Doe and Emma Godsell (psychologists from the University of Portsmouth), 'Secondary emotions in non-primate species? Behavioural reports and subjective claims by animal owners', *Cognition & Emotion*, 22 (2008), pp. 3–20. The surveyors asked 337 dog owners, all of whom had owned their dogs for an average of more than six years, to tell them how confident they were that their dogs experienced each of sixteen different emotions (there were actually seventeen, but one, disgust, was difficult to interpret because the term itself can be used in two different ways). Forty of these owners participated in the follow-up study on signs of jealousy.
3. Including Marc Bekoff, in his book *The Emotional Lives of Animals* (Novato, Calif.: New World Library, 2007), and also Jeffrey Masson, a philosopher at

the University of Auckland in New Zealand; see his book *Dogs Never Lie About Love* (New York: Three Rivers Press, 1998).
4. See Alexandra Horowitz, 'Disambiguating the "guilty look": salient prompts to a familiar dog behaviour', *Behavioural Processes*, 81 (2009), pp. 447–52.
5. See Mike Mendl *et al.*, 'Dogs showing separation-related behaviour exhibit a "pessimistic" cognitive bias', published on-line in *Current Biology*, 20 (Oct. 2010), pp. R839–R840.
6. Not over a hundred, as the urban myth would have it. Nevertheless, linguists do agree that the Central Alaskan Yupik language has between a dozen and two dozen such words, depending on the method of counting adopted.

CHAPTER 9. A WORLD OF SMELLS

1. The definitive observations were done on two Italian greyhounds called Flip and Gypsy, and a toy poodle called . . . Retina (only a vision scientist would call a dog that). The dogs were presented with three windows, two illuminated with one colour and the third with another, and trained to paw at the odd one out; if they got it right, they were given a tasty food treat. By varying the brightness of one of the colours, the experimenters could tell whether the dogs were really telling them apart by their colour: if they were seeing only in black and white, there would be one combination that would appear exactly the same shade of grey. The dogs could not always distinguish greenish-blue from grey, or orange from red, but they could always tell red from blue. See Jay Neitz, Timothy Geist and Gerald Jacobs, 'Color vision in the dog', *Visual Neuroscience*, 3 (1989), pp. 119–25.
2. The hearing range of humans extends up to 23 kilohertz, that of dogs to 45 kilohertz, and cats to 80 or even 100 kilohertz. In dogs, maximum sensitivity is reached between 0.5 and 16 kilohertz.
3. Of course, dogs also have a sense of taste, which apart from being rather insensitive to salt, and more sensitive to compounds called nucleotides that are common in blood – a relic of their predator origins – is much like ours. They discriminate between food flavours using a combination of odour and taste, just as we do.
4. Research done by Professor Peter Hepper at Queen's University, Belfast, and published as 'The discrimination of human odour by the dog', *Perception*, 17 (1988), pp. 549–54.
5. You can see just how stable the boundary layer is by watching the drops of water on the bonnet of your car as you drive away after a rain shower: quite a speed has to be reached before they are disturbed by the air rushing past.
6. Research conducted by Debbie Wells, a dog behaviour expert from Queen's

University, Belfast, and Peter Hepper, and published as 'Directional tracking in the domestic dog, *Canis familiaris*', *Applied Animal Behaviour Science*, 84 (2003), pp. 297–305.

7. Although our vomeronasal organ has disappeared, we still make a few of its receptors (V1Rs) – but they are now found in the regular olfactory epithelium. It is unclear what they are used for, but some scientists implicate them in the perception of human 'pheromones' that may affect our reproductive behaviour.

8. Deborah Wells and Peter Hepper, 'Prenatal olfactory learning in the domestic dog', *Animal Behaviour*, 72 (2006), pp. 681–6.

9. This study was done by my student Amanda Lea, who was able to establish the basics of such dog–dog encounters after a few dozen hours of sitting on park benches pretending to sketch dogs (in case anyone became curious as to what she was doing in the same place day after day). It was published as 'Dyadic interactions between domestic dogs during exercise', *Anthrozoös*, 5 (1993), pp. 234–53.

10. Stephan Natynczuk, then a student at Oxford University, and I spent many a happy hour collecting samples of anal sac contents from beagles, and then putting them through a mass spectrometer in order to demonstrate this gradual change scientifically. Every now and again we'd fail to line up the collection pot correctly and end up with a very smelly lab coat – or worse.

11. Sunil Pal, 'Urine marking by free-ranging dogs (*Canis familiaris)* in relation to sex, season, place and posture', *Applied Animal Behaviour Science*, 80 (2003), pp. 45–59.

12. Ádám Miklósi and Krisztina Soproni, 'A comparative analysis of animals' understanding of the human pointing gesture', *Animal Cognition*, 9 (2006), pp. 81–93.

13. The UK charity Medical Detection Dogs (http://hypoalertdogs.co.uk) has recently trained an Affenpinscher to alert its owner to onsets of hypoglycaemia. These flat-faced toy dogs are unlikely candidates for such a role, but the successful training outcome shows that the breed's sense of smell cannot be totally impaired.

CHAPTER 10. PROBLEMS WITH PEDIGREES

1. Federico Calboli *et al.*, 'Population structure and inbreeding from pedigree analysis of purebred dogs', *Genetics*, 179 (2008), pp. 593–601.

2. Research published by Danika Bannasch, a veterinary geneticist working at the vet school at Davis, California, with Michael Bannasch, Jeanne Ryun,

Thomas Famula and Niels Pedersen, 'Y chromosome haplotype analysis in purebred dogs', *Mammalian Genome*, 16 (2005), pp. 273–80.

3. During the week of Crufts' national dog show in 1989, Celia Haddon wrote in the *Daily Telegraph*: 'The question of what a scientist, tinkering in a laboratory, might be able to do with an ordinary cow, sheep or pig is regularly aired. But one form of genetic engineering is already going on, and has been changing the face of Britain's most popular domestic animal, the dog, for decades.' See also veterinarian Koharik Arman's article, 'A new direction for kennel club regulations and breed standards', *Canadian Veterinary Journal*, 48 (2007), pp. 953–65.

4. Summaries are available in several expert reports, including those commissioned by the Royal Society for the Prevention of Cruelty to Animals, http://www.rspca.org/pedigreedogs; the Associate Parliamentary Group for Animal Welfare, http://www.apgaw.org/reports-a-publications/pedigree-dog-report; and the UK Kennel Club in partnership with the rehoming charity Dogs Trust, http://dogbreedinginquiry.files.wordpress.com/2010/01/final-dog-enquiry-120110.pdf.

5. From the RSPCA report: 'Syringomyelia. The formation of cavities in the nervous tissue of the spinal cord. In dogs, this is often but not always accompanied by "referred" pain (perceived at a site adjacent to or some distance from the site of the cavity) or irritation. The dog is clearly in discomfort and tries to scratch at or near the shoulder or face, in the position from which they perceive the pain to originate.'

6. Published as 'Paedomorphosis affects agonistic visual signals of domestic dogs', *Animal Behaviour*, 53 (1997), pp. 297–304.

7. Steven Leaver and Tom Reimchen (University of Victoria in British Columbia), 'Behavioural responses of *Canis familiaris* to different tail lengths of a remotely-controlled life-size dog replica', *Behaviour*, 145 (2008), pp. 377–90.

8. Ray and Lorna Coppinger put forward this theory in their book *Dogs: A New Understanding of Canine Origin, Behaviour and Evolution* (London: Crosskeys Select Books, 2004).

9. http://www.the-kennel-club.org.uk/services/public/breeds/Default.aspx. Accessed 6 December 2010.

10. Ibid.

11. Ibid.

12. This study was published as a book, *Genetics and the Social Behavior of the Dog*, by John Paul Scott and John L. Fuller (Chicago: University of Chicago Press, 1965).

13. The dog's breed is often recorded by hospital staff from eyewitness accounts, or by police officers. Rarely is an expert in identifying dogs involved in such reports.

14. Taken from Stephen Collier, 'Breed-specific legislation and the pit bull terrier: 'are the laws justified?', *Journal of Veterinary Behavior*, 1 (2006), pp. 17–22.

CHAPTER 11. DOGS AND THE FUTURE

1. The following is part of a statement issued by the UK's Centre of Applied Pet Ethology: 'There are still huge numbers of "stamp and jerk" dog trainers and whisperers at large with their choke chains, spiked collars, shock collars, rape alarms, correction sticks and bullying attitudes . . . such dog trainers, whisperers and behaviourists are simply being "Cruel to be Cruel".' See http://www.coape.org/awsn.html. Accessed 21 April 2011.
2. For example, UK trainer Charlie Clarricoates, quoted in *Your Dog* magazine (Dec. 2009), pp. 44–6: 'We are seeing dogs now who are spoiled rotten, and never have any discipline, mainly because owners are force-fed incorrect impractical information . . . This moralistic attitude that you can only train dogs by loving them and being kind is ridiculous. There are some dogs you can't do this with because it doesn't work, even if you have a year with them.'
3. US veterinarian and behaviour specialist Dr Sophia Yin summarizes her stance on punishment as follows: 'Punishment isn't always inappropriate. It's just incredibly overused – and in most cases it's performed incorrectly . . . My goal is to use whichever techniques will work best with the least likelihood of side effects in the pet. If that best technique involves a punishment such as . . . a pinch collar "pop" or reprimand, or booby trap of some sort, or even an electronic collar, then I will use it. But it rarely does. Consequently I use punishment 100 to 1000 times less than a traditional trainer and relevant rewards 1000 times more.' See http://drsophiayin.com/philosophy/dominance. Accessed 20 September 2010.
4. See, for example, Bruce Johnston, *Harnessing Thought* (Harpenden: Lennard Publishing, 1995).
5. See, for example, a paper by Pauleen Bennett and Vanessa Rohlf, 'Owner–companion dog interactions: relationships between demographic variables, potentially problematic behaviours, training engagement and shared activities', *Applied Animal Behaviour Science*, 102 (2007), pp. 65–84.
6. According to Jean Donaldson, Director of the San Francisco SPCA Academy for Dog Trainers: 'Dog training is a divided profession. We are not like plumbers, orthodontists or termite exterminators who, if you put six in a room, will pretty much agree on how to do their jobs. Dog training camps are more like Republicans and Democrats, all agreeing that the job needs to be done but wildly differing on how to do it.' She goes on to say: 'dog training is currently

an unregulated profession: there are no laws governing practices . . . Provided it's in the name of training, someone with no formal education or certification can strangle your dog quite literally to death and conceivably get off scot-free'; see http://www.urbandawgs.com/divided_profession.html (accessed 24 September 2010). Likewise, the UK's Companion Animal Welfare Council concluded recently that 'there is no nationally accepted benchmark for qualification and skill in training or behaviour modification . . . With no minimum standard there can be no assurance of quality.' See *The Regulation of Companion Animal Services in Relation to Training and Behaviour Modification of Dogs*, published in July 2008, http://www.cawc.org.uk/080603.pdf, p. 5.

7. Gillian Diesel, David Brodbelt and Dirk Pfeiffer, 'Characteristics of relinquished dogs and their owners at 14 rehoming centers in the United Kingdom', *Journal of Applied Animal Welfare Science*, 13 (2005), pp. 15–30.

8. The bush dog is a rare social canid found in South America. Its stumpy tail, round head and furry feet would probably, if married to a suitable temperament, be rather appealing.

9. This list of desired traits is drawn from a paper by Paul McGreevy and Pauleen Bennett, 'Challenges and paradoxes in the companion-animal niche', *Animal Welfare*, 19(S) (2010), pp. 11–16. Pauleen Bennett and colleagues at Monash University in Australia presented further refinements of the ideas behind this list at the 2nd Canine Science Forum held in Vienna in July 2010.

Index

references in italics indicate either illustrations or boxed text